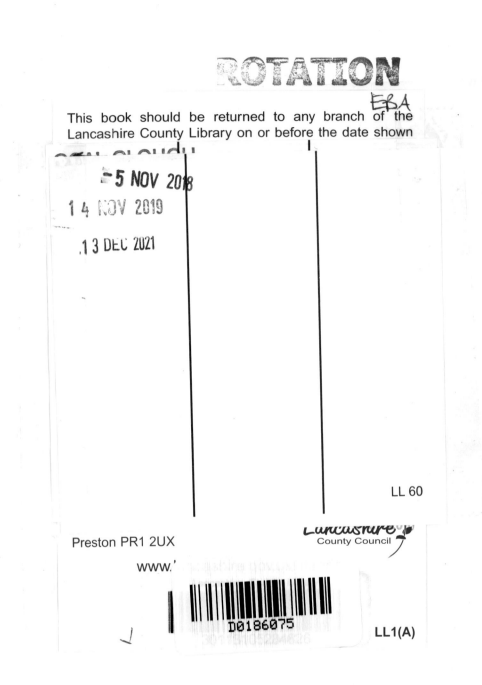

the GARDEN
handbook

the GARDEN handbook

IAN COOKE

NEW HOLLAND

First published in 2007 by New Holland Publishers (UK) Ltd
London • Cape Town • Sydney • Auckland

Garfield House
86–88 Edgware Road
London W2 2EA
United Kingdom
www.newhollandpublishers.com

Level 1, Unit 4
14 Aquatic Drive
Frenchs Forest
NSW 2086
Australia

80 McKenzie Street
Cape Town 8001
South Africa

218 Lake Road
Northcote
Auckland
New Zealand

10 9 8 7 6 5 4 3 2 1

ISBN 978 1 84537 670 3

Senior Editor: Corinne Masciocchi
Illustrator: Coral Mula
Designer: Sue Rose
Editorial Direction: Rosemary Wilkinson
Production: Hazel Kirkman

Cover photographs: Sea Spring Photos, © Joy Michaud 2001

Reproduction by Modern Age Repro House, Hong Kong
Printed and bound by Replika Press, India

CONTENTS

INTRODUCTION

 MANY YEARS AGO I WROTE AN ARTICLE entitled 'Who'd be a horticulturalist?', which was a light-hearted look at the woes and challenges of being a gardener and a warning against pursuing such a career. I guess I never listened to my own advice because here I am after nearly forty years in horticulture still having a passionate affair with the gardens I tend and falling in love regularly with fresh plants. And so it is with gardening, that whilst only some will make a career out of it, many will make it a lifetime's pursuit.

When asked to author this book, it felt a little like being asked to write down everything I knew about gardening. The subject matter is immense and the challenge was what to leave out rather than what to include. Nevertheless, I hope the end result has enough clarity and depth to be valuable.

Although this is not a personal book as such, it inevitably reflects my experience and techniques accumulated over many years. Put a group of gardeners together and they will often argue about the different ways of doing things, each claiming their methods are the best. So predictably the methods described throughout the book will usually be my preferred techniques! And of course I have to say they are the best!

At home I now have a tiny gravel garden, where I get my hands dirty and indulge my love of exotic plants. In the past I have tended gardens behind the nine houses I have lived in, all with their own delights and problems. One was a country garden beset with mosquitoes and small fallow deer. Another was a town garden with no access except through the house itself – quite a problem when you order a load of manure! I have struggled with sticky wet clay and also the lightest of sandy soils – great for growing carrots but not much else.

My work experience is varied too. My job enables me to garden on a grand scale at someone else's expense, although most of my time nowadays is spent behind a desk rather than a mower! There I have rolling acres, mature trees, meadows, flower beds and greenhouses. Over the years I have also looked after fruit and vegetable plots, historic gardens, and designed both private and public gardens.

Gardening is regarded by some as a very basic set of skills, and a therapeutic exercise at the very most. But creating gardens and cultivating plants is a pastime that draws people from a vast spectrum of backgrounds and ages. The designing and creating of a garden is in itself an art form and particularly challenging because of the living dynamic nature of the materials used. Growing and propagating some plants requires high levels of skill, knowledge and most of all patience. This is no quick fix hobby!

Over the years I have been in horticulture, I have seen many changes. Peat-based composts heralded a new revolution in growing but now we are moving away from these. From clay pots, we moved to plastic and now we are thinking of bio-degradable alternatives. Thirty years ago we sprayed everything in sight and had perfect crops but little wildlife. Winters nowadays are not so cold but spring and summer seem to come later. Garden fashions change, decking is out, gravel is in! This year's novelty plant is next year's compost. But still the almost universal love of plants and gardens remains – and grows – long may it be so!

understanding plants and gardens

GETTING STARTED

MANY OF US LOVE to 'dive' right into jobs without reading the basic instructions. However, take a rainy day or a cold winter's evening and peruse the first section of this book, which deals with a number of basic issues. When understood and practised, these will make you a better gardener and give a greater likelihood of success.

WHY GARDEN?

Why would anyone want to work outside getting cold, wet and muddy in winter and hot, sweaty and dehydrated in the summer? Cracked skin, aching backs and dirty finger-nails – that's often the image of gardening! And there's all the heartache of plants that don't grow, losses to slugs and birds and acres of healthy weeds and unmown grass just flaunting themselves! Well, there are indeed some strains, stresses and disappointments in gardening but overall, it is a very worthwhile pastime that brings endless joy and pleasure to millions of people.

People cultivate gardens for many reasons. There are those who do so out of necessity, purely because they own a house with a garden and like to keep it tidy. Others will enjoy the end result of an attractive garden, although not necessarily the work involved in keeping it tidy. Some still enjoy the mechanics of gardening, getting pleasure from digging, hoeing or mowing. Yet more gardeners enjoy collecting plants, and the end result in terms of the overall picture may not be important but the plants themselves are. Then we have the productive gardeners, those who enjoy growing fruit and vegetables for use in the kitchen. And, of course, there are the competitive gardeners, who have a constant urge to grow something bigger and better than anyone else's!

In general, gardening is a very healthy pursuit. Steady exercise taken in the open air has got to be beneficial. Gardening, if undertaken carefully, will exercise a wide range of muscles and provide a reasonable cardiovascular workout. Jobs such as digging or raking a lawn can be equated with cycling as a similar form of exercise.

However, all things in moderation, and it is unwise to attack any job heavily, particularly if you have not done it recently. Heavy jobs such as digging should be done for short spells, swapping to another activity for a break. Any jobs that involve lifting should be done with great care, being sure not to lift excessively heavy loads and to bend your knees rather than your back. Care should also be taken when working in the sun. Excess sun can cause sunburn, heatstroke and dehydration. When working on sunny summer days, always wear a hat and apply suntan lotion to exposed skin. In very hot weather, take frequent breaks from the sun and be sure to drink plenty of water.

WHAT TO GET FROM THIS BOOK

This is a general gardening handbook. It gives basic information about a great many topics, hopefully enough to carry out most of the routine activities in most ornamental and

SUN OR FUN

It is sometimes said that those in warm countries design gardens to relax in as it is too hot to work and those that live in colder climates design gardens to work in as it is too cold to relax!

kitchen gardens. You will possibly have bought this book because you have a garden for the first time and need some basic instruction. Maybe you've gardened for a while and need to learn a bit more about certain crops or plants. Or perhaps you are a reluctant convert having worked a garden out of necessity but like many others have discovered the joy of growing plants. Hopefully this book will contain valid information for a wide spectrum of gardeners. However, this is not a specialist book on anything in particular and those gardeners who want detailed or advance information will need to read further. If it inspires you to do that, then it will have achieved its purpose.

Some of the more complex topics and less common crops have been barely mentioned in order to avoid complicating this book, so for example, although we mention grape growing we do not discuss it in detail. However, you will find detailed cultural information on growing many other types of more common fruit.

We speak about many aspects of the ornamental garden and how to look after it but there are only limited suggestions of plants to grow – plants known to perform well and often the author's favourites! This is not a plant enthusiast's book as there are many other such books with exhaustive lists and descriptions of beautiful plants. There's a whole world of wonderful plants out there to discover.

FIRST THINGS

Many people find getting started on a task the most difficult aspect of all. Gardening is no different, particularly for those who are possibly tackling a new garden or approaching gardening for the first time. Where do I start? What comes first? What will I need? How do I do it? All very valid questions when faced with a new garden. Once started, the tasks often seem less daunting, some jobs achieved quickly and easily and remaining problems more approachable. We speak more about some of these issues on pages 72–75 where we consider some basics of garden design.

Assess any new garden carefully before starting work. What have you actually got? Is it open and sunny, or shaded, possibly by trees or a neighbour's house? Is it exposed to cold winds or maybe sheltered by a hedge? Remember that brick walls and fences do give some shelter but strong winds are merely buffeted around by them so there may be little wind shelter value. Brick walls are valuable as they trap the sun's heat and are useful sites for tender shrubs and fruits. In moving to a new area, you will need to ascertain the likely weather patterns in the area to gauge what plants are likely to be successful. A quick look at the neighbour's garden will also guide you as to what survives and thrives.

The soil is vital to any garden and we speak much more about this on pages 20–32.

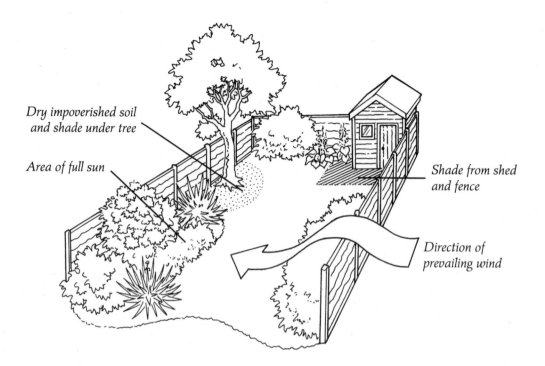

Dry impoverished soil
and shade under tree

Area of full sun

Shade from shed
and fence

Direction of
prevailing wind

Discover all the secrets of a new garden to help you make the best of all its different areas.

Initially we need some simple assessment of the soil conditions in order to predict what might be likely to grow. Is there a good depth of topsoil – at least a spit's depth (about 30 cm/12 in). Is it sandy, clay or a mixture? Does it look dusty and worn out or is it rich in dark organic matter? Is it waterlogged maybe? And of course what is the pH – acid or alkaline? All of these are essential considerations.

And then there is the basic equipment to get the jobs done. Good tools make a tough job easier but equally expensive tools can be poor buys if you are not sure what you need. Initially a new gardener should buy a simple kit of essential tools, to include a spade, fork, hoe, rake, broom and pair of secateurs. Many jobs can be done with these basic tools. More on tools and equipment in on pages 33–38.

Lawns require mowers and that's where things become more expensive. More elaborate tools should wait until you really need them and have had the opportunity to assess different options and maybe try some of the possibilities.

PLANT LIFE

PLANTS ARE ESSENTIAL FOR LIFE ON EARTH and form a critical part of the food chain. Some of the plants we grow in our gardens will be for food but the majority are grown purely for pleasure.

HOW DOES A PLANT WORK?

Plants are fascinating organisms and understanding their structure and how they work can be very useful to us when growing them. There is great diversity in the plant kingdom, from giant conifer trees down to tiny alpine plants, but most of them have many characteristics and functions in common. There are distinct differences and these help us to arrange them in groups, which in turn leads to naming. This section is all about botany, which initially sounds a little dry and academic but I hope as you read, you will appreciate some of the wonder of how plants function.

Most of the plants we want to grow in our gardens are the flowering plants with reproductive parts as recognisable flowers, followed by seeds. Then there are conifers, which have very simple flowers and bear their seeds in cones. Ferns and mosses are grouped separately and both reproduce by spores.

Plants are then grouped together into families according to certain similarities they may have and the families are further broken down into genera and species and this gives them the botanic names, by which we identify them (more about this on pages 54–56). Botanists who study plants in great detail have other more complex groupings but this classification is enough for us to understand garden plants.

LIFE CYCLES

Another way of dividing the plant kingdom is by means of life cycles. Annuals grow, flower, seed and die all within one season. For this reason they are always fast growing plants. Many bedding plants such as marigolds, sunflowers, nemesia and sweet peas are annuals.

Perennials are plants that live for a number of seasons, often flowering and seeding each year. The term 'perennial' is often simply used to refer to herbaceous perennials, which are plants that live for a number of years but die down each winter to the roots. Woody perennials are trees and shrubs that have a permanent framework and do not die down each year.

Biennials are plants that grow one year making a leafy plant and flower and seed the next year before they die. This includes plants such as *Digitalis purpurea* (foxglove), *Myosotis alpestris* (forget-me-not) and *Lunaria biennis* (honesty).

There are also a number of plants that are actually perennial (such as snapdragons, petunias or salvias) that are treated as annuals as they are so easy to grow from seed and perform best in the first year. Catalogues list them as annuals. Quite a few vegetables are actually biennials but this would not be of interest unless we wanted to collect seed from them.

HARDINESS

All plants vary in their ideal growing temperature and their ability to withstand cold. Books and catalogues will therefore often add the words hardy, half-hardy or tender to the description so we may have a hardy annual or a tender perennial and so on. Hardy generally refers to a plant's ability to withstand frost.

In some countries, such as the USA, where the climate varies considerably and temperatures can drop very low, there is a more complex system in place which divides the country into zones. Plants are then given a rating according to the zones in which they are likely to grow. So you will see the letter 'Z' (for zone) and a number after a plant name. The UK falls in between zones 7 to 9 whereas the USA straddles zones 2 to 10.

BULBOUS PLANTS

Many perennial plants have particular swollen parts, which enable them to store food materials and to survive from year to year. These are often underground but vary in their structure and appearance. The word 'bulb' is often used to mean any of these structures but they do have distinctions and individual names.

The most common is the bulb itself, with the most familiar example being the daffodil or the onion. If we cut one of these in half we can see that it is made up of white swollen sections, which are actually the bases of next year's leaves. Eventually these will grow out, become green in the light and look like normal leaves. Bulbs such as daffodils often have the flower bud pre-formed from the previous year.

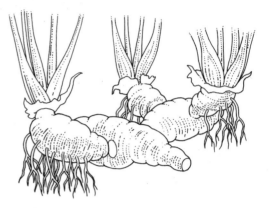

Rhizomes: a type of swollen stem

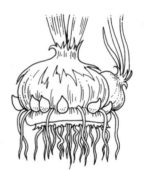

Left: a corm (another swollen stem)
Right: a bulb (swollen leaf bases)

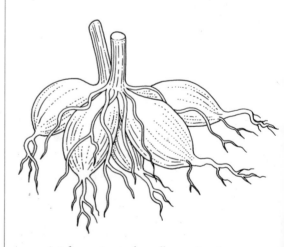

A tuber: a type of swollen rootsystem

Corms are the swollen bases of the stem and familiar examples include crocus and gladioli. Tubers are swollen roots and here we have the well known dahlia and the potato. Finally there are rhizomes, swollen stems that often run on the surface of the ground, such as *Iris germanica* (flag iris) or *Canna* (Indian shot), which grow just under the surface of the soil.

Bulbous plants are often lifted from the soil for propagation and distribution during their dormant season and should be stored carefully to avoid deterioration. It should be remembered that they are still alive and will not tolerate being abused. In general they must not be allowed to dry out to the extent that they shrivel. Most bulbous plants need cool, slightly damp environments for storage. Some, such as *Cannas* must not be allowed to freeze in winter. With all of them a watch should be kept for any signs of mould or rotting.

DECIDUOUS OR EVERGREEN

Deciduous plants are those that lose their leaves in the autumn, stay bare and leafless over winter and grow fresh leaves the next spring. Evergreens retain their leaves throughout the year. They do, of course, shed leaves all through their lives but this tends to be either spread over the year or sometimes in the spring when growth is restarting and fresh leaves are being produced. Some plants are semi-evergreen and retain some their leaves if conditions are suitable. In harsh winters or at times of stress, they will drop their leaves.

CLIMBING PLANTS

Some plants have very lax, elongated habits of growth and naturally scramble through other plants to get to the light. We call these climbers. In gardens, we often give them trellises or other formal supports, although there is no reason why we cannot let them grow through other plants.

Some climbers grow by means of twining their stems around a support, either clockwise or anti-clockwise. Runner beans and honeysuckle climb by twining. Other climbers, such as sweet peas, have some sort of tendrils, thin modified leaves which wrap themselves around suitable supports. Some tendril climbers, such as Virginia creeper, have sticky suckers on the end of the tendrils.

Clematis and nasturtiums are examples of another group that climb by twisting their long leaf stalks around a suitable support. A few climbers produce roots from their stems, which attach to any rough surface, and the most familiar of these is ivy. Finally there are those plants like climbing roses that have hooked thorns. As they grow, the shoots latch onto other branches or surfaces enabling them to scramble higher.

PLANT STRUCTURE

Most of our familiar garden plants have a similar structure made up of roots, stems, leaves, flowers, and eventually fruits and seeds. All of these parts of the plant are essential and have a job to do.

Roots These attach the plant to the ground, giving it anchorage. The roots also enable the plant to absorb water and nutrients from the soil. Some plants have large roots that penetrate either some distance around the plant or sometimes deep into the ground. These are called tap roots and the best examples are vegetables such as carrots or parsnips.

As well as these larger roots, all plants also have a fine web of smaller fibrous roots, which in turn are covered with root hairs. These are the important structures which absorb water and nutrients. When we transplant plants, great care should be taken not to damage these finer roots or to let them dry out.

Stems All plants have stems, although the trunk of a large tree would seem to be very different from that of a small alpine plant. Some plants such as primroses have a very short truncated stem which is hardly noticeable, as all the leaves seem to come from the same point. Plants such as these sometimes produce a special flowering stem to hold the flowers above the foliage. Stems give a plant structure and rigidity supporting the leaves and flowers. They are also complex and vital plumbing systems, carrying water, food materials and other natural chemicals to all parts of the plant.

Leaves The shape and appearance of leaves varies significantly and this is one of the characteristics used in classifying plants. As well as different shapes, they will also have different margins: smooth, curved or jagged. The veins in a leaf are the extensions of the channels in the stems that carry water and nutrients. Many different words are used to describe leaf appearance. Most leaves are green due to a pigment called chlorophyll and even plants with coloured leaves will contain some chlorophyll.

Flowers Very many garden plants are grown for their flowers and we often forget these are the reproductive parts of the plant. They can be very varied in their shape, size and colouring as well as other characteristics such as scent. Flowers have four main parts. The sepals are the outer casing, which is often green but may also be coloured and protects the flower when in bud. The petals are usually the brightly coloured showy parts of the flower. In the centre are the stamens (the male parts bearing pollen and the pistil) and the receptive stigma (the female part). Pollination is the transfer of pollen from the stamens to the stigma, which leads to fertilisation and seed production. Insects often do this, attracted to the flowers by their colour and the possibility of nectar. Wind can also do this with some plants such as grasses which have light feathery flowers.

The shape of flowers, the number of petals, sepals and other parts are used in classifying plants. Flowers may be borne individually on a stem or in heads with many flowers. They may be single with one row of petals or double with several rows. Petals are sometimes fused together into a tube or trumpet as with petunias. Sometimes plants have separate male and female flowers such as begonias and in other genera, such as holly, male and female flowers may be on separate plants.

Fruits and seeds These develop after pollination of the flowers. The structure containing the seed is correctly called a fruit and will contain one or more seeds. When we speak of fruits in terms of the edible types such as apples or tomatoes, we are actually speaking

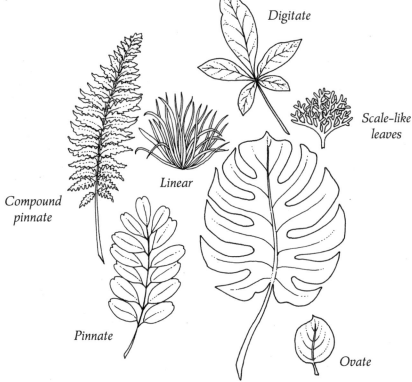

Just a few of the many common shapes that leaves take, some simple and others compound, bearing smaller leaflets.

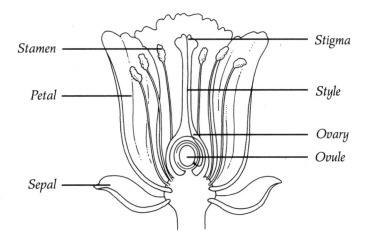

Most flowers, however different in appearance, will have these common components in some form.

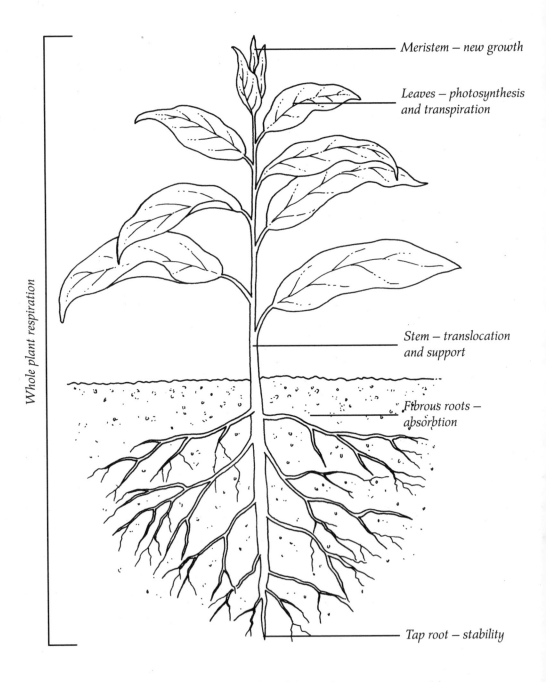

Meristem – new growth

Leaves – photosynthesis and transpiration

Stem – translocation and support

Fibrous roots – absorbtion

Tap root – stability

Whole plant respiration

A living plant is like a small factory, with each part taking on an essential function which in turn links with another part and a different process.

of succulent fruits. Other types are dry and sometimes papery or prickly and certainly not always edible. Seeds are shed from their parent plants in many different ways.

HOW A PLANT WORKS

Plants are like small factories that never stop with various different processes going on all of which interact together resulting in the growth and development of the plant.

Photosynthesis is the process by which leaves convert the sun's energy into carbohydrates, which are used for the plant's growth. During photosynthesis, carbon dioxide from the air is taken in to the leaves and oxygen is given out. This is why trees are so important for the quality of air in cities. Chlorophyll in leaves is essential for this process to take place. Light is also fundamental, which is why it is important to position plants to ensure they get the right amount of light. Trying to grow plants in a greenhouse in winter can be demanding, as whilst we may be keeping them warm, there will be insufficient light for photosynthesis and growth.

Leaves also carry out transpiration, which is the passage of carbon dioxide into the plant and oxygen out through small pores known as stomata. These also lose excess water vapour. When temperatures are high, a plant will continue to lose water by this process and if there is a shortage of water at the roots, this is when wilting occurs. When we take cuttings, we place them in a humid environment to reduce the water loss, as at this stage they have no roots to absorb more. We also shade newly transplanted seedlings until new roots have established to slow transpiration.

The other major vital process that takes place in a plant is respiration, which is the process by which it breaks down carbohydrates to release energy for growth and life itself. This happens all the time whilst the plant is alive. This also happens to dormant plants, bulbs, seeds and even fruit. Many can survive for long periods of time just slowly respiring stored foods but eventually when this is used up it will die. Respiration is faster at higher temperatures so when storing seeds or fruits we generally aim to keep them cool.

Many other processes take place in plants such as diffusion, which is the means by which water and nutrients pass from cell to cell. Most plants grow towards the light and this is called phototropism. Some plants are able to respond to the time of year by measuring the length of day and night and this is called photoperiodism. This is why chrysanthemums naturally flower in the autumn, when the days are short and the nights long.

SOILS AND FERTILISERS

SOIL IS THE VERY BASIS from which gardens grow. It is uniquely important but also often misunderstood and neglected. Soil provides anchorage for plants and the essential source of moisture, air and nutrition.

TYPES OF SOIL

Gardeners often speak of topsoil, which is the rich, well cultivated uppermost layer of soil, in which most plant roots grow. This is generally around 30 cm (12 in) deep, although it may vary considerably according to whether it has been well cultivated or neglected. Subsoil is the material below topsoil, which is generally poorer, more compacted and less rich. By cultivating soil deeply and adding soil improvers, the depth of topsoil in a garden can be increased. This in turn will result in increased plant growth.

Soils are made up of solids, liquids and air, and the proportions of these are quite critical. A good soil will have 50–60% mineral solids, about 5% organic matter and 35–45% air and water. The space for air and water is very important and when a soil is compacted, say with heavy wear or vehicles driving over it, the spaces for air and water are squashed out. This makes it much more difficult for plants to grow adequately. Cultivating a soil opens it up for air and water to penetrate.

The mineral components of a soil are generally made up of three basic types: clay, silt and sand. Stones may also be present. Clay particles are minute, silt slightly larger and sand largest, and visible to the naked eye. A good soil is one that contains a mixture of all three of the main constituents and gardeners often call such a mixed soil a loam.

You can determine the type of soil you have by rubbing a small sample between your wetted fingers. A sandy soil is easy to ascertain as the sample feels rough and gritty and does not stick together. A clay soil feels sticky and a larger sample of it will actually roll into a shiny ball. Silty soils are more difficult to determine by this test but generally feel silky and smooth. With a loam you may be able to feel all the constituents in the mixture. Depending on the proportions, we may speak about having a sandy loam if the proportion of sand is high or a clay loam at the other end of the scale, and so on.

Understanding the type of soil we have is important in knowing how to cultivate and what types of plants are more likely to thrive and be successful.

Sandy soils are generally free draining, easy to cultivate and tend to warm up quickly in the spring, making them good for vegetable production. In particular root crops such as carrots will grow well. Sandy soils do not retain water well, so tend to need more irrigation in the summer. They are also often poor soils, needing more nutrients adding and in regular small dressings.

Clay soils are heavy, generally difficult to cultivate and regarded as more of a challenge. They can be wet, poorly drained and therefore often slow to warm up in the spring. They do, however, retain more

pH TESTING

It is important to know the pH of the soil in your garden. Testing kits are readily available from garden centres. A small soil sample is taken from various areas and mixed together to give an average. The soil is then shaken up with a testing reagent and water in a small tube. The reagent changes colour according to the pH and this can be checked off on a colour chart supplied with the kit.

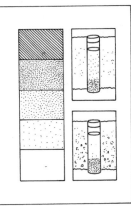

A small colour chart is provided with a soil testing kit, which enables you to determine the soil pH from the colour of the sample fluid.

moisture through the summer and are generally regarded as rich soils. They are good for fruit and permanent plants such as roses.

Silty soils are not so common, although occur in certain areas and in particular near to rivers. They generally behave more like sandy soils but are richer and less prone to drying out. They are also good soils for growing vegetables.

SOIL pH

Soils can also be acid or alkaline, and are measured on a scale called pH. In the middle of the scale at pH7, the soil is said to be neutral – neither acid nor alkaline. Above pH7, soils are alkaline and below they are acid. The ideal pH for many plants is pH6.5, just slightly acid.

Some plants are very sensitive to pH and will only grow at certain levels. For example,

there is a whole range of plants such as rhododendrons, heathers and camellias, known as *calcifuges*, that are acid loving and will not thrive in soils with a high pH. Others such as vegetables in the brassica family (cabbages, etc.) need a high pH to grow successfully.

As well as controlling what will grow in the soil, pH has an effect on pests and diseases. For instance, brassicas are less likely to get the disease clubroot if the pH is high. pH may also control the availability of certain plant nutrients.

Altering pH

The pH of a soil does not remain constant. The very action of rain and natural cycles within the soil, slowly make it more acid. From time to time it may be necessary to add lime or chalk to a soil to neutralise the acidity. A soil testing kit will usually also contain information on how much lime to use.

The most common garden lime is hydrated lime (calcium hydroxide), although chalk (calcium carbonate) can also be used. Lime should ideally be added to the soil in the autumn as the response is slow and may not be fully effective until the next spring. It is difficult to reverse the effects of liming so small quantities should be used and the effects monitored before adding more. Always wear rubber gloves, a dust mask and eye protection when applying lime as it can be an irritant.

Never apply lime at the same time as farmyard manure as the two react resulting in the release of excess ammonia, which will scorch roots and wastes the effect of both.

Should you wish to make a soil more acid, for example if you wanted to grow rhododendrons, this is possible but more difficult. Certain materials such as peat and flowers of sulphur will slowly make the soil more acid. Again, this is a slow process. It is probably easier to buy in a quantity of acid compost, often sold as ericaceous compost, in order to grow choice plants.

LIFE IN THE SOIL

Good soil is not a dead inert material but a living, thriving community all of its own. There are many small creatures, some visible such as earthworms, wood lice and centipedes, and other microscopic bacteria and fungi, which live within the soil and contribute to a healthy condition. In general they should be encouraged.

One of the main activities of soil organisms is breaking down dead materials within the soil and converting them to

SOURCES OF ORGANIC MATTER

- Garden compost
- Recycled green waste (from your local authority)
- Farmyard manure
- Chicken manure
- Spent mushroom compost
- Leaf mould
- Composted seaweed
- Composted bracken
- Spent hops or brewer's grains (from a brewery)

All of these can be valuable and may vary in price according to whether there is a local source. Farmyard or chicken manure must be well rotted before use or it can damage the roots of plants. Mushroom compost is good but is quite often alkaline so should never be used with plants that need an acid soil.

organic matter or humus. Organic matter in the soil is vitally important and adding this is one of the best ways of improving almost any type of soil. There are many different sources of organic matter but they will all be originally derived from living materials, either plant or animal in origin.

GARDENING ORGANICALLY

Some gardeners may choose to garden on an organic basis and this means growing as naturally as possible, without the use of any chemical fertilisers, pesticides or weed killers. This is quite possible and for many people a matter of strong personal belief. All gardeners should respect wildlife within the garden and the living aspects of the soil in particular. For those who feel less strongly, a moderated approach using a mix of organic principles and modern fertilisers together with a minimum of pesticides is often an acceptable compromise.

COMPOSTING

Composting is nevertheless a valuable process for all gardeners, whether traditional or organic in thinking. A compost heap provides a means of disposing of the majority of our garden and kitchen waste, without having to send to landfill. The end product is then a valuable commodity for enriching the soil – it's a double winner! A compost heap can be made in as little as a square metre, although it is better to have two, separate ones. This enables you to have one rotting down whilst you have the other

building up. Two heaps about the size of a cubic metre would be ideal for most small gardens. Larger gardens will need bigger heaps to deal with all the waste. To keep it tidy, a compost heap can be made within a bin of some sort. Proprietary bins made of plastic are available from garden centres or in some areas free from your local authority. Alternatively, a very usable bin can be made from old wooden pallets. Three sides will form a suitable enclosure; the fourth side needs to be loose so that access to the heap is possible.

Many different types of waste can be used in a compost heap. Some rough, loose material is useful at the bottom to keep the heap well drained. If you've had a previous heap, there are usually some tough remains that may not have been rotted properly and will be a useful base for the next one. Alternatively, use some rough prunings or

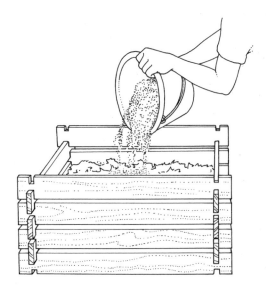

Notched and spaced timber slats can be used to make a good well-aerated compost container which can be extended as it is filled up.

hedge trimmings chopped up. A good heap is made up of a mixture of materials. Some wastes such as hedge clippings can be quite woody whereas others such as grass mowings are very soft and lush. Mixing various materials such as these together helps the different types to decompose. Small domestic shredders are now readily available and make it possible to process woody material such as prunings or tough hedge trimmings into smaller components that will decompose more evenly and quickly.

A compost heap will be constructed as materials become available but ideally different types of material should be mixed as added. If the constituents are dry, water should be added, as decomposition will not take place if it is dry. Compost activators are available, which can be added to encourage the natural organisms to work but these are not usually necessary if the heap is a good mixture of different ingredients.

About six weeks after the heap has been completed, it is a good practice to 'turn' the heap. This means taking the half-formed compost out, mixing it up, letting fresh air into the heap and stacking up again for the process to complete. Where there is space, this is where a second bin comes in handy. The compost can be forked out of one bin, shaken up and re-stacked in the next one. This process is not essential but certainly helps in producing good compost in a short space of time. A foul smell from a compost heap usually means that it is too wet, usually from too many lush materials such as wet grass mowings. Shaking it out and adding drier materials will usually help to get it back on course.

Compost is ready when it resembles a crumbly dark brown material in which you can barely recognise the original constituents. It should smell earthy but not unpleasant. This may take between three to six months depending on the time of year.

PROBLEM SOILS

We have already emphasised the importance of the soil to any garden and yet so often gardeners have to struggle with a problem soil. The following are some of the most familiar problems along with suggestions on dealing with them.

Compacted soils This is a common situation with a new garden. Contractors building new houses do not understand soil

MATERIALS TO ADD TO A COMPOST HEAP

- ⚘ Weeds (not perennial weeds)
- ⚘ Grass mowings
- ⚘ Autumn leaves
- ⚘ Dead plants and crops
- ⚘ Dead flower heads or cut flowers
- ⚘ Rootballs or used potting compost
- ⚘ Vegetable peelings from the kitchen
- ⚘ Tea leaves and coffee grounds
- ⚘ Torn up newspaper
- ⚘ Animal manures, such as bedding from pets
- ⚘ Hedge trimmings (chopped or shredded)
- ⚘ Prunings (if shredded)

Avoid perennial weeds, diseased plants and cooked foods or meats, which will attract vermin.

and the need to respect and protect it. Heavy machines will often have been used in the construction works and the soil will have become very compressed. Improving soils such as these is a slow and tough job. They need cultivating as deep as possible to let air into the soil, allow it to drain naturally and let roots penetrate easily. This is done by digging as deep as possible and breaking up all the compacted layers. The traditional technique of double digging is ideal, although it is slow and back-breaking work. Whilst cultivating the soil, add copious amounts of compost and sharp sand or gravel to try to keep the mixture open for the future.

Badly drained soils This problem is often associated with compaction but may occur on its own. Soils and often lawns stay permanently wet and are difficult to cultivate or use. This may be because the water table is too high. In a situation such as this, we need to open up the soil once again with cultivation, adding sharp sand for drainage. Ideally we would run perforated pipe drains through an area such as this, to take the water away completely. This is only possible if there is a ditch or pond into which the excess water can be drained.

Tired, worn-out soils An old garden around an old house, possibly in a city centre, will often have a dry, dust-like soil. This will have resulted from years of cultivation, sometimes with heavy tree cover stripping the nutrients from the soil. Such soils should be enriched with large quantities of organic matter to try to bring life back into them.

Toxic soils Occasionally one may come across an area of soil which just will not grow anything and it is possible that the soil may have become contaminated in some way. Common contaminants are oil and weed killer. Diesel or petrol from a vehicle or heating oil can penetrate the soil easily and render it useless for any sort of growing. Ideally such soils should be dug out and replaced with new soil. You would need to discuss the disposal of contaminated soil with your local refuse department, as there are strict regulations with regard to such disposal. A slower technique would be to keep the soil loosely cultivated to allow the residues of toxins to decompose. Test sowings of something simple such as cress will show whether the soil is able to support plant life. If the contamination is unknown, great care should be taken and using such soils for growing edible crops would not be recommended.

No topsoil Sadly, some gardens on new developments will have very little topsoil. They may have been turfed to give a 'green' appearance but will have no more than a few scant inches of topsoil. Such gardens are hard work! Initially it is worth digging a trial pit to see what's below the surface. It may be that the natural topsoil is buried under a cover of subsoil and builders' rubble. Sometimes hardcore or other stone materials may have been used in the construction to give a firm surface to work on and these may be mixed in with the topsoil or in a separate layer beneath the surface. A decision will need to be made as to whether it is feasible to remove unwanted materials or to bring buried topsoil back to the surface. Alternatively one has to work with the soil that's there. In this case it is important to cultivate carefully, breaking up any compaction and adding generous amounts of organic matter.

SOIL CULTIVATIONS

Any technique by which we move or turn the soil is regarded as cultivation. This will include, digging, forking, hoeing and raking. Soils should never be cultivated when wet. This is particularly important for clay soils, which are sticky and can easily be damaged if cultivated wet.

However, the most valuable technique is digging and is the basic technique for preparing soils for almost any type of growing. Digging is carried out using a spade, although with very heavy or compacted soils a fork may be easier. In digging we take a spadeful of soil and invert it. This has the effect of burying any unwanted vegetation and bringing to the surface a layer of fresh soil. The whole process improves drainage and aeration of the top layer of soil. Digging can be done at any time, although it is particularly valuable to dig clay soils before the winter as cold, winds and frost will help break up the surface and make it more friable for spring plantings.

Single digging

The basic method is single digging using a spade. To do this we should ideally take out a small trench the width of the area to be cultivated and transport the surplus soil to the far end of the plot. Digging then proceeds turning the soil into the open trench, inverting the soil, burying weeds and leaving

BUYING TOPSOIL

For various reasons you may occasionally need to buy topsoil, possibly because a new garden has little or because landscape alterations require areas to be topped up. Good topsoil can be difficult to buy and particularly difficult to assess. Always insist on seeing a sample before buying. Remember the simple tests for assessing a soil on pages 20–21. A good topsoil will be a loam with a mixture of sand, silt and clay and will be dark in colour showing the presence of organic matter. Check to make sure it does not contain the roots of pernicious weeds such as couch grass or bindweed.

The cheapest topsoils available are manufactured and often available from demolition or builders' merchants. They have often been made with a high proportion of ground-up brick and concrete. At an initial glance, they will appear attractive as they are often very finely sieved. In use, however, they pan down hard to a badly drained and lifeless material that is very difficult to cultivate. It is rarely necessary to buy a soil that has been screened and in fact a soil with a mixture of lumps and stones indicates that it is more likely to be good proper topsoil taken from the top of a field.

a fresh layer of soil on the surface. Digging proceeds working backwards to the end, where the surplus soil goes into the final trench. Compost or other organic matter can be added to the open trench before covering with soil. Gardeners often avoid making a trench and digging in this situation becomes a muddle.

Double digging

Double digging is a traditional and laborious technique that breaks up the soil to twice a spade's depth. It is very valuable on land that is compacted or has not been previously cultivated. Growers of exhibition vegetables will also value this technique. The process is started with a double width trench, say 60 cm (2 ft) wide. The soil is taken out and moved to the end of the plot as with single digging. The trench that is created is wide enough to work in and the base is then broken up, usually with a fork, down to another spit's depth. Organic matter can again be added before the topsoil is inverted into this trench, creating a second trench and so on.

NO DIG GARDENING

Sounds ideal, doesn't it! This is a technique whereby we give the soil minimum disturbance but apply a thick dressing of fresh garden compost each year and allow the worms and other organisms to incorporate it into the soil. This works very well with permanent plantings of shrubs, rose and other perennials. It can also work with the vegetable garden as we can sow directly into the new layer of compost.

The basic soil must be well cultivated and free from any drainage problems before embarking on this technique and it is essential not to compact the soil by walking on it. This therefore works best with small beds that can be tended from either side. The compost must be well rotted and weed free.

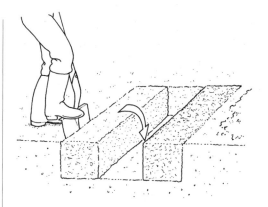

Single digging involves just turning over the top spit of soil and is adequate for most purposes.

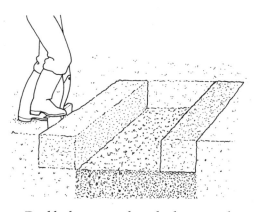

Double digging involves also loosening the second spit and is ideal for neglected gardens or new borders.

Other cultivations

A fork is more generally used for 'tickling' the surface of the soil, removing large weeds and breaking up clumps of soil. If forking amongst existing plants, avoid disturbing their roots systems. Raking is generally used as a technique for preparing level fine soil for a vegetable garden seedbed or for laying turf. A rake may be used to gather up unwanted debris such as stones or leaves from the surface. When raking use long steady but light strokes and avoid gathering up heaps of soil. Hoeing is primarily a method of weed control. The most common hoe is a Dutch hoe, which has a flat blade and is pushed through the soil. It slices off the weeds just below the surface and also leaves a layer of fine soil on the surface which is often claimed to act as a mulch and retain moisture.

FEEDING PLANTS

All plants need nutrients to grow and develop. The three main elements needed by plants are nitrogen, phosphorous and potassium (sometimes called potash) and generally referred to as NPK from their chemical symbols. These are required in large quantities for growth. Generally one thinks of nitrogen as the nutrient that promotes leaf growth, phosphorous for roots and potassium for flowers or fruit.

In addition, plants all require a range of other elements in differing levels. Magnesium (Mg), calcium (Ca), and sulphur (S) are the next most important. Finally there are those that are required in minute quantities and are usually called trace elements. These include iron (Fe), manganese (Mn), copper (Cu), zinc (Zn), boron (Bo), molybdenum (Mb) and chlorine (Cl).

There are many types of fertiliser that will contain varying amounts of all or some of these for different purposes. It is virtually never necessary to add sulphur as it is normally present as part of other compounds such as ammonium sulphate. Nowadays there is a bewildering range of fertilisers available for use and products will be described in many different ways.

USING A ROTAVATOR

The use of a rotary cultivator to quickly cultivate large areas seems very attractive, particularly to those with limited time and such machines can be very valuable but they do have problems.

Rotavators are heavy pieces of equipment and handling them to cultivate neglected soil can be hard, shoulder-wrenching work – not a job for the frail! Rotavators also smash through the soil and can quickly turn good soils into either dust or a sticky mess. They should only be used when the soil is moist but not wet. Make several passes over the area, aiming to go a little deeper each time. Any perennial weeds in the area will just be chopped up into small fragments multiplying the problem so avoid rotavating weedy ground.

Chemical or inorganic fertilisers These are factory produced, generally cheap and the type of fertilisers widely used in agriculture, for vegetable or fruit production or for fertilising lawns.

Organic fertilisers These originate from some sort of natural product and include fertilisers such as bonemeal or dried blood. They will generally be more expensive and slower in reaction than chemical fertilisers as the material has to break down in the soil to release the nutrients.

Straight fertilisers These are simple chemicals providing one of two nutrients, for example superphosphate – a phosphorous fertiliser. These are generally rather outdated and rarely used nowadays as their use means stocking and applying a number of different fertilisers.

Compound or balanced fertilisers These have a blend of different nutrients within them supplying all of the plant's needs at a certain time. One of the most common would be 'Growmore', a cheap balanced chemical fertiliser widely used for vegetable production.

Slow-release fertilisers These are generally the 'Rolls Royce' of fertilisers and will have all the nutrients required bound up in a small pill, which breaks down slowly within the soil, feeding the plants over a predictable span of time. Such fertilisers are very useful in providing a whole season's nutrients in one application. Larger pellets or plugs of slow-release fertiliser are available for pot plants and even for young trees.

Liquid feeds Some fertilisers are soluble and can be supplied as a liquid feed. They may be sold as a concentrated liquid that is diluted or as a powder, which is dissolved before applying. In both cases they must be diluted with the correct amount of water before using. Liquid feeds have the advantage of being immediately accessible to the plant and so giving a rapid response. They are particularly valuable for pot plants, summer planters or hanging baskets and fast-growing crops such as tomatoes. Liquid feeds should never be applied to a plant that is dry as root scorch may occur.

WHAT'S ON THE PACKET

By law all fertilisers have to be packaged with the analysis of contents on the outside. It will usually have a six-figure code, maybe 15-30-15, which refers to the relative proportions of NPK. It will probably also have a detailed analysis of the percentage of each nutrient. This is useful to determine whether trace elements are present or not.

The packet should also have a rate of application or for dilution in the case of liquid fertilisers. You should always read the instructions and never exceed the rates recommended. In fact applying a half rate application then repeating at a later stage can be useful if there is any concern about causing scorch.

Whenever handling fertilisers it is wise to wear rubber gloves. Fertilisers can cause dermatitis or make the skin very dry. When applying large quantities, for example in the case of an allotment or lawn, it is wise to wear a dust mask to avoid inhaling the finer particles.

Foliar feeds These are similar to liquid feeds but instead of applying to the roots, they are sprayed directly on to the leaves and rapidly assimilated. Great care needs to be taken not to scorch the foliage. They are more likely to be used to correct minor trace element deficiencies in fruit trees, where it would take a long time for root applications to work.

Many of the above explanatory terms can be used together because they describe different aspects about a fertiliser. So, for example, we could have a slow-release, inorganic fertiliser like many modern commercial products or an organic balanced fertiliser such as blood, fish and bone – a very smelly mixture of traditional constituents!

WATER IN THE SOIL

An adequate supply of water is essential for healthy plant growth. The amount required will depend on different plants. For example, a tomato crop in the full flush of summer growth inside a greenhouse will have a massive daily requirement of water. By contrast, there are many plants such as succulents and grey leaved plants, that have a low water requirement and many gardens are designed nowadays to avoid the need for artificial irrigation. Such 'dry gardens' as they are often called are fashionable and environmentally sound. Water is a valuable commodity and when using in the garden we should be aware of how to avoid wasting it.

A good well-structured soil will have plenty of open spaces within it, which not only allow for air to penetrate but are also capable of absorbing water. Good soils act as a sponge holding water in reserve ready for use by plants. Clay soils with tiny particles and tiny air spaces hold the greatest amount of water. Sandy soils have larger pores and although they fill up easily with water, this drains away quickly and is therefore not held in reserve for the plants. In general you will have to water a sandy soil more often than a clay soil.

When it rains or when we irrigate a soil, all the spaces become filled up with water and the soil becomes saturated. When the rain or irrigation stops, the excess water runs away leaving the soil holding water within its finer pores. This stage, where there is both air and plenty of water within the soil, is known as 'field capacity' and is the ideal condition in which roots function and plants grow. As plants grow they remove the water from the soil until a stage is reached where they can remove no more and the plant starts to wilt. Ideally we should try to keep soils at field capacity, although in many garden situations this is not always possible.

If the excess moisture cannot drain away after rain or irrigation, the soil remains water-logged. This may be because the soil is compacted and the water cannot flow freely through it or because the general water table is too high. The water table is the level of natural water within the soil. Moisture is able to rise within soils by means of capillary action, so for example clay soils, which have strong capillary action, may be saturated for up to 2 m (6 ft) above the water table.

Under waterlogged conditions, roots do not thrive as there is no air present and may die if waterlogging persists. In this situation, with dead roots, the plant cannot take up water and so will wilt, which seems contradictory in a waterlogged situation.

IRRIGATION

Applying water to garden areas is known as irrigation and may be necessary in dry seasons or with plants in greenhouses or containers that hold limited quantities of water. In general, the principle should always be to apply generous quantities of water to allow the soil to become fully charged. Repeating this need not take place until the soil is showing signs of drying. Frequent applications of water are not recommended as they only dampen the surface and do not penetrate to the roots.

Some plants may have critical water requirements that vary with the seasons. For example raspberries must have adequate water when the fruits are swelling or they just shrivel. Tomatoes must have enough water when the flowers are ready for pollination or the fruit does not set, and potatoes must have generous supplies of water when the tubers are swelling. These are just a few examples.

Apply water to garden areas thoroughly using a hose to get soils completely moist down to root levels. A good sprinkler with coarse droplets will help. It is best to irrigate in the evening or at night rather than in bright sunshine or windy conditions, when a proportion of the water will be lost by evaporation. Professionally-planted trees often have a watering unit, which is a perforated pipe buried at the same time as the tree is planted. Watering then takes place directly into this tube putting the water exactly where it is needed below the surface, around the roots. On a small scale we can mimic this by scooping out a shallow depression around important plants that we want to water and so directing the water to the right area. Alternatively plant pots can be partially buried around choice plants and then filled with water, which percolates directly into the rooting zone.

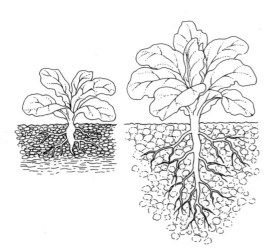

Compacted soils result in restricted root growth and poor top growth (left) compared to a thriving plant where roots can fully penetrate the soil (right).

Directing water to a flower pot buried next to a new plant enables the water to get directly to the root system.

MULCHING

This is a gardening technique that has many values. It refers quite simply to the spreading of some material over the surface of the soil. This is often a bulky organic material such as mushroom compost, shredded bark or leaf mould. It can be something inert such as gravel, ornamental stones or even coloured glass chippings. In the kitchen garden or nursery areas we might even use polythene or a purpose-made horticultural fabric.

In general all of these materials are valuable in that they help to retain moisture in the soil by reducing evaporation from the surface. Mulches should always be applied when the soil is already moist so that we trap the water within the soil. Organic mulches will slowly break down and as they do so will provide nutrients and act as general soil improvers. Sometimes in the past they were regarded as important sources of nutrients and so for example soft fruit bushes or roses would be annually mulched with farmyard manure. A mulch should be applied between 7.5–10 cm (3–4 in) deep. Shallow mulches are not effective.

All mulches also act as weed suppressants and prevent the germination of most weed seeds. Gravel and other inert materials will not have soil improving abilities but are very effective as weed smotherers. All mulches also help to regulate soil temperatures keeping them cool in summer and warmer in winter.

RAINWATER

For most plants there is little advantage in using rainwater as opposed to tap water, however, rhododendrons, camellias and other lime haters will benefit from rainwater, which will have a low or neutral pH.

However, in this era of water shortages, we should emphasise the environmental value of storing rainwater in a water butt and reducing the use of town water. Various techniques and pieces of equipment are available to divert rainwater into a storage butt. It should be emphasised that such stored water is however stagnant and may contain plant diseases so should not be used in greenhouses or with any young seedlings.

TOOLS AND EQUIPMENT

A BAD WORKMAN BLAMES HIS TOOLS was the phrase my father always used if I got something wrong! Whether or not it's true, a good gardener needs a combination of skills and the right tools to do the job. Visit a good garden centre and you will discover an alarming array of tools, most of which you do not need to buy. A few basic tools will enable you to do the majority of basic tasks and you can add to these as interests develop. Good quality tools will inevitably last longer and perform better than cheap ones but it may not be wise to spend large sums of money until you are sure what you want.

THE BASICS

The basics for all gardening are a spade, fork, rake, hoe, trowel, secateurs and probably a wheelbarrow, depending on the size of your garden. Spades vary in the length of the handle which is quite key to comfortable work. The handle may be either shaped as a 'T' or a 'Y' or a 'D'. The shaft of the spade will be either wood or metal. Although metal will last longer, it makes using the spade heavier and therefore much harder work. A stainless steel blade will make digging much easier but will be more expensive. There is a smaller size spade available, called a border spade, which is lighter and may be more suitable for those with less strength. Handle the spades on display until you are comfortable with one.

A fork is probably the second most useful tool and is used for a myriad of jobs. Again a variety is available including the smaller border fork, which is a very useful tool for working in confined areas.

The most useful rake is a standard steel-headed rake that can be used to break down soil, level and create a tilth. A wire-toothed rake, sometimes called a 'springbok', is useful if you are going to have to rake leaves in the autumn. Fancy proprietary variations exist.

Hoes come in many different styles. The Dutch hoe is the most useful for simple weeding and it is used with a pushing action, whilst walking backwards. There are some fancy versions of it where the blade is wavy edged or where both sides are sharpened. It is often forgotten that to efficiently control weeds with a hoe, the tool should be kept sharp. If you are growing vegetables, then a draw hoe will be needed, partly for drawing out drills for seeds and also for earthing up potatoes. Most hoes come in various widths. Hoes with short handles, called onion hoes, are very useful for close work such as in rock gardens.

A trowel is a small tool but choose it carefully, selecting one that has a smooth handle that fits comfortably in your hand. A poorly designed trowel can soon cause a blister on the palm of your hand. Some are marked with dimensions, which can be useful with gauging the right depth to plant bulbs. In general it is always useful to know the length of the trowel you are using as it can be a useful handy measure when planting things like bedding plants.

A wheelbarrow may or may not be an essential depending on the size of your

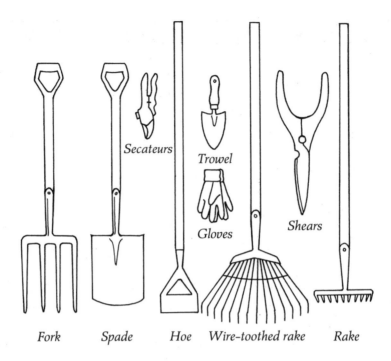

Secateurs

Trowel

Gloves

Shears

Fork   Spade   Hoe   Wire-toothed rake   Rake

Most of the common garden jobs can be done with a remarkably small 'arsenal' of equipment that need not cost too much. If you are not sure of something, buy a cheap item and then buy a more expensive one when you are clearer on choices.

garden. Many people make do with a bucket, a trug or a garden sheet with four handles at the corners for carrying. Sheets are good for light bulky materials such as hedge trimmings. Small garden barrows have hard tyres which are adequate but do not help with moving heavy loads. A simple builder's barrow from a DIY store or builder's merchant is a sound investment for larger gardens. If transporting materials is a real issue, there are also barrows with large wheels like balloons and also ones with two wheels sometimes called garden carts.

Secateurs and other pruning tools will be dealt with under the section on pruning (see page 57). Those with a lawn will need a pair of edging shears and if doing any lawn repairs a half-moon edger. A watering can is always useful and plastic ones will be the lightest and longest lasting. When buying hose pipe, do buy good quality reinforced hose that will not kink and a reel to wind it on as it's always a good investment.

You should always have a stout pair of gardening gloves to protect your hands when doing tough jobs. Having also spent a lifetime with dry chapped gardening hands, I am also a fervent user of the disposable vinyl gloves for all garden jobs. Use a good skin cream on your hands before and after a gardening session. Some people may also find the use of a kneeling pad or even a kneeling stool with handles useful. Other tools may be required for specific job.

GARDEN MACHINERY

Probably the greatest advances in recent years have been in the variety and complexity of garden machinery. You can get a machine for doing almost any garden job imaginable, although some of these will be inappropriate for the amateur gardener. Some machines you will need to own, for example a lawnmower, which is very much an essential if you have a lawn. Others you may only use occasionally, such as a rotavator or lawn spiker and will be most economical to hire, as and when you need them.

Machines will either be based on a petrol engine or need an electrical supply. With a petrol engine, you will need to make sure you use the correct fuel. Some machines will need a mixture of petrol and oil which is known as two-stroke mixture and must be mixed to the correct proportions. Remember all fuels are flammable. Electrical equipment

LOOKING AFTER TOOLS

Good tools are worth looking after. Always wipe the mud off tools before putting away under cover. If you wash them, don't forget to dry, to avoid them going rusty. Ideally you should finish off with a quick wipe with an oily rag to protect the metal. Keep secateurs and any other cutting tools sharpened ready for use.

must be connected to a circuit protected with a residual current device (RCD). Modern installations include this at the fuse box but if you are unsure, use an RCD adapter with the plug. Be particularly careful with cables to make sure they are never damaged and keep them well away from any cutting blades. Never use electrical equipment in the rain.

GIMMICKS AND GIZMOS

Do beware of highly advertised gadgets that promise to do all sorts of things in wonderful ways! For example, tools with multi heads that fit on single handles and gadgets that promise to do the work with a fraction of the normal energy. The weekend newspapers and gardening magazines are full of adverts for wonder inventions. Over the years improvements have been made in tools but there are no miracle-working tools. By all means consider anything new but as always, buyer beware!

Lawnmowers

Some mowers are based on a cylinder with cutting blades, which generally gives a very neat close-cut finish. Cylinder mowers usually have a rear roller, which gives the traditional striped effect and normally have a grass box to collect the clippings. The more blades it has on the cylinder, the neater the finish. Five is the normal for a quality lawn. The blades on cylinder mowers are easily damaged and need re-grinding annually which can be an expensive job.

Rotary mowers have a horizontal rotating blade. They generally don't give such a close-cut finish but are good for long and rough grass. Some have a rear roller and may have

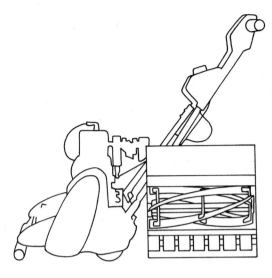

Cylinder mowers are the 'Rolls Royce' of mowers and produce an excellent cut and striped finish, collecting the mowings as you go.

Hover mowers are very good for banks and more general grass areas but rarely collect the clippings or leave stripes.

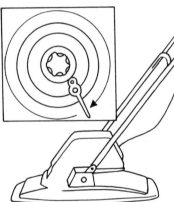

Petrol-engine rotary mowers are usually powerful machines that are good for cutting rough and long grass. They may have a grass box or bag and some have a roller to stripe the grass.

a grass box. Rotary mowers are also sometimes based on a hovercraft principle and the mower floats over the surface on a cushion of air. Hover mowers do not collect the mowings or leave stripes but are very good for sloping banks.

Ride-on versions of both cylinder and rotary mowers are available for those with large grass areas. Such machines often double as garden tractors and can be used to tow small trailers or operate other implements.

Strimmers

These are machines with a rotating head consisting of a tough but flexible nylon thread. They are good for trimming edges, around obstacles and corners inaccessible to a mower. If the nylon line is damaged, another section is easily fitted so it can be used in fairly rough situations. A strimmer is carried or sometimes attached to a harness worn over the shoulders that takes the weight. Strimmers can be powered by electricity or by a small two-stroke petrol engine. Petrol strimmers can sometimes be fitted with a metal brushcutter blade which enables it to tackle very tough weeds including brambles and woody weeds. When using a strimmer, you should always wear goggles as it can cause stones or other debris to fly. Some strimmers can be fitted with metal blades for tough work and in this situation, boots with steel toe caps are a wise precaution.

Rotary cultivators

These are sometimes simply called rotavators. Some mention of their use and the effects on soil is mentioned on page 28. Rotavators are always powered by a petrol or diesel engine so are always relatively heavy powerful pieces of equipment. Some have rubber-tyred driving wheels with the rotors mounted behind. Generally these are the best machines for heavy deep cultivation, especially when trying to break up compacted soil. Some of the smaller ones just have small wheels for transport, which are removed when using the machine. These are driven through the soil by the rotors themselves and are less powerful but will stir up soil that has been previously cultivated, producing a reasonable tilth. Some cultivators have a variety of attachments but multi-purpose machines are less likely to do any job as well as a bespoke machine.

SAFETY

All machines are powerful pieces of equipment and as well as doing a job, can easily inflict injury if they are not respected.

- Always check a machine over before starting
- Never remove the guards on a machine
- Always turn off a machine and immobilise before attempting repair or adjustment
- Remember petrol is highly flammable
- Always use an RCD with electrical equipment
- Keep cables away from cutting edges
- Use appropriate protective clothing, steel toe-capped boots, gloves, goggles and ear protectors
- Ensure safety of others in the area, especially children

Hedge trimmers

These are essential for anyone with a large hedge. They can be powered by a petrol engine, mains electricity or a battery. Those with a petrol engine will be powerful but heavy and noisy. With mains electricity, you are limited by the source and length of cable which is also a safety hazard. Battery power may seem desirable but they lack power for tough work and may run out of power before finishing the job with anything other than a small hedge.

Trimmers with a longer blade will do the job quicker but will be heavier. Some have double-sided cutting blades but these are less easy for the amateur to handle. The spacing of the teeth controls the type of cut. Widely spaced teeth will be good for a rough hedge such as thorn, that is perhaps cut once a year, whereas closely spaced teeth will be needed for a fine finish on, say, box or yew. Always wear gloves, goggles for eye protection and ear protectors when using hedge trimmers, and make sure to turn off the power at the mains when not in use.

CHAINSAWS – A WARNING!

Chainsaws are available to the amateur for both purchase and hire. However, they are very powerful pieces of equipment that are capable of causing great injury and it is advisable that they are never used without proper training and the full protective clothing, which is rarely available from hire shops. In particular, the amateur gardener should never attempt tree surgery with a chainsaw. Never use a chainsaw from a ladder – the professional doesn't so neither should the amateur. If it's too big to cut with a handsaw or beyond reasonable reach from the ground, DON'T DO IT!

Other machines

Powered spikers and scarifiers are available for autumn lawn maintenance and these are probably best hired. As everyone is likely to want them at the same time, book in advance! Post hole borers can be useful if you are building a fence. There are also various blowers and vacuum devices that can be used for leaf collection.

PLANT PROPAGATION

GROWING YOUR OWN NEW PLANTS can be one of the most exciting and fascinating aspects of gardening. Seeing the end results of fully grown plants that you have nurtured from a small seed or a frail cutting can be very rewarding and very cost effective compared to buying from a nursery or garden centre. Having spare plants can also be very useful as it provides opportunities to exchange plants or contribute to local plant sales.

There are many techniques of propagation, some quite simple, others more complex. Many gardeners do some of these, such as sowing seeds or dividing perennials as routine jobs. Others are more complicated and may need special equipment and skills or the use of a warm environment such as a greenhouse. Understanding some of the basic principles of propagation will give a greater level of success and encouragement to try more ambitious methods.

COMPOSTS AND HYGIENE

Whilst talking about propagation we will often speak about different composts – these are the growing media that we particularly use for growing plants in containers. Seed composts have very low nutrient levels and are used for seed sowing. Potting composts will have more nutrients and are used for pricking out and potting young plants. A cuttings compost can easily be made by mixing sand and peat, or peat and fine bark. Proprietary mixes are available. There are also many multi-purpose composts available, which do not perform perfectly for any one function but will be adequate for most purposes and avoid the need for lots of different bags. They have low nutritional levels so additional liquid feeding must start at an early stage.

Traditionally most potting composts were made from a mix of loam (soil), peat and sand. A range of standard mixes were developed called the John Innes Composts and these are still available and very good for some uses. There is a John Innes Seed Compost then three potting composts with increasing levels of nutrition. For short, they are often labelled JIP1, JIP2 and JIP3. The latter is good for tubs and outdoor planters.

Then there was a move towards composts that were not based on loam and these were quite simply called loamless composts. They were often based on peat, sometimes mixed with other materials together with a balance of fertilisers. These composts were lighter to carry, easier to water and gave predictable results. In recent years there has been a move away from peat-based composts for environmental reasons and now non-peat composts are available based on materials such as coir, bark, wood chips or other recycled materials. Although these can produce acceptable results they are nowhere near as easy to use and the results can be disappointing. Peat-based composts generally remain the most popular, predictable and effective.

Cleanliness is essential for plant propagation. Young seedlings or rooting cuttings are very vulnerable and can easily

THE PEAT DEBATE

For some years, there has been much debate about the use of peat in horticulture and great concern about the loss of the sphagnum bogs due to the harvesting of peat. The arguments are however not clear and many would suggest that the harvesting of peat for horticulture is a minor use compared to others. Also although most would agree that the loss of peat bogs is of concern, there is an opinion that the loss on a worldwide scale is minor.

The alternatives to peat such as coir, bark and other products still need much research and particularly where we are considering potting and propagating composts. Not all alternatives are as environmentally friendly as they might seem at face value. Coir, for example, has to be shipped long distances with the inevitable use of fossil fuel. Although most would agree that we should limit our use of peat to essential purposes, it is still the best material for growing media and shouldn't be immediately vetoed.

fall prey to a number of damping-off or rotting diseases. Although it may be possible to control these, it is better to avoid and this is done by good hygiene. Always use clean pots and fresh compost. Never be tempted to use rainwater out of a water butt or storage tank for seedlings or propagation. It is very likely to be contaminated with various fungal infections.

GROWING FROM SEED

Seed is the most common way by which plants reproduce and spread themselves in nature. It's is an entirely natural process that happens in gardens, forests and fields throughout the world. Seed of many cultivated plants is readily available and provides probably the cheapest and easiest way of producing new plants, particularly where large quantities are required.

A seed is an amazing structure, in that within an often quite tiny structure there is all that is required to initiate a new plant. Seeds have their own store of foods that enable them to remain alive, often for long periods of time until they are ready to germinate. When the new seedling germinates and starts to grow, it contains all

F1 HYBRID PLANTS

Any gardener perusing a modern seed catalogue will soon see the term F1 hybrid. These ranges of seed, generally available for vegetables and bedding plants, provide plants that are very uniform and may have other desirable characteristics such as early flowering, high cropping or even disease resistance. They are often more expensive than other seed but the results are virtually always worth the extra cost. F1 hybrid seed is produced under controlled conditions, whereby two known parent plants are crossed to produce the 'first filial generation'. It may have taken the plant breeders many years to get to the situation with the two parents that produce the F1 hybrid, hence the high cost.

The same cross has to be repeated by the seed producers each time to produce these. Therefore seed saved from F1 hybrids will not show the good characteristics of the F1 hybrid itself and may in fact be very disappointing so do not save seed from F1 hybrids.

the genetic information needed for it to grow into a full mature plant. Seeds do not always provide offspring that are identical to their parent plants. Indeed the ability to produce something different is the very basis of plant hybridisation, which enables the plant breeders to continually produce new and better plants than previously.

Generally most seeds require three basics for germination – water, warmth and air. A few seeds require light and some require their dormancy to be broken in a specific way before they will germinate but more about the difficult ones later!

OUTDOOR SEED SOWING

If we are sowing vegetables or hardy flower seeds in the soil outside, we will need to prepare a seed bed to give suitable conditions for sowing. Soil will initially have been dug or forked over. It will then need to be raked down to a fine level seed bed. Seeds do not actually need any nutrients for the initial germination process, although a pre-seeding fertiliser may be applied at this stage and raked in as part of the final seed bed preparation.

In order to give those ideal conditions for germination, the soil should be moist and the surface suitably open and loose to allow air to penetrate. Warmth will be determined by the date when we sow the seed and the natural warmth in the soil at that time. Many new gardeners are anxious to get started and often sow seeds too early before the soil has had time to warm up in the spring. A later sowing, when the soil is naturally warm, will usually catch up an earlier sowing, which will struggle or die in a cold soil.

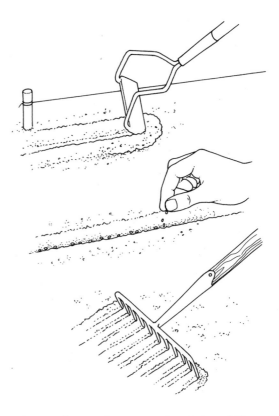

Most outdoor seed sowing is done into a drill created using a draw hoe and then covering the seeds with a light raking.

Seeds should always be sown at the correct depth, which is usually very shallow. As a rough guide, the amount of soil over a seed should be no more than twice its diameter. Large seeds such as beans, with a diameter of about 1 cm ($3/8$ in) will need to be covered with 2 cm ($3/4$ in) soil. With tiny dust-like seeds no more than 2 mm ($1/8$ in) across, the depth of covering must be no more than about 4 mm ($1/4$ in). If the seed is buried too deeply, the tiny germinating seedling will not have enough food reserves to reach the surface and the light before it dies.

When sowing outside, it is possible to broadcast seeds freely over the surface and just rake into the soil. This, however, is not ideal as the depth of covering is very vague and the resulting seedlings will be very difficult to differentiate from weeds germinating at the same time.

It is therefore far better to sow seeds outside in a seed drill. This is a very narrow and shallow slit cut in the soil. This can be drawn with a stick alongside a plank or with a draw hoe alongside a garden line stretched tightly across the soil surface. The depth of the seed drill can be fairly accurately gauged for the seed and after sowing the seeds are covered by lightly raking the soil back into the drill. When the seeds germinate in a neat straight row, it is then fairly easy to separate weeds from the plants you are intending to grow.

SOWING SEED IN CONTAINERS

Although we are generally thinking here of sowing seed in a glasshouse, it is also possible to raise plants in this way on a warm windowsill or in a cold frame. The containers used will be seed trays or, for small quantities, small flower pots. It is important to use a proprietary seed sowing or all-purpose compost as garden soil is not suitable for use here. Such a proper growing media will have been carefully blended to have all the right proportions of materials to give ideal conditions for germination.

Carefully fill the container to overflowing, tap on the bench to lightly consolidate and then strike off the excess with a ruler or slat of wood. The surface is then further lightly

firmed using a suitable presser board or the base of another plant pot. The compost should then be thoroughly watered using a watering can with a fine rose so as not to disturb the level surface of the compost. Allow excess water to drain away and the unit is ready for seed sowing.

Seeds can be sown with a pinching action from the hand or from a sheet of folded paper. Whatever way is used, be sure to sow thinly and evenly. Leave space for each tiny

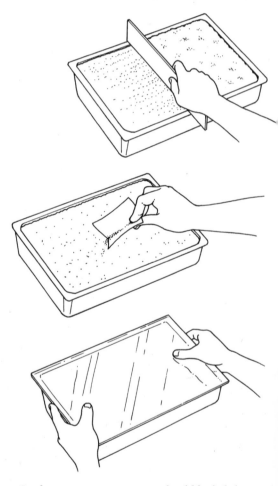

Seeds sown into containers should be lightly sown and then covered with glass and paper to encourage germination.

seed to develop into a seedling when it germinates. After sowing, the seed should be covered remembering the basic principle that the covering depth should not be more than twice the diameter of the seed. The covering in this instance is most easily applied by shaking through a small garden sieve. Don't be tempted to use a kitchen sieve, which has far too small a screen size! Normally we would finish off the process by covering with a sheet of black polythene to keep out the light and help retain the moisture. Remember that some seeds may require light and so should not be covered, although the packet will usually remind you of this.

Seeds sown in this way should be placed in a warm place such as a propagator, a heated greenhouse or a kitchen windowsill. Never be tempted to sow seeds too early. Many tender seeds such as bedding plants will require a temperature of around 21° C (70° F). This will normally require a heated greenhouse or propagator, although successful results for many plants can be obtained in an unheated greenhouse if sowings are delayed until mid spring. The germination temperature does vary from plant to plant so it is always worth checking the packet for any specific requirements.

Check sown seeds daily. If the compost shows signs of drying, water gently using a watering can with a fine rose. The black plastic should be turned each day so that the dry surface goes back onto the compost to avoid a build up of excess moisture on the surface. As soon as there is any sign of germination, the black plastic should be removed. For the first day or so seedlings should be kept in light shade to avoid

DAMPING OFF DISEASE

This is a problem that particularly affects young seedlings which suddenly wilt, topple over and die. It is caused by various fungi that are often present in dirty conditions. Seed trays and pots should always be washed before use and new clean compost should always be used for seed sowing. Water from water butts and tanks should never be used for seedlings as this is often infected. Keep seedlings in warm, well-lit areas and with some ventilation when the weather is suitable. A copper fungicide can be used as a preventative drench when watering.

scorching. When fully emerged, place them in full light to ensure that they grow into sturdy seedlings.

PRICKING OUT

This is the process by which seedlings are separated and moved on into other containers where they can grow into young plants. It is best done at an early stage, as soon as you can handle the small seedlings. The containers will either be further seed trays or small pots. These will be filled, this time with a potting compost or again a multi-purpose compost. Seed trays will take generally 35 or 48 seedlings (seven rows of five, or eight rows of six seedlings) evenly spaced and will enable more plants to be grown in a small area. Pots will be used for individual seedlings and will produce fewer but better quality plants.

After filling and tapping to lightly consolidate, the seedlings are gently separated and

DORMANCY

Some plants produce seed, which will not germinate immediately because it has a dormancy factor. This means that the seed needs particular conditions to break the dormancy before it can go ahead and germinate. Seeds of many hardy plants such as holly or rowan need a period of cold or actual freezing before they will germinate. This means that seed must be sown in the autumn and left outside exposed to the cold over winter. Such seed will then often germinate freely in the spring. Make sure rodents or birds don't steal the seed by protecting with wire netting.

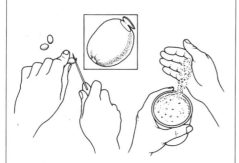

Scarification and stratification are both ways of overcoming a plant's natural dormancy.

Other seeds such as most legumes and also cannas have very hard seed coats and would naturally be very slow to germinate. We can speed this up by scarifying the seed. This means that in some way we gently break through the hard seed coat to allow water to penetrate and germination to start. Some seeds can be nicked with a knife whereas others will need a small file, sandpaper or a hacksaw to penetrate through the hard seed coat. Following this with soaking in water is also often beneficial for many seeds.

carefully levered out using a plant label or old fork. A hole is dibbed in the new container and the roots of the seedling gently transferred. Seedlings should always be handled by their leaves only and never the stem, which is too fragile at this stage. Gently cover over the roots and lightly firm into place. In general seedlings should always be pricked out at the same depth as before and not buried. There are a few exceptions to this such as tomatoes, which are pricked out down to, but not burying, their seed leaves.

Water the seedlings lightly and grow in a warm, light environment such as a greenhouse or sunny windowsill.

Make an adequate hole for the roots and handle seedlings carefully by the leaves only when pricking out.

CUTTINGS

Many plants can be easily propagated by taking cuttings, which generally involves the removal of a piece of a plant, which is then induced to produce its own roots and become established as an independent plant. Sharp knives, secateurs, suitable rooting composts and a selection of pots and trays are the basic requirements. Hormone rooting powders can also be very useful and speed up the process of rooting, particularly with difficult subjects. These are synthetic products but are based on natural auxins that exist in all plants. Ideally, many cuttings will prefer to be rooted in a heated propagator within a greenhouse but successful results can be achieved with a cold frame or on a windowsill.

STEM CUTTINGS

The simplest type of cutting is a softwood tip cutting and is used for propagating many plants such as hardy shrubs, fuchsias, chrysanthemums and pelargoniums. This is prepared by removing the soft tip of a shoot. It is reduced to about 7.5 cm (3 in) with about three leaves or pairs of leaves. The base of the cutting is trimmed just below a joint which is correctly known as a node. Some of the lower leaves may be removed to leave a bare stem.

Such a cutting can be dipped into hormone rooting powder and then inserted into a pot of cuttings compost. Several cuttings can usually be inserted around the edge of a pot. For larger quantities, seed trays can be used. Such cuttings have no roots and so we must ensure that they remain as moist as possible. This is done by either placing them in a closed propagating frame or within

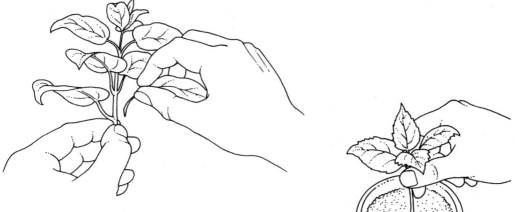

Remove the lower leaves from a softwood tip cutting cleanly to avoid leaving 'snags'.

Dip the cutting in a hormone rooting powder before inserting in rooting compost.

a plastic bag. Softwood cuttings are usually prepared in spring or early summer when growth is soft and young, although within a glasshouse this may be possible throughout the year.

Semi-ripe cuttings are very similar to the above except they will be taken in late summer or early autumn when growth has started to ripen and is less lush. Semi-ripe cuttings are often used for evergreen shrubs and for conifers. Conifers are slow to root and can be encouraged by removing a sliver of bark at the base of the stem before dipping in rooting powder. This is called wounding and exposes more of the cambium tissues, the part of the stem that produces roots.

WEANING

A rooted cutting is a new plant capable of life on its own but is still fragile. You should slowly acclimatise rooted cuttings to normal conditions, removing them from the propagator but still keeping lightly shaded and damped over for a few days. When nicely established, they can be potted up separately in potting compost in individual pots. Again keep shaded and damped over until settled in their new pots.

HARDWOOD CUTTINGS

These are prepared from leafless stems in the autumn and winter months and are used for deciduous plants such as some shrubs and also soft fruits such as currants and gooseberries. They can be prepared from about late autumn to mid winter by cutting up stems into sections about 20 cm (8 in) long. These should be trimmed just above a bud at the top and just below a bud at the bottom.

WINDOWSILL PROPAGATION

Many houseplants and common shrubs can be easily propagated on a shady windowsill with simple equipment. A plastic bag can be used to cover a pot of cuttings with the base secured with an elastic band. The bag should be removed on a daily basis and turned inside out so that the cuttings do not stay excessively wet.

Alternatively the base of a plastic soft drinks bottle can be removed and used as a tiny propagator to cover a small pot of cuttings. Again it should be wiped out each day to avoid a build-up of excess moisture. Cuttings of many plants can easily be rooted in two to three weeks in this way.

Hardwood cuttings can be lined out in a narrow trench partially filled with sharp sand.

As they have no leaves they do not require fussy conditions for rooting so can be inserted in a trench in the garden. Lining this with sand helps to avoid the cuttings rotting if the winter is wet. They should be deeply inserted, about 15 cm (6 in) apart, leaving no more than two or three buds above ground. Be sure to insert them the right way up and gently firm the soil round them. They will not root and grow away until next spring but growth is often fast and young plants will be ready for transplanting the following autumn.

LEAF CUTTINGS

This technique is generally used for various fleshy-leaved houseplants. Individual leaves from African violets or peperomias are detached and used as cuttings. The leaf stalk roots and a new plant develops from the base. With *Begonia rex* (King begonia), the whole leaf is pinned down and new plantlets form where the leaf veins touch the compost. Alternatively the leaf can be cut up into small postage-stamp sized squares which are used as individual cuttings.

Leaf cuttings from plants such as African Violet are inserted with the petiole intact.

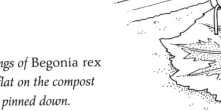

Leaf cuttings of Begonia rex *are laid flat on the compost and pinned down.*

Trim the top of a root cutting squarely across the stem and the base at an angle.

Insert root cuttings ensuring you have them the right way up with the slanted cut at the base.

ROOT CUTTINGS

A few fleshy rooted perennials have the ability to produce new plants from sections of root. Oriental poppies and phlox can be propagated in this way. This technique takes place in the dormant season. Sections of root between 2.5–5 cm (1–2 in) are prepared. Thick roots such as poppy can be inserted vertically in a pot of compost. Thinner roots such as those of phlox are laid on the surface of the compost and given a light covering. They will require a little protection such as an unheated greenhouse or cold frame. New plants will be produced in the spring.

LAYERING

This is rather like taking a cutting but without severing the shoot from the parent plant, so is much easier to carry out. It is useful for many hardy shrubs, especially those which are otherwise difficult to propagate. Magnolias and clematis can be rooted this way. A suitable shoot is bent down to the ground. At the point where it will touch the ground, a small incision is made in the stem to partially sever it. Hormone rooting powder can be dusted over the cut. The shoot is then pegged down and the cut area gently buried, ideally in a suitable rooting compost, which must then be kept moist. Layers may take several months to root according to the time of year they are started. When rooted, the stem connecting the layer to the parent plant is first severed. A few weeks later the plant can be lifted and transplanted or potted for growing on.

Strawberries are also often propagated in this way, although they are much quicker to root, often taking only a few days. They are therefore often layered directly into small pots of compost (see fruit growing section pages 168–169).

AERIAL LAYERING

With some plants there may not be a suitable shoot near to ground level so we have to perform the layering procedure higher up the plant. Sphagnum moss was traditionally used for this procedure but is becoming increasingly difficult to obtain so a multi-purpose compost can be used. Once again, the stem is nicked and the small wound packed with either moss or compost to stop it closing.

A polythene sleeve is then constructed around the stem and packed with the rooting media. Make sure it is moist, then seal the polythene securely above and below the rooting site. Rooting is often slow and may take many months. When roots start to show against the polythene, the air layer can be severed from the parent plant and potted up on its own.

Layers are pinned into a pot of compost which must be kept moist to encourage rooting.

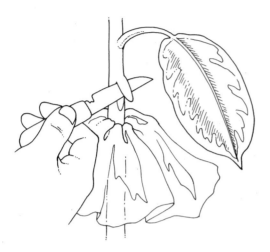

*Partially sever the stem to encourage roots
when aerial layering.*

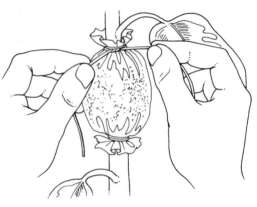

*Wrap the cut portion with a polythene sleeve
containing rooting compost or damp moss.*

DIVISION

Herbaceous perennials, ornamental grasses,
bamboos and some houseplants are propagated by dividing (in fact anything that has
a clump showing many shoots coming from
ground level are propagated in this way). Big
clumps of plants will require a spade to chop
them up or two forks placed back to back
to force them apart. Small clumps can be
pulled apart by hand or cut with a knife.
The resulting divisions should be replanted
or potted to grow on. Never allow them to
dry out.

Division is usually done during the
dormant winter season with most hardy
plants so no special conditions or equipment
will be needed. If leafy houseplants such as
Spathyphyllum (peace lily) or ferns are divided,
then the resulting offspring must be kept
damp and shady until re-established.

GRAFTING AND BUDDING

These are complex methods of propagation
that are used by professional nurseries
generally to produce trees or rare shrubs. This
may be because a fancy cultivar of a plant is
difficult to propagate by any other means or
because we want to produce a special form
such a weeping standard tree or a fruit tree
on a dwarfing rootstock.

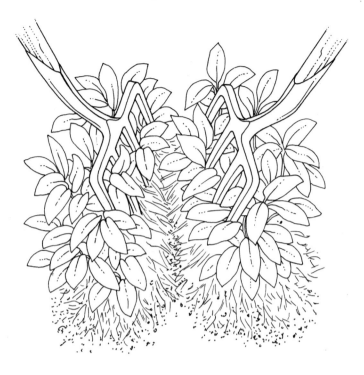

Large clumps of herbaceous perennials are best divided by levering with two forks to avoid damaging the roots.

Propagators will take a piece of the plant that is wanted and join it to a rootstock. The rootstock will often be the basic wild form of a fancy tree or it may be a specially produced rootstock. Either way it will always be closely related. When a single bud is used for this it is called budding, whereas a shoot that is attached is called a graft. Roses are normally grown by budding, and fruit trees by grafting. The end result will be a composite plant consisting of the rootstock of one plant joined to the top growth of another. In later life, with even quite mature trees, you can often see the join, which is called the union.

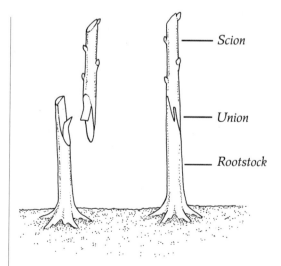

This type of graft which is commonly used for apples is called a 'whip and tongue' graft.

Scion

Union

Rootstock

51

PLANTING

CHOOSING AND BUYING NEW PLANTS can be a very pleasurable exercise. Some gardeners will spend hours perusing books and catalogues and then track down chosen plants. Others will fill their gardens with impulse purchases and then go on to buy more! Both are nevertheless plant lovers.

TYPES OF PLANT

There are of course many places where plants can be purchased and the choice is endless. The quality does of course vary and the maxim 'you get what you pay for' is just as true here. Plants come in many different shapes and containers and a few terms are worth understanding.

A 'bare root' or 'open ground' plant will be a plant, often trees, roses and sometimes shrubs that have been grown in a field. They are dug up and the soil shaken from the roots. It is imperative that the roots never dry out and so bare root plants should always be wrapped. Bare root plants must be planted in the winter.

A 'rootballed' plant is similar but has been dug with some soil and roots intact and these wrapped in sacking or plastic. It is a technique often used for trees, conifers and evergreen shrubs such as rhododendrons. They are usually planted in winter but the season is a little less critical as there is less disturbance to the roots.

Left: the roots on a 'bare root' plant must be protected and kept moist at all times.
Centre: 'rootballed' plants have their roots wrapped so are easier to transport and less likely to dry out.
Right: container-grown plants can be planted at any time providing they are kept watered.

'Container grown' means that the plant has been grown in a pot of some sort, generally for all of its life. Container growing is used for many different types of plants and particularly for shrubs. 'Containerised' means that the plant has been moved to a container. Trees are often field grown then containerised for garden centre sales. Both types can be planted throughout the year.

Bedding plants are sold in trays, small units or pots. The individually grown plants are more expensive but the quality is always better. Many plants are offered by mail order as plugs and this can be a very economical way of obtaining good plants at a reasonable price. They are, however, only part grown and you must be prepared to grow them on.

WHERE TO BUY

Traditional retail nurseries where plants are grown on site and sold direct to the customer are far less frequent these days. Where they exist they can be a source of good plants and usually very good advice, direct from the people who grow them. Prices will nevertheless reflect this and they are unlikely to be the source of a good bargain!

Many nurseries sell through specialist plant fairs that are run throughout the country, particularly in the spring, summer and autumn. These will often be located at a public garden or stately home at a weekend. Here you will find the cream of small nurseries, all offering the best they have at any one time. These are really good events at which to buy plants, particularly if you have become a bit discerning. Although prices may not be cheap, you have the opportunity to compare different sellers at close quarters in one area. Quite often several nurseries will have the same plants and you can check which are best or cheapest.

Garden centres offer an amazing range of products and plants for the garden. Very few will grow their own plants but usually stock good quality plants. Prices tend to be competitive, although it is less likely that you will obtain anything unusual. It is all likely to be very basic although garden centre chains may have newly introduced plants as they are released. Some advice may be available.

Mail order can be very uncertain but bear in mind that any plants that are going to be sent through the post are unlikely to be very large or have much soil attached to the roots. I know of at least one person who received a 'whole hedge-full of plants' in an envelope through the letter box! Plugs are nevertheless usually available by mail order. Mail order does carry the risk of postal delay but suppliers will usually send another batch if your delivery arrives dead.

Many readers may have discovered eBay, the online computer auction, and this too has a gardening section. Some unusual plants can often be offered and there is some assurance over supply in that eBay sellers are rated and you can see if past customers have been pleased. As I write this there is on offer evergreen box plants, raspberries, bamboos and amazingly both tea and cocoa plants! Remember though that unless the seller happens to be local, whatever you buy has to come through the post.

Plants are also offered in all sorts of other places, car boot sales, garage forecourts, greengrocers and bazaars. Buy with care in any of these non-specialist situations.

LOOKING FOR A GOOD PLANT

All plants are different but a few basic principles will help you assess the value and health of a plant. Firstly, any plant should have good, healthy green leaves that do not show signs of pests or diseases. Remember, of course, that some plants are grown for their yellow or other coloured foliage. Any plant that has a tired faded label has also probably been on display far too long and should be avoided.

It is often difficult to assess the roots of a plant but if you can gently knock the plant out, there should be a good proportion of strong young white roots showing. When the pot is full of old brown roots, it is an indication that the plant has been around rather too long. Whilst looking at the roots, keep an eye open for vine weevils, which are small white grubs. They are serious pests that live on the roots of plants and can cause the total collapse of the plant.

The biggest plants are not always the best. Look for plants that are stocky and sturdy and have a number of branches or sideshoots. These will ultimately give the best garden display.

HOW TO READ PLANT LABELS

New gardeners often complain that they do not understand botanical names and indeed Latin names can be daunting. Some would argue that we should make greater use of

The sad looking plant on the left exhibits all the symptoms of having been around too long and will not be a good purchase. A strong and healthy plant that is fresh from the nursery, like the one on the right, is likely to be a good purchase.

common names but these are not precise. For example, the word 'daisy' could refer to any number of similar plants from the common lawn weed through to exotic plants such as the gerbera, all of which have a similar multi-petalled form. The common name sycamore refers to a different plant in Scotland to England! It is therefore well worth any gardener who has more than a cursory interest, understanding how plants are properly named.

Most plants will have two or possibly three Latin names that give them their precise botanical name. No other plant will have that name and the name is recognisable by gardeners and botanists, regardless of language, throughout the world. For example:

Betula pendula (silver birch)

The first word is the genus and is always spelt with a capital letter.
The second word is the species and is in lower case.
Now there are of course many different birches and so we can also have:

Betula nigra (black birch or river birch – note two common names for one plant but one botanic name!)
Betula papyrifera (paper birch)
Betula ermanii (Erman's birch)

The species word is a describing word and tells us a bit about the type of birch so quite simply pendula means weeping, nigra means black, papyrifera means paper and describes the white bark, whereas ermanii tells us the

plant was named after Erman. Species names are quite useful in that they often tell us about the conditions the plant needs or about how it is going to perform in the garden.

The above plants are all natural forms that have originated in the wild. Some plants have a third name such as
Betula pendula 'Golden Cloud' (silver birch with golden foliage)

SOME USEFUL SPECIES NAMES

aquatica	growing by water
argentea	silvery
capensis	of the Cape, ie: South Africa
fastigiata	narrow and upright growing
floribunda	free flowering
foetida	strong smelling
grandiflora	large flowered
hookerii	named after Sir Joseph Hooker
horizontalis	spreading
lutea	yellow
nana	dwarf
odorata	sweet scented
praecox	early
rubra	red
sempervirens	evergreen
sylvestris	of woodland origin

This is a cultivar name and refers to a cultivated variety, which means that it originated in cultivation, possibly a garden or nursery rather than in the wild. Cultivar names are always given capital letters and enclosed within single quotes. These are usually in the language of the country in which the plant originated but are often translated when a plant is imported.

Many people use the word variety when they really mean cultivar. A true variety is a variation on the basic form that has occurred in the wild. So we have white bluebells as well as the normal blue form. Continuing our example with birch we could have *Betula utilis var jacquemontii*. This is the Himalayan birch of which the plain species has brown bark but this variety has white bark and so is distinct. A variety name has all lower case letters and no quotes.

PLANTS TO AVOID

There are a number of plants you should avoid growing in your gardens as they are likely to be invasive and easily take over, denuding the soil of nutrients, shadowing other plants or generally taking up too much space. A few of these are clearly recognisable as weeds but were originally imported and distributed as ornamentals. Giant hogweed, Japanese knotweed and Himalayan balsam are obvious ones.

Some basic shrubs can take up a great deal of space, things like *buddleias*, *philadelphus* and *forsythia*. In small gardens you should make sure that you seek out good, modern, compact, free-flowering cultivars. Be very careful with bamboos in a small garden. Although many are well-behaved clump forming plants, a few such as *Sasa veitchii* are very invasive and become very difficult to remove. Avoid forest trees such as sycamore, oak and horse chestnut in small gardens and particularly near buildings. They will soon become far too big and risk damaging drains and foundations.

Some herbaceous plants such as *Lysimachia*, Michaelmas daisy, ornamental grasses and valerian will spread rapidly. The variegated form of ground elder is a pretty little plant but just as invasive as its green cousin. A few annuals can be very permissive and cast their many seeds everywhere such as *eschscholtzia*, annual grasses and forget-me-nots. One should always be a little careful of gifts of plants unless you know what they are. Anything which a neighbour has to give away in large quantities is likely to be very vigorous and may not be worth the space.

CARING FOR PLANTS

MANY OF THE TASKS we do in the garden are centred on a plant's wellbeing, making sure that there are the right conditions for growth, development, flowering and fruiting. Throughout this book there are many recommendations on how to achieve this with all the different plants and crops we discuss. As well as this there is also the need for us to protect our plants from the depredations and damage from pests, diseases and weeds.

PRUNING

Throughout this book, various pruning techniques will be discussed for individual plants. There are, however, a few basic principles that apply to all pruning. In general don't prune plants unless there is a valid reason for it. Plants do not naturally get pruned! Only prune if the plant has genuinely become too big for its situation or if there are cultural reasons, encouraging bigger flowers or more fruit. You will rarely kill a plant by bad pruning but you can sure make a mess of it!

Pruning is normally carried out using secateurs for smaller shoots or loppers or a bow saw for larger branches. Always keep these tools sharp and make clean cuts that will heal quickly. Whenever possible, prune to just above a bud and ideally to a bud that is facing to the outside of a plant.

Thinning normally refers to selective pruning whereby we will remove a number

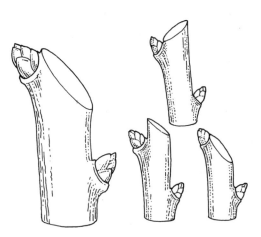

Always prune with a clean cut just above a bud and sloping away from it as in the correct example on the left.

of shoots but still leave the overall shape of the plant. Spur pruning is used for wisteria and fruit bushes and involves trimming sideshoots to encourage fruiting or flowering buds. Stooling means to cut a plant right back to ground level and is used for plants such as dogwood where a massive vigorous regrowth is needed. Root pruning is sometimes carried out on fruit trees to restrict their growth and encourage fruiting. This is done by digging a trench all round the tree and severing a proportion of the main roots.

WEEDS

SOMETIMES GARDENERS SPEND MORE TIME dealing with weeds than they do caring for cultivated plants and this can be very disheartening. Traditionally, weeds are usually thought of as 'plants in the wrong place'. Indeed in the countryside, many of the plants that we think of as weeds would simply be seen as wild flowers. Bluebells in a woodland are a beautiful sight but in a small garden can become a persistent problem weed.

Some plants such as bindweed were originally introduced as ornamental plants but we would now regard as persistent weeds. Equally some plants such as lantana, that we would cultivate with great care in our greenhouses are regarded as weeds in Australia, for instance.

Nowadays the division between weeds and wild flowers is even more difficult as it is fashionable to cultivate many native plants for their wildlife benefit. Some would encourage gardeners to cultivate patches of brambles or nettles because of their wildlife potential. Whilst this is undeniable, it is not surprising when such weeds spread to beds, borders and vegetable plots.

WEED GROUPS

Weeds come in basically two groups, annual and perennial weeds, which need controlling in different ways. You will recall that annuals complete their life cycles in a single year and produce large quantities of seed to perpetuate themselves. Annual weeds include familiar things like groundsel, annual nettle, chickweed, shepherd's purse, annual meadow grass and hairy bitter cress. Annual weeds are often a problem because of the sheer weight of numbers. They can be controlled relatively easily but there are always more waiting to grow from seed laying dormant in the soil.

Perennial weeds survive from year to year by means of persistent roots which remain

PROBLEM WEEDS

Japanese knotweed has become a major problem in some areas in recent years. It grows to over 2 m (6 ft 5) tall with very deep persistent roots and spreads voraciously, smothering everything around. Even small portions of chopped up root will grow into a new colony. It can be controlled with sprays of the chemical glyphosate. This must be used when the weed is growing strongly in spring and summer and repeated at frequent intervals. It is likely to take more than one season to eradicate.

The second weed to treat with great caution is giant hogweed. This was very fashionable some years ago as a garden plant and indeed it is attractive with enormous white flower heads at the top of a 3 m (10 ft) architectural plant with huge cut leaves. This weed should be treated with great caution because it is very toxic, causing painful skin rashes and potential eye damage. It is a biennial and so dies after flowering but will produce numerous seeds. Occasional plants should be dug up wearing protective gloves and then burnt. Large quantities of the weed can be sprayed out with glyphosate, to which it readily responds.

in the soil. Examples will include couch grass (twitch), ground elder, nettles, bindweed, creeping thistle, docks and dandelions. Some such as bindweed have deep far-spreading roots, which in time infest large areas. Perennial weeds can be difficult to control.

WEED CONTROL

There are a number of techniques for controlling weeds, all of which have different values. Some will be of more use with certain weeds, others of greater value in different parts of the garden.

Hoeing

This age-old technique is of value in both the ornamental and vegetable garden. The Dutch hoe is the easiest to use and should be slid along shallowly so that it severs the weed at the point just between root and shoot. If weather conditions are dry and weeds are small, they can be left to dry and shrivel up. In damp weather, there is the danger that some weeds may re-root and so raking up is advisable. Big weeds can be raked up for the sake of tidiness. Hoeing is really only effective with annual weeds. Perennial weeds can be controlled by repeated hoeing over time as the continual removal of the shoots will weaken the plant until it eventually dies but this is a slow process.

Mulching

A good mulch of a material such as bark chippings should be 5–7.5 cm (2–3 in) deep to be effective as weed control. It is a useful technique in that it prevents weed seedlings appearing. It will generally only be successful with annual weeds, as established perennial weeds have enough energy to push their shoots through. However, heavy duty black polythene or an old carpet can be used as a weed blanket over a neglected area. It must be left in place for at least a season during which time weeds will have attempted to grow and will die in the dark under the covering. Such techniques can be useful for clearing weed infested vegetable plots. Always dispose of the weed blanket in a responsible manner.

A good sharp hoe will sever weeds at ground level just between the root and stem.

WEED KILLERS

Herbicides, as they are more correctly called, are available to deal with a range of weed problems. Contact herbicides, also called foliage-acting herbicides, have an instant effect, killing weeds that they touch. They are not taken into the plant so do not kill roots and are therefore less effective against perennial weeds. They are not selective and so will also kill any cultivated plants that become contaminated. For example, you should take great care when spraying a path alongside a lawn.

Translocated herbicides are taken into the weed and moved throughout the plant including its rootsystem. They take longer to be effective but they kill the entire plant and so are very valuable for controlling deep-rooted perennial weeds. The most common material is glyphosate, which is sold under a variety of trade names. When used correctly it is a very safe product and is neutralised as soon as it touches the soil so there is little risk to pets and wildlife. It will, however, just as effectively kill cultivated plants so care must be taken in application.

Selective herbicides are a variation on translocated ones. Here we have 'clever' chemicals that only control certain weeds and do not harm cultivated plants. The most common example of these are the selective lawn herbicides that can be sprayed on to turf areas and will kill the weeds without harming the grass. There are others but they are more commonly used in commercial horticulture and agriculture.

Finally there are residual or soil-acting herbicides. These are chemicals that are applied to clean soil in the spring. The chemical remains in the surface of the soil and kills any weed seedlings that try to emerge. They can be used on bare ground, gravel areas and in rose and shrub beds. Once applied the area should not be cultivated as the 'chemical seal' will be broken and the effect lost. These are most commonly used by professionals in nurseries and in agriculture.

PESTS AND DISEASES

SADLY ALL PLANTS SUFFER from various pests, diseases and other problems. Even the best of gardeners will have to contend with these from time to time. Identifying the cause of the problem is the primary concern and then deciding what course of action to take. Making the right decision is not always easy, although it is important to take some action as some pests can wreck good plants in a short space of time.

THE GOOD AND THE BAD

A book such as this can only attempt to deal with a small proportion of the pests and diseases that may occur but often these are variations on a basic problem. For example there are many different types of aphid (greenfly and blackfly) that attack different crops but there will usually be a similarity, enough to identify and the treatment is often the same. The pests and diseases listed here are commonly occurring. Some others will be mentioned in particular connection with certain plants or crops in the relevant sections of this book.

The control of pests and diseases has become far more difficult for the amateur gardener in recent years as the range of pesticides available for dealing with plant pests is severely restricted. This of course is a good thing for both safety and environmental reasons and indeed many gardeners may wish to choose alternative, non-chemical treatments for pest and diseases.

Many of the insects and other creatures that live on plants and in our garden are not pests and may indeed be beneficial in the garden. Ladybirds, lacewings, spiders and centipedes are all garden friends and act as natural predators. Bees are of course pollinating insects. Larger creatures such as frogs, toads and hedgehogs are valuable too in controlling slugs.

CONTROLLING PESTS

The traditional method of controlling any pest or disease was by means of a chemical control. A poison was sprayed onto the plants which simply killed the pest. The side effects were possible contamination of the plant and the environment and also sometimes destruction of other beneficial creatures such as ladybirds.

Nowadays we try to use a minimum of pesticides and wherever possible look for alternative ways of controlling pests. We can often reduce the effects of pests and diseases simply by growing plants well, feeding them to make them healthy and able to withstand pests and diseases. A weak poorly fed plant is much more likely to succumb to attack.

There are also various cultivars, particularly of vegetables but also some flowers that are resistant to diseases and sometimes pests. These are well worth growing. Certain techniques such as crop rotation and companion planting are also effective and are described elsewhere in this book. The use of other creatures, which act as parasites or predators is becoming well established and this is referred to as biological control. These are usually available mail order from specialist firms.

PESTICIDES

When all else fails, you may still have to use a chemical pesticide but you should always aim to use the least toxic chemical and use it in a safe and reliable way. If it is used responsibly alongside other techniques we call this integrated control. This book does not give specific recommendations as regulations surrounding the availability of pesticides to amateur gardeners has meant that there has been a lot of change in recent years. Also availability of chemicals will vary from one country to another.

Most of the chemicals available on garden centre shelves nowadays have relatively low toxicity and if used in accordance with the recommendations and precautions, can be used quite safely. Many products are based on natural products such as pyrethrum and derris or simple materials such as soft soap.

Pesticides are described as contact or residual. Contact pesticides kill by means of contacting the pest as they are applied and have an instant knock-down effect. Residual pesticides are taken in by the plant and remain inside the tissues for a while, killing the pest as it feeds on the plant. These are best for any pest that lives inside the plant. Fungicides can also be residual and have a long lasting effect.

PESTS

Pests are small creatures that live in or on plants eating them for food. Some may be very obvious such as slugs and snails. Other pests include greenfly and smaller still are microscopic pests such as eelworm, which live within the plants but still have devastating effects. Some pests carry other diseases. So for example greenfly on their own are an annoying but relatively harmless pest but the virus they can carry and spread can be devastating.

Slugs and snails These are probably the most hated of all pests because the damage they do is so devastating, eating large holes in leaves or even the whole plants. Both slugs and snails leave slimy trails, if there is any doubt of their guilt. Once damaged, plants can be disfigured for a whole season or be severely checked in their growth. Soft lush plants such as *hostas*, vegetables and bedding plants are often attacked. They are particularly active in wet weather and feed at night.

CONTROL Slug pellets can be used. Scatter sparingly and remember they are very toxic so care should be taken with children and pets. Alternatively, scatter sharp sand around plants, set up beer traps to drown them or collect at night by the aid of a torch.

Aphids These include greenfly, blackfly and also woolly aphid found on fruit trees. Aphids feed on a wide range of plants both outside and under glass. They are small, often winged insects up to about 5 mm (^{1}/4 in) usually found on the undersides of leaves and around young growths. They feed by sucking the sap out of the plant which weakens it and often turns the leaves yellow. They also leave behind a sticky excrement called honeydew, which then turns black and is called sooty mould. Aphids spread viruses.

CONTROL Contact insecticides such as soft soap products will give an immediate knock-down effect. Winter washes can be used to control the eggs of overwintering aphids on fruit trees. Various biological controls are available.

Red spider mite This is a pest that 'creeps up quietly' and is often not noticed until there is a massive infestation. Red spider mites can affect garden plants such as fruit trees but they are more commonly seen on indoor plants either in a greenhouse or in the house. These are tiny creatures less than 1 mm ($1/16$ in) and so visible only as a coating of fine dust underneath leaves. For this reason they are often missed until the attack is well established. This usually shows as a dull yellow mottling of the leaves, which become brown, brittle and drop. With a bad attack a fine mesh like a spider's web is formed around plant tips.

CONTROL This is a difficult pest to control. It can be deterred under glass by maintaining a damp atmosphere but this will not control an established infestation. Most insecticides will not control red spider mite and a specific for this pest must be obtained. Alternatively biological control by means of the predatory mite Phytoseilus is very successful. Removal of infected leaves or cutting down of badly infected plants may be the best solution in some situations. You will need to know how the plant will respond to such drastic treatment.

Mealy bugs These are generally only a pest of indoor plants such as houseplants, cacti and succulents. Other plants may be affected including grape vines under glass and other tender fruits such as citrus. The pest looks like little blobs of cotton wool around 5 mm ($1/4$ in) across. The actual creature is much smaller hidden in this waxy white coating which protects it and makes it difficult to control. They tend to hide in crevices on plants such as under the bark of vines or around the spines of cacti.

CONTROL Some contact pesticides may be effective. On a small scale the use of methylated spirits on a small paintbrush to dab at individual pests is very effective. There is a very effective biological control called Cryptolaemus.

Whitefly This pest is commonly found on glasshouse plants such as tomatoes and fuchsias but also outside on crops such as brassicas. There are actually two separate pests but in basic appearance they look very similar. The creature itself is like a tiny white moth, which flies off in large numbers when disturbed. They feed by sucking the sap from plants, living on the undersides of the leaf. They also leave behind sticky honeydew and sooty mould as aphids do. They breed rapidly so numbers and damage can escalate fast.

CONTROL Contact insecticides such as soft soap are reasonably effective as are some of the synthetic pyrethroids. The trick with whitefly is to spray frequently at about four-day intervals, changing the chemical used for control to avoid a build up of resistance. Under glass, the parasite Encarsia is very effective, particularly on individual crops such as tomatoes or cucumbers. Yellow sticky traps can also be used in greenhouses to catch whitefly.

Scale insects   This is not a particularly common pest but can sometimes be found on house or greenhouse plants and occasionally outside on trees and shrubs such as bay. The creatures are like little yellow, brown or grey blisters on the undersides of the leaves, up to 6 mm (¹/4 in) across. They are largely immobile.

CONTROL A contact insecticide can be used for control. In small quantities on indoor plants they can be removed by hand.

Leaf miner   This is a pest that lives inside the leaf and creates a distinct pattern leaving twisting whitish tunnels as it moves through the leaf feeding. With a bad attack, the tunnels will end up linked together into large blister-like patches which go yellow and brown. It affects some trees, shrubs and perennials, especially chrysanthemums and celery.

CONTROL This is rather difficult as the pest is inside the leaf and many pesticides will not control it. For insecticides to be really effective, they need to be systemic and taken into the plant where the pest is feeding. When there are relatively small quantities of damage, either destroy the individual creatures with your thumbnail or pick off infected leaves. Remember though that removing too many leaves will slow down the plant growth.

Typical tunnelling from leaf miners that live within the leaf tissues.

Vine weevil   This pest has become noticeably more prevalent in recent years and can be found on a wide range of plants, particularly plants in greenhouses and nurseries so it can sometimes be brought in with new plants from a garden centre. The adult vine weevil is an ugly greyish beetle with long antennae that eats notches out of leaves. It disfigures plants but rarely causes major damage. The larva, which is the young stage, is a small white grub, up to 1 cm (¹/2 in) long with a brown head. This stage causes major damage as they live on the roots of plants and infected plants wilt and can die. Established plants in the garden can usually withstand an attack but young plants, with small root systems in pots will be badly affected.

CONTROL If vine weevil is suspected in a potted plant, the simplest treatment is to tip it out and examine the roots. If infected, wash the roots thoroughly, removing the infected compost and grubs. Repot in fresh compost and keep in a damp atmosphere until re-established. Surprisingly plants will often recover from such drastic treatment. With a more widespread problem, it is possible to use a chemical root drench or alternatively a biological product based on a nematode that parasitises the weevil and is very effective.

Caterpillars These come in a whole host of sizes and colours, often camouflaged to hide in the plants they are feeding on. Cabbage white caterpillars are common on brassica crops and tortrix and winter moth are pests of fruit trees. Damage occurs in the summer.

CONTROL On a small scale, hand picking is both effective and very safe. Contact insecticides can be used. A biological control based on the bacteria Bacillus is also available.

DISEASES

These are distinct from pests in that they will be caused by another organism such as a fungus, which is the most common, a bacteria or a virus. Diseases may attack any part of the plant, including the root system, so the effect may not be observed until the plant is badly infected. Sometimes the effects may be clearly visible as a mould on the leaf surface, or a distortion whereas other diseases may be inside the plant and only show as the plant's health declines. Some diseases, like pests, can be fatal to plants.

The control of diseases is slightly different

to the control of pests in that many diseases such as mildew or botrytis are very difficult to eradicate once they are established on a plant. The emphasis is therefore on prevention. Initially it is good practice to modify conditions where plants are growing to deter diseases. However, with some plants and situations where diseases are particularly likely to occur, some gardeners will choose to use a preventative spray of a fungicide to protect the plant. For example this is often done with roses to protect them from powdery mildew or with seedlings in a greenhouse to protect them from damping off disease. The spray or drench will need to be repeated at intervals to maintain the protection.

Powdery mildew Many plants suffer from this, particularly roses, lupins, apples and peas. It is immediately visible as a white mealy deposit over leaves and sometimes flower or fruit. Strangely whilst it is most prevalent on plants in dry conditions, it spreads from plant to plant in damp weather and by means of water splashes. So a rainy spell followed by dry weather is an ideal set of conditions for a mildew outbreak.

CONTROL Do not let susceptible plants go short of water. With important crops, use a protective fungicide spray as a routine precaution. Vary the fungicides to avoid resistance developing.

Rusts There are many different types of rust affecting different plants. Rust usually appears as bright orange or brown patches on the undersides of leaves with a yellow spot showing on the upper surface. Such an infection on hollyhocks or snapdragons has probably been seen by many gardeners.

CONTROL Affected leaves can be removed and burnt or a protective fungicide spray used if susceptible plants are being grown.

Botrytis (grey mould) This fungal infection can attack almost any plants although soft lush young plants are most likely to succumb. It is also most prevalent under poor conditions such as a cool greenhouse, early in the year when the light is poor and growth will be weak. It shows as a grey fuzzy mould on leaves, shoots or in the growing points of plants. The tissues underneath this rapidly go mushy and rot. It spreads rapidly.

CONTROL Avoidance is as always best, which in this instance means trying to grow strong healthy plants. In greenhouses, good ventilation and air circulation helps. A fungicidal spray can also be used as a protection where the problem is expected.

Armillaria This is also known as honey fungus because of the groups of honey-coloured toadstools that are eventually produced. This devastating disease attacks trees and shrubs. Initially it will show as a general yellowness of leaves, followed by wilting. Quite quickly the plant will start to die and large trees can go from appearing healthy to death within a single season.

The presence of this disease can be confirmed in two ways. Scrape the bark near ground level and check for the presence of a white mould that smells of mushrooms. Alternatively dig down to the root system and look to see if there are any black thread-like growths. These give the disease the name 'boot lace fungus' which is sometimes used. It easily spreads from plant to plant through the soil, so for example on privet, which is particularly susceptible, you can see the disease working its way down a hedge.

CONTROL This is very difficult. Initially infected plants should be dug up and burnt. There is a soil drench that can be used to prevent further spread and this is worth using if there are other valuable trees or shrubs nearby. Soil infected with armillaria can only be used for non-woody plants such as annuals, herbaceous plants and vegetables for some years. Replacement of the soil is possible but large quantities will usually have to be dug out and it is difficult to be sure that all the fungus has been removed.

Virus diseases These can attack a wide variety of plants, although they are less likely on annuals as viruses are less commonly seed transmitted. They are most likely to occur on plants that are perennial and those like dahlias or pelargoniums that are regularly propagated, meaning that the disease is also multiplied every time the plant is propagated. Viruses cause a wide variety of symptoms, which include distortion of leaves or flowers, spotting, mosaic patterns or streaking and reduction in flower size, vigour or cropping potential. Viruses rarely kill plants completely but they can so distort or weaken a plant, that it is no longer attractive or productive.

CONTROL Viruses are almost impossible to control. In general garden terms, if a plant has acquired a virus it is infected for life. This is not entirely true as there are sophisticated techniques by which specialist nurseries can produce virus-free stock under laboratory conditions. So for example you may see virus-free stock of old favourites such as the 'Royal Sovereign' strawberry offered for sale. Sometimes gardeners may feel that a virused plant has recovered as it may appear to be growing well. This is likely to happen in good summers or when growing conditions are good and the plant is able to grow well in spite of the virus, which is still there but masked. In a poor summer, the plant will once again appear sickly. Virus-infected plants should ideally be dug up and destroyed.

Viruses are usually spread by sap-sucking insects such as aphids, so these should be controlled to avoid the spread of the virus. Viruses can also be passed from plant to plant on a propagating knife. So where plants are propagated by cuttings, the knife should ideally be sterilised between cuts, by passing through a flame or with a suitable disinfectant. This is particularly important where a gardener may have a susceptible collection of plants such as dahlias or cannas.

One pest that produces similar symptoms to virus is eelworm. These are tiny microscopic worms that live inside the leaves and cause distortion. They are particularly likely on phlox, onions, chrysanthemums, narcissus and penstemons. Things are never simple!

BENEFICIAL INSECTS

Not all insects are enemies! Many of the insects that live in our gardens are beneficial and feed on others that we would call pests. The ladybird is probably the most common example and eats many aphids each day to stay alive. Lacewings, bumble bees, mason bees, centipedes and hover flies are also friends. As well as these small creatures, there are frogs, toads and hedgehogs, all of which eat vast quantities of slugs. By minimising the amount of pesticides we use, we can encourage these beneficial creatures and move towards a situation where pests are held in check by natural means.

CULTURAL PROBLEMS

Just to complicate issues, there are a host of other problems that can adversely affect plants, that have nothing to do with pests or diseases. These are all to do with the situations in which plants grow and when these are less than ideal, plants will start to suffer and show various symptoms.

ORNAMENTAL VIRUSES

Just occasionally viruses can cause changes in plants that are attractive. The wonderfully striped and flamed parrot tulips are infected by break virus which causes the attractive patterning. Back in the 17th century these fascinating bulbs were a novelty and changed hands for exorbitant figures, although the true origin of the patterns was then unknown. Variegated *Abutilons* such as 'Thompsonni' with its blotchy yellow leaves are also infected with a different virus, which causes the coloured leaves but is specific to *Abutilons*.

SAFETY MEASURES WHEN SPRAYING

- Always wear suitable protective clothing: gloves, goggles and a dust mask.
- Keep children and pets away whilst spraying
- Never eat, drink or smoke whilst spraying.
- Select the right chemical for the pest and read the instructions carefully.
- Always dilute to the correct rate and never mix chemicals unless the manufacturer suggests this.
- Do not spray in windy or very hot conditions as scorch can result.
- Early morning or evening is best to avoid bees.
- Dispose of excess chemical by spraying out on bare soil and not by flushing down the drain.
- Wash out sprayer thoroughly after use. Never use the same sprayer for weed killers as pesticides.
- Wash clothes after spraying.
- Wash or shower thoroughly after spraying.
- Make sure all chemicals are stored securely, away from children.

Yellowing between the veins (shown here as shading), is called interveinal chlorosis and often indicates a shortage of iron.

Nutritional deficiencies

Probably the most common are nutritional problems. Both a lack or an excess of certain nutrients will cause plants to suffer and show altered characteristics. A lack of nitrogen will show as yellowing leaves and slow stunted growth. Yellowing can also be phosphorus deficiency but this is very rare as most soils have sufficient phosphorus. Potassium deficiency will show as blue, yellow or purple tints, especially at the edges of the leaves which turn brown and die. These are easily corrected with a suitable fertiliser dressing. Liquid or foliar feeds are the quickest ways to correct deficiencies.

A deficiency of iron is very common on alkaline soils and shows as yellowing between the leaf veins (interveinal chlorosis). It readily shows with plants such as rhododendrons growing on chalky soils. It is corrected with sequestered iron which is readily available in garden centres. Shortages of other minerals and particularly trace elements are less common. Some can give odd symptoms such as a shortage of molybdenum on brassicas, causing a condition known as whiptail, which shows as narrow deformed leaves, which are not much more than a rib.

Climatic conditions

Gardeners always blame the weather! And indeed plants are very sensitive to changes in conditions or excesses. High temperatures will cause scorch as will frost, high winds or shortage of water. Excess water causes roots to die, resulting in wilting. Low light will cause plants to be thin, spindly and pale. Plants growing in greenhouses are often particularly likely to suffer from these excesses.

the
ornamental
garden

BASIC LANDSCAPING

LANDSCAPING ON EVEN A SMALL SCALE can be a very exciting process. Seeing either a blank plot or an overgrown garden transformed into something new, fresh and attractive can be a thrilling experience. This is particularly so when you have been closely involved, either with planning the garden or in its construction and planting.

DESIGNING YOUR PLOT

Planning landscape changes needn't be a complex process. You don't need to be a draughtsperson with a drawing board, although there is no reason why you shouldn't put ideas down on paper if this helps. Some people like to plan new features in a garden on the site itself. Borders and lawn edges can be marked out with canes or a hosepipe and possible new trees marked with a temporary stake. You can then stand back and survey the effect before constructing the real thing.

Certain gardens need particular care in planning. A small garden, just like a small kitchen, needs very careful thought to make sure you can get in everything you want without it being cramped. Make sure you choose small versions of things and in particular dwarf forms of plants to maximise your space. Large gardens need to be planned with low maintenance in mind or they soon become a heavy drag on your energy and wallet! Long, thin gardens can end up looking like railway carriages. Break up the space by dividing the garden into a number of smaller 'rooms' of different shapes and sizes.

It's always fun to dream about your ideal garden and with a little care, it is amazing how much can be fitted into even a small space. Don't forget the realities though. How much time do you want to spend in your garden, both constructing and looking after it? Are you lucky enough to have a generous budget or does this need to be planned very economically? And of course all those basic essentials such as room for the bins, maybe the washing drier and such things as children's swings, play areas or sand pits.

RENOVATING AN EXISTING GARDEN

When taking over an existing mature garden, the greatest problem is often being patient for long enough to find out what is really there. Ideally you should leave such a garden a full season to see what is growing, ascertain the good and bad features, see if any bulbs emerge and identify the problems. Having said that most gardeners are impatient to get started on an overgrown garden and are unlikely to wait a full season. Nevertheless do clearly analyse what is there. Wherever possible retain as much as possible of an existing garden as established trees and shrubs will give a valuable air of maturity.

Old plants can often be rejuvenated by careful pruning (see page 85 for pruning overgrown shrubs). Climbers and wall shrubs can usually be pruned back to a framework and tied back to their supports. Neglected lawns can usually be brought back into shape with a thorough renovation programme (see page

122). Unless they are very small, trees should be skilfully pruned by a professional. Fruit trees and bushes can also usually be pruned and may be brought back into bearing.

Neglected gardens may be harbouring various pests and diseases. Plants such as fruit bushes and roses that will not have been sprayed may have developed various problems. If they do not appear healthy or fail to crop, throw them out and buy new ones.

Weeds may be a problem if the garden has been neglected for some time. Initial hand weeding will probably be necessary amongst other plants although this can be tedious and hard work. If perennial weeds are present, the use of glyphosate can be very valuable but remember it will kill anything it touches (see pages 59–60 and 117).

The soil in a neglected garden will probably need improving, particularly if you are going on to plant new features. Clearing away weeds and the remains of old plants will all have reduced the fertility of the soil and this will need to be enriched with fresh organic matter and nutrients. A soil that has not been cultivated for a long time may also be hard and compacted and need loosening to improve aeration and drainage. Looking at the plants that are thriving in an existing garden will give an indication of the pH. Healthy rhododendrons will suggest an acid soil. Pink hydrangeas will suggest alkaline.

Many neglected gardens, particularly old ones, will often yield items or materials of value. Underneath the weeds and undergrowth there may be old bricks, edging tiles or paving stone that can be re-utilised. You might even be lucky enough to find old pots or garden ornaments.

TAKING OVER A NEW GARDEN

Acquiring a brand new garden with a new house may sound an ideal start to gardening but it can have its own set of problems. New gardens are often turfed, which leaves them looking neat and green but this may hide a whole host of soil problems. Always check the pH of the soil in a new garden before investing in plants that may fail to thrive (see page 21).

With such a new garden, always investigate the soil under the turf. There should be a good layer of dark topsoil, ideally at least 30 cm (12 in) but developers often use considerably less under turf and you may only have a shallow layer. Dig down further to see what is below this. It is quite likely to contain bricks and other remains from construction, which although a nuisance, can be removed. The greater problem is if you have a compacted pan or a thick layer of sticky clay.

When preparing planting areas in such soils, this needs to be broken up or loosened to allow drainage and root penetration. It will also need improving with organic matter. Lawns laid over such problems may always be weak and fail to thrive. Deep spiking will help but it may be necessary for a really good lawn to strip the existing, properly cultivate, improve the whole area and relay.

New gardens will also have little shelter and in cold areas may be either frost pockets or wind tunnels. Establishing some tough shrubs and small trees will help to shelter the garden and give it a warmer microclimate which is important if you are intending to grow more tender plants.

New gardens, particularly if you are a new gardener can be daunting. Start small with modest projects. Gardens grow and develop over the years and you can easily add extra features and make it more complex in time.

GARDEN STYLES AND THEMES

All the best gardens have been designed in some way. This does not necessarily mean that a professional has been involved or that a plan has ever been drawn. It simply means that the owner has thought through what he or she wants to achieve in the garden and has made positive moves to achieve this.

Some people like gardens that are informal, based on gentle curves, flowing shapes and a more natural appearance. Nothing will be in straight lines and plants will be grouped in soft loose groups to look almost as if they happened by chance. Others will like formal gardens that will be rooted in geometric shapes and straight lines, all very strict and stark. Neither are right or wrong, purely a matter of taste. Certain plants will more readily fit in with either style.

Gardens may also be based on various chosen themes. For example you may want a garden that is full of scent throughout the year and so you might select plants that have perfumed flowers or aromatic foliage. You might live in a traditional style cottage and want to create a classic country cottage

An informal style will have natural curves and flowing shapes that try to mimic nature.

garden full of a mixture of flowers, fruit and vegetables all tangled together in a happy profusion. The exotic garden is a fashionable theme and it is amazing how many plants can be grown to give an appearance of an urban jungle. An abundance of ideas are available in design books to help you achieve these and many other themes.

COLOUR SCHEMES

Some of the most effective gardens are based on colour schemes. These may be for the whole garden or just for part of it with colour borders and beds. Colour schemes can be based on one or more colours. For example, you might choose to have a yellow border and fill it with plants with yellow flowers and golden foliage. More complex colour schemes will involve two or more colours such as a red and white garden, selecting plants with red and white flowers, maybe white variegated foliage and possibly dark red leaves that some plants exhibit.

Other more complex colour mixes would be based on themes such as hot colours with reds, yellows and oranges or conversely pastel shades with pale blues, pinks, primrose shades and whites. Clever gardeners may want to add other features to match, such as pots or stained timberwork. However expecting white peacocks to wait patiently in a white garden may be too ambitious!

This formal garden has geometric shapes and straight lines, making it all very crisp.

GARDEN FEATURES

As well as the general components of a garden, its beds, borders, lawns and other surfaces, we will probably want to include certain features, which have a special attraction for us and will act as focal points within the garden. These may be small, such as a container of plants, or quite large and elaborate, such as a garden pool or rock garden.

WATER GARDENS

Many people admire water in the garden and it is not surprising that many want to add a water feature. However, water in the garden can provide problems and ponds are not always easy to manage. There are many possibilities, from still to moving water with cascades or fountains. Lots of different plants can be grown in and around pools and there's the whole range of fish and other wildlife that water makes possible. If you embark upon a water feature, you must realise that construction can be time-consuming and hard work and that the end result will need regular care to keep it in top condition.

Assuming that you have decided to make a pond, the first decision will be its location. Generally pools should be in open sunny positions away from trees. The next question will be the choice of material to be used for lining the pool. This can be either concrete, butyl or a pre-fabricated shell made of glass-fibre or plastic. Concrete will probably be the most long-lasting but also the most expensive and construction will need to be precise and thorough. Badly constructed concrete pools easily leak or can be fractured by frost.

POOL CONSTRUCTION

The plastic or fibreglass shell is an attractive option, usually providing different depths with pre-formed shelves for aquatic plants. With these prefabricated pools it is essential to very carefully dig out a hole almost exactly the same shape and size as the shell. If this is not so, when the pool is filled with water, the weight will put uneven pressure on the unsupported areas and can cause fractures.

Probably the easiest and cheapest way to construct a pool is to use a butyl liner. This can be used for almost any shape of pool but is particularly effective for informal ponds. The hole is dug slightly larger than the desired size of the pool. The sides should be

Excavating for a garden pool and creating shelves and different levels for aquatic plants.

sloping, and shelves and deeper areas can be created. The main area of the pool should be no shallower than 45 cm (18 in) particularly if fish are to be introduced. Any large stones or other sharp protuberances must be removed. The base should then be covered with a thick layer of soft sand. If this is dampened, it will help to keep it in place on the sloping sides. This can also be covered with

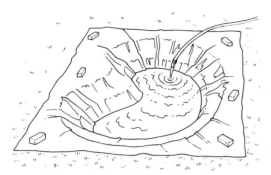

*Allowing the butyl liner to fill with water
pulls it naturally to the exact shape
without folds and creases.*

*The edges can be hidden by stone paviers
or coping stones.*

sections of old carpet or layers of thick damp-ened newspaper. It all helps to make a thick layer protecting the liner from sharp objects protruding from the underlying soil.

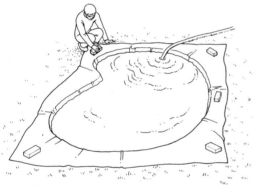

*After filling, the edges can be cut, leaving an
overhang of about 30 cm (12 in).*

The liner is then laid loosely over the hole and lightly anchored at the sides with weights such as bricks. Start filling the pool with a hose, allowing the weight of the water to gently drag the liner into the exact shape of the pool. This technique fits the liner to the shape of the pool far better than trying to fold it before filling. When the pool is full and the liner taut, excess material can be removed from the sides and the edges masked and anchored with paving stones, turf or planting.

AQUATIC PLANTING

Although pools can be constructed to have pristine clean water, this will entail the use of expensive filters or chemicals to keep the water free from algae. Most pool owners prefer to grow plants in and around the pool to achieve a more natural effect and keep the pool water clean by natural means.

Aquatic plants come in various groups according to the conditions they like. Oxygenating plants are submerged aquatics that grow from the bottom of the pool and release oxygen into the water, which is essential if fish are being kept. Marginal plants live in shallow water at the side of the pool and are often planted in baskets placed on shelves or on bricks lifting them up off the base. Water lilies and a few other floating aquatics will have their roots on the base of the pool and their leaves on the surface of the water. With these plants the correct depth of water is critical. Fortunately there are many different water lilies that can be selected for everything between very shallow pools down to ponds up to 90 cm (3 ft) deep.

PLANTING AQUATICS IN BASKETS

The simplest way of growing most aquatics in a small garden pond is to use aquatic baskets, which are like square plastic pots but made of a mesh so that the water can easily pass through and roots pass out. The basket is lined with a square of hessian or similar fabric to stop the soil washing out and then filled with a heavy clay-based soil. Slow release aquatic plant feed tablets are available and can be added but are not essential.

Aquatic baskets are lined with permeable fabric and filled with a clay-based soil mix.

Plants are planted into the top of the filled basket in the normal way and firmed in. Any loose hessian above the top of the container should be trimmed off. Finally the surface of the soil is finished with either coarse gravel

Plants are placed in the centre of each basket and the soil topped up to nearly the rim.

or cobbles to prevent the soil being washed away and also prevent foraging fish or wildfowl disturbing the plants until they are rooted in.

The basket is finished off with coarse gravel or cobbles to prevent the soil washing away.

Aquatic plants can be planted any time between mid spring to late summer whilst the water is warm, although spring plantings will establish best. Containers can then be carefully lowered into the water. Marginal plants can go immediately into their final locations usually with just a few centimetres of water above the roots. Water lilies need to be placed in shallow water initially and then as they grow moved to deeper water until they are down to their recommended depth. Oxygenating plants are often supplied as little bunches of shoots with a lead strip wrapped round them. Although you can just throw these into a pool, unless there is soil on the base they are unlikely to root and thrive. It is better to plant these in baskets also. Although they do not initially have roots, they will quickly form them.

There are also a few floating plants that do just that, floating on the surface with their fine roots dangling in the water. *Stratiotes aloides,* the water soldier, is hardy but sinks to the bottom of the pool for winter. Water hyacinths and water lettuce are also some-times offered. Both are tender but can be fun additions to a pool for the summer. They will not overwinter outside.

As well as the above groups, there are also bog plants that simply love soil conditions that are constantly moist such as you would find beside a natural pond or stream. You can recreate these conditions alongside a pool by creating a separate area alongside the pool that is constantly fed by enough water to remain moist.

SOME EASY AQUATICS

Most aquatic plants are easy to grow providing they are planted at the right season and in the right depth of water.

Shallow marginals

Lysichiton americanus – curious bright yellow flower and large leaves
Mimulus cardinalis – brilliant-coloured monkey flowers
Carex elata 'Aurea' – a golden grass-like plant
Typha minima – a small bullrush

Submerged oxygenators

Ceratophyllum demersum – very delicate dark green foliage
Callitriche hermaphroditica – starwort – delicate rosettes of leaves

Water lilies

Nymphaea 'Escarboucle' – popular, red flowers, 45–60 cm (18-24 in) depth
Nymphaea 'Helvola' – a miniature, creamy yellow flowers, 15–20 cm (6–8 in) depth
Nymphaea 'Gladstoniana' – vigorous, white flowers, 1.2–1.8 m (4–6 ft) depth

MINI AQUATIC GARDENS

For those with very small gardens but a yearning to try aquatic plants, you can create a small water feature in a large tub. For this you will need a tub without drainage holes, or you will need to line it with a butyl or polythene liner. This can simply be a series of marginal plants submerged to the correct depth in pots and surrounded by water or you can even grow a miniature water lily in a shallow tub. Remember that such conditions will be fragile and the water can quickly evaporate in summer and will need regular topping up. In winter such a small volume of water will easily freeze and crack the container. It is best to empty the water and start again the next year.

Tiny water features such as this make excellent seasonal summer features.

Bog plants

Osmunda regalis – the royal fern – lush leafy plant with divided foliage
Iris sibirica – delicate typical iris flowers in blue or white, and narrow foliage
Primula japonica – Japanese primrose with red or white flowers

POND PROBLEMS

Most of these are weed problems of some sort. Green algae is probably the most common problem that a pond owner will have, particularly when the pond is new. Cutting out the light by means of water lilies and floating aquatics helps. Sophisticated ultraviolet filtration units are possible but expensive. Submerging bags of barley straw is also an effective deterrent but needs to be started early in the year. Do not be tempted to clean out the pond and start again because fresh tap water encourages the algae and the whole process will start again.

Blanket weed is another type of algae that forms in long stringy threads, particularly in hot weather. This can be pulled out using a wire rake. Duckweed is a tiny floating plant, no more than a centimetre across but it spreads rapidly. It is commonly introduced on the feet of birds. It is very difficult to control so should be removed as soon as it appears.

A similar problem plant is *Azolla* or floating moss, which is a tiny reddish plant sometimes sold as an aquatic. Avoid it as it spreads rapidly. Canadian pond weed, *Elodea canadensis*, is sometimes sold as an oxygenator but is too vigorous for most ponds.

Occasionally, ducks can take over a small garden pond and nest nearby. The result, as far as the pond is concerned, can be disastrous as they will fill the pond with excrement and forage on all plant life until it dies. This may be tolerated because of the brood of fluffy ducks that eventually result. Herons and cats may be a problem with ponds with fish stocks. These three problems can be alleviated by netting the pond. This can be either a simple plastic mesh stretched across temporarily or a more permanent wire netting structure with a wooden frame. Neither are particularly attractive.

OTHER POND LIFE

A new pool is best left to thoroughly settle down and for the plants to establish before fish are introduced. A stockist will advise on the best types and the correct quantities for the size of pond you have. Ramshorn snails can also be introduced and these act as scavengers removing some of the waste materials within the pond.

MOVING WATER

Small pumps are easily available now with fountain or waterfall kits. Most are very safe and work on low voltage but they should still be used with an RCD device and any new electrical sockets should be installed by a competent electrician. For those with tiny gardens, kits are available to create small bubbling fountains set amongst cobbles and rocks. They have a small reservoir, pump and fountain. You add the cobbles or boulders to give the effect you want.

GARDEN FURNITURE

Increasingly, gardeners like the idea of 'living outside' so some garden furniture is desirable. The weather in temperate climates is not always conducive to this but it's worth a try – nothing quite like a cool beer sitting in the sun on a warm summer's day. Garden furniture can be timber or metal. Timber will need treating with oil occasionally. Most metal furniture is aluminium and needs no attention. Some furniture might be painted and will require intermittent repainting. As well as being practical garden furniture can be very attractive and a feature can be made of items such as garden seats strategically placed in an alcove and facing a suitable attractive view.

PERGOLAS AND ARCHES

Various structures can be made, usually using timber as supports for climbing plants and to add height to the garden. The cheapest structures will be rustic trellises using unpeeled timber in a traditional style. Such constructions will only last a few years but will be relatively cheap. Sawn square preserved timber will give a more formal appearance and should last many years but will inevitably cost far more. Most garden centres and DIY stores will have a selection of pre-fabricated structures part assembled.

ROCK GARDENS

Gardeners often admire rock gardens in large estates or at flower shows and the effect of a well built and planted alpine garden can be stunning. However, they can be not only expensive and hard work to construct and maintain but are one of the most difficult garden features to make look convincing in a small garden. Most rockeries end up looking like the proverbial 'dog's grave', a mound of soil spotted with stones.

A good rock garden needs a natural slope for construction. There are various types of stone available. Sandstone and limestone are probably the most easily available. Nowadays stone is quarried and so it will take some time to weather, grow mosses and look natural. Some hollow artificial stone products are available and in time do mellow reasonably.

Stone should be positioned with at least 50% hidden within the ground to look natural. The strata (original lines) of the stone should be matched up as you build to create a natural effect. A good rock garden will have varying features to create different growing environments – rock faces, ravines, crevices, screes and plateaus. Handling stone is a heavy and risky process. Use leather gloves, ideally steel toe capped boots and handle carefully using crowbars and levers to minimise strain. Alpine plants and the planting of rock gardens is also dealt with on page 103.

On a small garden scale, very good alpine gardens can be made in sinks or troughs. These can either be purchased ready made or an old china sink can be covered with hypertufa to give a natural looking trough that will weather with time.

Carefully placed rocks should show the strata all running in a similar direction for a natural effect.

WOODY PLANTS

Gardeners in temperate climates inevitably complain about the weather but we can nevertheless grow an amazing range of wonderful plants from around the world. Over the centuries, plant hunters have brought back vast quantities of plants from all continents, which we now accept as familiar residents in our gardens. Nurseries and plant breeders have also worked on these, giving us an even wider range of exiting novelties to grow. Whatever else may be in your garden, it is likely that plants of some sort will fill much of the space and that growing them will be a large part of the attraction.

WOODY PLANTS

These provide the bones or skeleton of the garden giving it structure, shape and interest even in the depths of winter. Trees and shrubs are the obvious plants here but there are also conifers, bamboos and climbers, all of which are woody perennials with lots of variety and interest.

SHRUBS

I remember growing up thinking there were just four different types of shrub: forsythia, deutzia, philadelphus and weigelia. These were the four enormous plants in my father's front garden, which I had to prune each year. They never flowered, just made leaves to sweep up and masses of flowerless growth to cut again the next year! The conclusion was that shrubs were boring and hard work, but nothing could be further from the truth.

Amongst the woody plants we call shrubs, there is an amazing world of plants that will give us flower, coloured foliage, berries or interesting bark for any day of the year. The word 'world' is appropriate as the shrubs that grow in our temperate climate have come from all around the globe. Although we may complain about our weather, it is an ideal climate for growing a very wide range of plants.

Shrubs are technically woody plants with a number of branches that give a 'bush' appearance. Shrubs are very valuable in the garden as they give a permanence and framework to a garden for the whole year. The likely lifespan for shrubs would be from five to ten or more years, so although shrubs may initially appear expensive, overall they are a very good investment and a cheap way to fill a garden. They are also relatively low maintenance.

A good planting scheme should make full use of the wide range of shrubs available. Evergreens are particularly important for winter colour as well as those with coloured stems and also berried shrubs for autumn. There is plenty of choice with regard to flowering shrubs. Use some with scented flowers or aromatic foliage to add extra interest.

Special shrubs

Euonymus fortunei 'Sunspot' – low growing, evergreen with gold spotted foliage
Potentilla fruticosa 'Goldfinger' – golden yellow flowers, very floriferous
Mahonia x 'Charity' – yellow scented flowers in winter, evergreen, tall

Lavandula x intermedia 'Grosso' – grey foliage, blue flowers and scent, low

Hebe 'Great Orme' – masses of pink flowers, evergreen

Choisya 'Aztec Pearl' – white flowers, scented, evergreen

Lonicera nitida 'Lemon Spreader' – tiny golden evergreen leaves, dwarf

Cotinus coggygria 'Royal Purple' – purple foliage, smoky-looking pink flowers

Pyracantha 'Orange Glow' – tall evergreen, white flowers, orange berries

Skimmia japonica 'Rubella' – low evergreen with pink flowers throughout winter

Planting shrubs

Although a few shrubs may be available as open ground or rootballed plants, the majority of shrubs are offered as pot-grown specimens. Winter planting is always best as it gives the plant time to make new roots before the next season's shoot growth. However, container-grown shrubs can be planted at any time of the year, providing you are prepared to keep them watered in dry spells.

A shrub border will probably be in place for ten or more years so it is well worth good preparation in the initial stages. The site should be free of perennial weeds as these can be difficult to control when growing through shrubs (see page 73). Thorough digging and incorporation of plenty of organic matter is essential. Before planting, add a high phosphate pre-planting fertiliser such as bonemeal and mix well in.

All shrubs, whether pot-grown, open ground or rootballed, should be planted with the root systems only just below the soil surface. Loose soil should be firmed around

Place containerised shrubs in their proposed location before planting to assess the final effect.

Dig out a good size hole with adequate space for the root system to develop easily.

Position the plant in the hole so that the root system is roughly at the same level as it was in the container.

the roots with your boots and the surface raked level. Finishing off with a good, thick mulch of bark or other organic matter will help to keep new shrubs moist and speed establishment.

Most good shrub catalogues and books give you an idea of the mature spread of a shrub as well as its height. This enables us to space them to allow for ultimate growth.

Remember that a shrub with a spread of 2 m (6ft 5 in) next to one with a spread of 1 m (3 ft 2 in) requires an average distance between them ie 1.5 m (4 ft 9 in). Shrubs placed at the right density for their ultimate size will look quite sparse in their early years and it is quite acceptable to plant other quick growing plants such as herbaceous perennials, bulbs or bedding plants in between to fill the gaps. Alternatively many gardeners will plant shrubs in groups much closer than needed for quick effect with the aim of thinning at a later stage when the planting starts to thicken out.

Shrub pruning

This is probably one of the least understood jobs in the garden. So often shrubs are badly pruned by both amateurs and even more so by professional gardeners who should know better. Commercial landscapers and local authorities often prune shrubs with hedge trimmers into shapeless blobs and the result is ugly to say the least! In general if there is no particular reason for pruning or you do not know the correct technique, then they are better left alone. If they block windows or paths, they can be pruned, otherwise let them grow naturally.

Having said that there are some that will give better displays with regular pruning and I will try to simplify the techniques to enable them to be easily understood. Much depends on how the plant grows, when it flowers or if the display is from foliage or coloured stems.

Slow growing shrubs

Plants such as *Rhododendron, Camellia, Viburnums, Daphne, Ilex* (holly) *Amelanchier*

(snowy mespilus) and *Hamamellis* (witch hazel) should generally not be pruned. The occasional leggy or misplaced shoot can be reduced but otherwise do not prune.

Foliage shrubs

Generally these will require little pruning but a different effect can be achieved by pruning quite hard to encourage vigorous leafy growth. Plants such as *Cotinus* (smoke bush), coloured leaved elders, and eucalyptus all respond well to cutting hard to the ground. This process is known as stooling and is done in early to mid spring to promote strong growth with large leaves.

Coloured stem shrubs

The same technique is used for plants such as *Cornus* (dogwood), the white stemmed *Rubus* and coloured stemmed willows. By pruning hard in mid spring we get vigorous regrowth, which is brightly coloured the next winter.

Late summer flowering shrubs

These have the whole of the summer to grow and produce flower buds and so can be pruned in the spring each year. This group includes *Buddleia* (butterfly bush), *Ceratostigma, Perovskia, Caryopteris,* hardy fuchsias, *Ceanothus* 'Gloire de Versailles' and *Hydrangea paniculata*. These are pruned fairly vigorously back to a short permanent frame-work. Vigorous growth will follow, which then matures and flowers the same season.

Early flowering shrubs

These should be pruned immediately after flowering to allow them to grow and make flower buds before autumn. The buds will remain dormant through the winter and then burst into life to flower immediately the next spring or early summer. The pruning technique here is not so harsh and this group should only be thinned removing the oldest flowered wood and leaving young shoots to mature for next year. This group includes *Forsythia, Weigelia, Ribes* (flowering currant), *Philadelphus* (mock orange) and winter jasmine.

Pruning old overgrown shrubs

Sometimes shrubs grow so big that they eventually totally outgrow the space allocated to them and become problems. Trimming and regular pruning rarely solve the problem, often spoil the shape and display of the plant and need to be repeated regularly. In such a situation it is well worth hard pruning back to a stump 15–20 cm (6–8 in) high. Follow this with a good balanced feed and a mulch.

Such a plant will grow back into a natural shape and soon resume its flowering pattern. With just a few shrubs such as rhododendrons, one has to be careful if the plant has been grafted that such pruning does not go below the graft line or merely the rootstock will grow back. Relatively few shrubs are grafted so it is not a common issue.

BAMBOOS

These dramatic architectural plants are actually woody grasses and have the added benefit of being evergreen. There are a few with variegated or gold foliage and also those with black or golden canes. They are easy to grow but have the reputation of being invasive. A few species are and if buying, you should be careful to choose 'clump-forming' species. Alternatively they can be successfully grown in large pots or tubs. They require very little attention.

Stooling consists of hard pruning, removing all shoots almost to ground level.

Hard pruning back to a framework for late summer flowering shrubs such as Buddleia.

Thinning old flowered wood from early flowering shrubs to leave new wood to grow on for next year.

HYDRANGEAS AND LILACS

Mop-headed hydrangeas do not easily fall into any group but are generally very lightly pruned, removing just the old flower heads, behind which can usually be seen a pair of fat buds which will be next year's flowers. This is normally left until mid spring as the old flower heads protect the buds in harsh weather.

Lilacs are pruned in a similar way by just removing the dead flower head back to the next two buds. In this case it is usually done in mid summer, straight after flowering.

Beautiful bamboos

Phyllostachys nigra – 'black bamboo' with rich dark stems, green leaves, tall

Fargesia murieliae AGM – elegant small green foliage, tall screening plant

Pleioblastus auricomus – golden foliage, dwarf groundcover bamboo

Phyllostachys vivax 'Aureocaulis' AGM – vivid golden canes, green stripes

CLIMBERS AND WALL SHRUBS

Climbers, or climbing plants, have many values in a garden. This is particularly so in a small garden, where it can be useful to take the display upwards, when space is otherwise restricted. Walls, fences, trellises, arbours and pergolas all provide suitable supports for climbers. Wall shrubs are often included with climbers. These are simply taller shrubby plants that grow well against walls and are often trained against a support.

Back on page 15 we spoke about the various ways in which climbers support themselves and it is useful to remember this when choosing which ones to plant. Most will require a small diameter support to cling to, such as a trellis or wires stretched across a wall. Sometimes if the support is too large such as a pergola post or a brick pillar, the climber will need additional help to grow by being tied in to the main supports. Ivy, Virginia creeper and climbing hydrangea are the only common ones that will cling on their own to a brick or stone surface. Ivy and other self-clingers will also need encouragement by pressing the stems against the wall using a support such as a bamboo cane.

With climbers, it is particularly important to choose plants for the right situation. In particular, walls will have very specific microclimates, either sunny and warm, shady or sometimes dry.

When climbers are planted to grow against a wall, the roots should be positioned at least 30 cm (12 in) away from the wall, as the soil at the base of the wall will be very dry and inhospitable to a new plant. The shoots can easily be encouraged back to the wall with canes or string. When planting roses or other climbers to scramble through old apple trees, the plant should go in next to the trunk. Most of the feeding roots of the apple will actually be further out, near the extremities of the branches so in the centre, the new plant will have less competition. Shoots can be tied in and encouraged to explore and colonise the tree.

MOVING A LARGE WOODY PLANT

Sometimes we may have a large specimen of some sort – shrub, bamboo or even a small tree – that is just in the wrong place but is thriving and too good to just throw away. In this situation it is quite possible to move it if some careful precautions are taken.

Ideally, prepare for this in the winter, a year in advance by digging around the roots at least 20 cm (8 in) away from the stem. This will sever any major roots. Refill the trench you have created with some good soil or old potting compost.

A year later, during the winter, you are ready to move the plant. You can reduce the top growth by up to a third if you wish as this will reduce the shock to the plant. Dig around the plant again, slightly further out from last year's trench and you should find a band of strong new fibrous roots which must be carefully protected. Go all the way round the plant and then dig carefully under it, trying not to damage the root ball. When the whole structure is loose it needs to be physically moved to its new location.

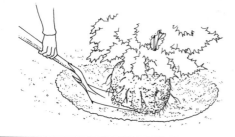

It may be useful to wrap the roots with polythene if it is likely to be out of the ground for more than a few minutes. Big rootballs can also be very heavy so handle carefully, possibly sliding it on a board.

Reposition the plant in its new location and refill with good soil, staking carefully with a diagonal stake to avoid breaking up the rootball. Water thoroughly. If the plant is an evergreen, spray it over with an anti-transpirant, which can be obtained from most garden centres, primarily stocked to prevent needle drop in Christmas trees.

HEDGES

Most people think of privet with the very mention of the word hedge but these living walls can be much more interesting. Hedges are really no more than rows of shrubs usually located to give shelter, privacy or a boundary. They are often trimmed to a precise formal shape making a living wall, although they can be left to grow more naturally, in which case they would be described as an informal hedge.

All sorts of shrubs can be used for hedges, although the best ones for trimmed formal hedges will be foliage plants, possibly evergreen such as yew, box or beech. Although the latter is deciduous, it holds the crisp brown leaves over winter providing some attraction. Informal hedges will often be flowering plants such as *Escallonia* or berrying plants such as *Pyracantha*.

Planting a new hedge

The site for a new hedge should be well prepared, as you would for any shrub planting. Ensure that the hedge is planted in a straight row, by using a planting board. This is a length of wood about 1 m (3 ft 2 in) long with three nicks in it: one in the centre and one at each end. First stretch a line and then mark the position of each plant with a bamboo cane. The board is positioned so the central nick is around the cane where the plant is to be and two additional canes are placed in the end nicks. The central cane and planting board can then be removed and the hole dug for the new hedge plant. The planting board is then repositioned using the two end canes and the plant accurately positioned in the central nick before replacing

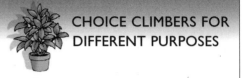

CHOICE CLIMBERS FOR DIFFERENT PURPOSES

Sunny walls

Fremontodendron californicum – large golden yellow flowers in mid summer

Solanum crispum – masses of small white flowers, sometimes called the potato crisp climber

Passiflora caerulea – passion flower with intricate blue and white flowers

Shady walls

Garrya elliptica – long, grey tassels in mid winter

Jasminum nudiflorum – yellow flowers in mid winter

Chaenomeles speciosa 'Nivalis' – similar to white apple blossom, in late winter

Self clingers for walls

Hedera colchica 'Sulphur Heart' – evergreen, huge leaves with golden centres

Hydrangea petiolaris – climbing hydrangea with white lace-cap flowers

Parthenocissus tricuspidata – green foliage and brilliant autumn colours

Scramblers to go through trees

Clematis montana – vigorous, masses of pink flowers in late spring

Wisteria floribunda – long tassels of blue pea-like flowers

Rosa 'Wedding Day' – very vigorous, plenty of white dog-rose style blooms

the soil and firming in well. The whole procedure continues down the row.

Hedges can be planted as a single or double row, in which case the second row of plants is usually staggered. Most hedging

Good hedges have a top that is narrower than the base. The third example would split open with heavy snow.

plants are spaced about 45 cm (18 in) apart. Dwarf species such as lavender or box can be closer at about 30 cm (12 in) and vigorous species such as yew, pyracantha or roses up to 60 cm (2 ft) apart. Varying the distance merely alters the speed of achieving a dense hedge and closer spacing will speed this up.

Trimming hedges

As a young hedge grows it should be regularly trimmed both on top and at the sides to encourage it to branch out and become bushy. Although this may seem as if it will slow down the achievement of the ultimate height, the end result will be much thicker and denser. A hedge that is not trimmed in the early years will usually be thin, patchy and bare at the base. As the hedge grows try to achieve a shape that is narrower at the top than the bottom. This helps the hedge to shed snow in cold weather. A broad flat-topped hedge will collect snow, which then tends to bear down on the hedge and spread the shape even more.

Formal hedges should be trimmed between one to three times a year. If little time is available you can get away with a single trim in mid to late summer but this is not ideal and the work will be tough. It is better to trim in mid summer and early autumn to give a neat finish. Hedge trimmers or shears will give a tidy effect for most hedges. To give a precise finish, use a string set between two stakes to give a guide for the top of the hedge and possibly a wooden template to show the shape of the hedge.

Plants for hedges

Taxus baccata – (yew) traditional evergreen, slow growing but classically good.
Buxus sempervirens – (box) evergreen, another classic for a low hedge.
Lonicera nitida 'Baggeson's Gold'– fast, small golden leaved evergreen.
Fagus sylvatica – (beech) deciduous, include some purple ones for interest.
Rosmarinus 'Miss Jessop's Upright' – silver grey and fast, but short lived.
Berberis x stenophylla – evergreen, loose growing, orange flowers.
Escallonia 'Donard Star' – evergreen and pink flowers.
Cotoneaster lacteus – semi evergreen, white flowers, red berries.
Crataegus x prunifolia – deciduous, red berries, prickly and good autumn tints.
Rosa 'Bonica' – a good flowering hedge, pink rose blooms.

Anything with very large leaves such as laurel is better cut with secateurs to avoid damaging the leaves which then go brown and unsightly. Raking up the trimmings can be a tedious job, which can sometimes be made easier by trimming onto a garden sheet that can be rolled up.

Flowering or berrying hedges should be pruned as you would the shrubs that

REJUVENATING AN OVERGROWN HEDGE

Old neglected hedges can often be brought right back into shape again by heavy pruning. Even yew will respond to this, although most conifers such as Leyland's cypress will not. As heavy pruning can be quite a shock to the plant, this process is usually done in two stages, over two seasons.

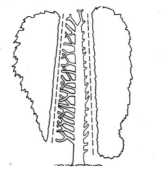

The first year, trim the top back to slightly below the desired height and one side right back to the framework of the hedge plants. Leave just short side shoots to regrow. Feed and mulch the hedge generously. The side that has been left green and unpruned will feed the plant and encourage regrowth. Assuming that has been successful, the other side can be hard pruned the following year.

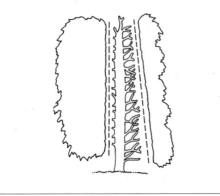

comprise them, but usually quite lightly. For example an escallonia hedge should be pruned after flowering, just lightly removing the longer growths and tipping other shoots to retain the shape. This is best done with secateurs. A rose hedge would be pruned as one would roses, but aiming for a uniform effect.

BONSAI

Many gardeners will be fascinated by bonsai. These are small miniature trees that have been shaped, often into gnarled contorted shapes, growing often in shallow glazed containers possibly with a small rock underneath the tree. Growing bonsai is a very specialised art and the most beautiful specimens will have taken many years of trimming and training to achieve their shapes. They can be very valuable.

If you buy a bonsai tree, remember that virtually all of them are grown from hardy tree species that have merely been dwarfed. They should therefore be grown outside throughout the year.

ROSES

Roses are favourite flowers for many people, although taste has changed in recent years with changes in gardening fashions. Formal beds of bush roses are less popular and there is an increasing interest in shrub and ground-cover roses together with the old fashioned styles. Roses are more likely nowadays to be planted as part of mixed plantings with shrubs and herbaceous perennials. Breeding in recent years has produced a wealth of different cultivars and it is exciting to see scent being bred back in.

Planting roses

Roses need an open, sunny but sheltered site and a rich soil. Although they will grow in most soils, they thrive on a slightly acid, well-drained loam or clay-loam. You should prepare the soil well by single digging in advance, incorporating generous amounts of organic matter such as farmyard manure. Roses do not thrive in a soil that has grown roses before. Rose growers speak of 'rose sickness' and although this is not specific, it is thought that they are prone to any build up of pests and diseases from the past. If replacing the odd plant in a bed, this is possible by digging out the old soil and replacing with new. Use a dressing of bonemeal or a pre-planting fertiliser before planting.

Most roses are available as open ground plants in the winter, although container-grown roses are available in the summer. A good rose bush will have several strong branches and a mass of fine fibrous roots. Make sure the roots never dry out by keeping

Plant rose bushes in a good size hole and position so that the union will be just covered by soil.

TYPES OF ROSE

- **Hybrid tea roses** – bushes, large, often individual blooms produced, high quality, good for cut flowers.
- **Cluster-flowered** (Floribunda) roses – bushes, large clusters of smaller, sometimes single blooms, a mass of colour, so good for garden display.
- **Standard roses** – a rose budded onto a tall stem.
- **Climbing roses** – tall, lanky plants with permanent framework used over trellises and pergolas, etc.
- **Rambler roses** – similar to climbers but fresh branches produced each year and often smaller, single flowers.
- **Species roses** – the original wild types, often tall, straggly and single flowering season but often with the added display of rose hips.
- **Shrub roses** – similar to species but includes both old and modern cultivars, generally tall and often single flowering season.
- **Old English roses** – modern shrub roses, bred to look and smell like old roses but with good modern characteristics.
- **Groundcover roses** – low growing, spreading plants, producing masses of small flowers.
- **Miniature and patio roses** – small plants for containers and confined spaces.

them wrapped until you are absolutely ready to plant it. The union is the point where the bush was originally budded and can be clearly seen at the junction between branches and root. Dig a hole big enough to spread the roots out and then backfill carefully around the roots treading down the soil as you fill the hole. The union should be just buried. Bush roses need to be spaced about 45–60 cm (18 in–2 ft) apart. Shrub roses will need 90 cm–1.2 m (3-4 ft). The procedure is similar for standard roses, which will need a small stake.

Newly planted bush roses should be pruned quite hard to about 7.5 cm (3 in) above ground. Cut to outward pointing buds. Treat standards in a similar way, like a 'bush on a stem' but new climbers and ramblers should just be lightly tipped.

Author's favourite roses

There are so many thousands of roses that a short list in a book such as this can barely touch the surface. Those listed are the favourites of the author!

'Graham Thomas' – a lovely yellow new English rose
'Nevada' – shrub rose, huge white single flowers
'Climbing Cecile Brunner' – tiny but perfect little fully double pink flowers
R. banksia 'Lutea' – climber, small double yellow flowers, prune lightly

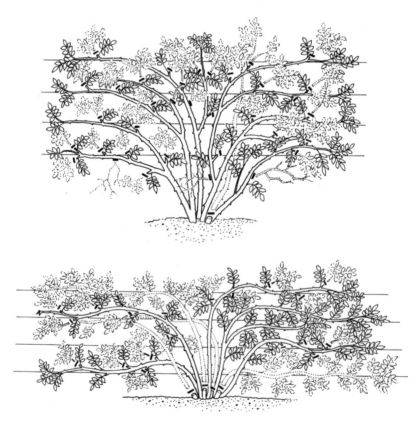

Top: climbing roses retain their main framework with just the side-shoots being reduced.
Bottom: rambling roses have last year's flowered wood removed back to the base each year.

R. filipes 'Kiftsgate' – very vigorous rambler, masses of white flowers

'Etoile de Hollande' – deep red climber, very strongly scented

'Max Graf' – widely spreading groundcover rose with single pink flowers

'Crimson Fire' – shrub rose, single red flowers and fine hips

R. sericea 'Pteracantha' – shrub rose, huge red thorns, small white flowers

Routine care of roses

Keep roses free of weeds, ideally with a mulch or very shallow hoeing. Roses need feeding generously. The first feed should be given in the early spring before growth starts. A balanced fertiliser such as Growmore can be used or a more sophisticated rose fertiliser that will contain trace elements. A second feed should be given after the first flush of flower in early summer to stimulate regrowth and more flowering. If it is dry at this time

ALTERNATIVE ROSE PRUNING

Over the years much mystique has built up over the skills needed for rose pruning. In recent trials, established rose bushes were pruned in a very rough way with hedge trimmers. The end result was initially not very attractive but the display the following season was just as good as those pruned in a conventional way. So much for skills! Groundcover roses are easily pruned in this way.

of the year, the fertiliser should be lightly hoed into the surface and well watered in.

As roses are budded onto a rootstock, sometimes a shoot will appear alongside a rose bush that has come from the stock. The leaves are distinctly different and the shoot will appear from the roots. Cutting them off with a pair of secateurs will only stimulate the production of more suckers. Using a stout pair of leather garden gloves, pull the sucker, which should detach from its point of origin. If you are unsure of this, you can scrape the soil away from a sucker to see where it comes from and grip low down. Hoeing or forking a rose bed is inclined to break the roots and stimulate suckers, so avoid deep cultivations.

As flowers fade after the first summer flush, the dead-heads should be removed down to a suitable bud just above a leaf. The bud should be pointing outwards. This will encourage the bush to regrow and produce a second flush. In the autumn, as the last flowers fade, shorten all the tallest branches. This leaves less growth to catch the wind and cause wind-rock.

ROSE CUTTINGS

Although roses are usually propagated by budding, which is a complex technique, a few extra plants can be raised by taking hardwood cuttings. These are prepared in autumn and can be done at the same time as the autumn trim.

Select healthy stocky shoots and prepare to about 23 cm (9 in), cutting above the top bud and below the bottom bud. Treat with hormone rooting powder and line out in a row about 15 cm (6 in apart). They will root slowly the next spring and make small bushes that can be transplanted a year later. Shrub roses are particularly effective when propagated this way.

Roses are prone to aphids, black spot and powdery mildew. For top quality roses, it is necessary to spray regularly as a preventative before the problems occur.

Routine annual pruning of roses

Most roses need pruning every year, although shrub and groundcover roses can be left to grow naturally for two or three seasons before needing attention. The main pruning takes place in late winter, although rose specialists often debate the precise time. Bush roses are pruned fairly hard to leave an open, vase-shaped bush with the topmost buds pointing out. Any weak or diseased wood is removed entirely.

Cluster-flowered roses are pruned slightly less hard but you should try to remove at least one old branch completely each year. This encourages new growth from the base. Sharp secateurs should be used and the cuts should slope away from the bud to shed water. Standards are treated like bushes on stems.

Climbing roses should be allowed to develop a permanent framework that covers the trellis or support. Each spring the side shoots are cut back to about 15 cm (6 in) and it is these that will become the flowering shoots in the summer. Occasionally prune out one of the main stems to encourage new replacement growth from the base.

Rambler roses are totally different. Each year the plant will produce a mass of very vigorous growths from ground level. These mature and flower in their second year. Pruning each year then consists of cutting out all the flowered shoots right down to ground level and tying in the new shoots for next year. Ideally this is done in late summer or early autumn, as soon as flowering is complete, but it can be left until winter.

Shrub roses can be left alone for a few years. After a while they become congested and the general vigour and flowering may decline. Prune them by removing a few selected branches as low as possible in the bush. This will encourage new growth and fresh vigour.

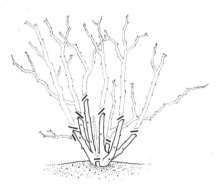
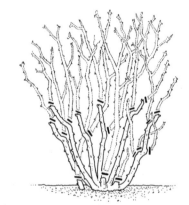

Left: hybrid tea roses are hard pruned, removing all small or crossing branches.
Right: cluster-flowered roses are pruned more lightly but we also remove some stems right down to ground level.

TREES

All gardens should have at least one tree! Amongst the huge range of trees that exist, there is one suitable for almost every situation, including even the smallest of gardens. Trees give impact, maturity and height to a garden and often act as a focal point. Trees may have many other valuable features such as flowers, coloured foliage or attractive fruit. Trees will also act as a haven for wildlife and birds in particular and of course trees are valuable for the part they play in returning oxygen to the air we breathe.

Not everyone likes trees in gardens, however, and this is usually due to bad experiences with trees that have become problems. When choosing a new tree always be careful to choose one that will not become too big. Such problem trees will ultimately take over a garden, casting it into shade and robbing the soil of moisture and nutrients, making it almost impossible to grow anything else.

Trees come in many forms, which roughly fall into four categories: rounded, weeping, fastigiate and pyramidal. In small private gardens we would often choose a fastigiate or pyramidal tree to avoid taking up too much space but there are slow and small trees amongst each group.

Catalogues will usually give estimates of the likely height and spread for a tree and this is invaluable when choosing a suitable species. Many people worry about the possible threat a tree might have to the foundations of a house. In general terms, plant at least 6 m (20 ft) from any buildings and avoid large parkland or forest trees such as willow, poplar, ash, oak and beech.

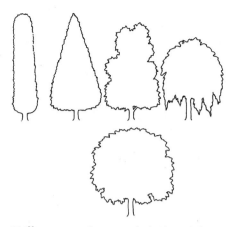

Differing tree shapes include, from left to right, columnar, fastigiate, upright, weeping and rounded.

Tree planting

A traditional saying suggests that we should spend a 'penny on the tree and a pound on the hole'! The underlying principle is that we should invest time and money in preparing the planting location for a new tree. So often people buy expensive trees, which are planted without due attention and then fail to thrive.

Choose your location for a new tree carefully. It needs to be seen as a focal point of the garden or part of the garden, such as a border or bed and needs adequate space to grow and develop. It can be useful to position something temporary such as a bamboo cane or timber stake in the proposed location and then consider for some days looking at it from various vantage points in the house and garden. Try to imagine it as a mature tree and adjust the position until it looks right.

The best time for tree planting is during the autumn although bare root trees can be planted right through the winter months and container grown trees at any time of the year.

Summer planted trees will need frequent watering. If you buy a bare root tree, you must ensure that the roots never dry out. At all stages until you plant the tree, the roots should be wrapped in polythene. If you are not ready to plant, heel the tree into a temporary location, which simply means digging a hole and covering the roots with soil to keep them moist.

Ideally, the site for a new tree should have the soil broken up a metre deep and as much in diameter. This seems a lot of soil to cultivate but a tree will be in place for perhaps 50 years or so and will probably be one of the most expensive plants in the garden. Dig out the soil a layer at a time, finally breaking up the bottom spit with a fork so that it will be well drained and roots will be able to penetrate with ease. As the soil is returned to the hole, it should be enriched with organic matter such as garden compost.

Retain the topmost layers of soil for using around the tree roots and enrich with a pre-planting fertiliser. Traditionally this has always been bonemeal, although there are other alternatives. A suitable fertiliser would have low nitrogen and high phosphate levels to encourage root growth. Mix the correct amount in with the retained soil.

The stake is hammered in before planting the tree. There are several different ways of staking trees suitable for different conditions. A tall tree with a slender stem will require a single tall stake to which it can be closely secured. A tree with a stout stem can be secured with a short stake. Some authorities would suggest this is better for the tree as it can flex in the wind and develops a stronger stem. Container-grown trees will require a

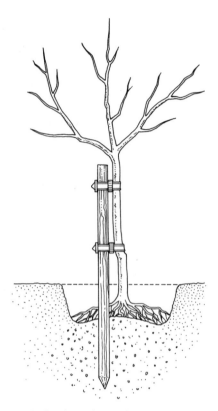

A newly planted tree showing well prepared soil, a stout stake and the stem carefully tied at two points.

stake at an angle or two stakes and a cross bar to avoid damaging the rootball.

Carefully offer the tree to the stake turning it round until the best side is facing the right way. If the tree is pot grown, gently tease out some of the long roots to allow them to grow away easily. At this stage make sure the tree is roughly at the same level as it was in the nursery. This can be checked with a cane laid across the hole from side to side. Replace the soil around the roots feeding it carefully in to make sure all roots will be in contact with the soil. Gently firm the soil in place by treading as the soil is filled in.

TOP TEN TREES

Pyrus calleryana 'Chanticleer' – tailored upright tree, white flowers in late winter and good autumn colour

Betula pendula 'Youngii' – a weeping birch that makes a rounded umbrella shape

Gleditschia triacanthos ' Sunburst' – very small tree with golden foliage

Prunus 'Amanogawa' – pencil thin and upright with bright sugar-pink cherry blossom

Sorbus 'Sheerwater Seedling' – a variation on rowan with orange-red berries and good autumn colour

Amelanchier canadensis 'Ballerina' – a form of the snowy mespilus with clouds of small white flowers in spring and bright autumn tints

Acer davidii – a snakebark maple with attractively striped winter bark, good summer foliage and autumn colours

Malus 'Golden Hornet' – apple blossom, followed by golden yellow crab-apples

Pyrus salicifolia 'Pendula' – a small weeping tree with delicate silver foliage

Ginkgo biloba – the maidenhair tree, a curiosity with fan shaped foliage that turns gold in autumn. Ultimately tall but slow growing and sparse foliage, which casts little shade.

The tree is then secured to the stake using a plastic tree tie, being sure to use the rubber buffers provided to prevent the tree from rubbing against the stake. The tie is nailed to the stake to prevent it slipping down.

Finish off with a mulch of bark chips to retain moisture and discourage weeds. Wild rabbits are very fond of damaging the bark of young trees and if this is likely, a spiral tree guard should be added.

Caring for young trees

Young trees do not need a great deal of attention but they should nevertheless not be neglected. In dry summers they will need watering particularly during the first summer after planting. Any suckers that develop from the main stem should be removed and the base of the tree kept free of weeds. Each spring a general or high nitrogen fertiliser can be applied to encourage steady growth.

Young trees need very little pruning and should generally be left unpruned. However, if the tree develops more than one leader (dominant main shoot) then these should be reduced to one, choosing the most centrally placed one to grow on and pruning back the others. As the tree grows, the tie should be loosened to prevent it strangling the tree. At some stage, probably about three years after planting, when the tree appears strong enough to stand on its own, the stake and tie can be removed completely.

CONIFERS

These are a fascinating group of plants and, if carefully chosen and strategically placed, make fine and elegant focal points. Most are evergreens with golden, blue-grey or green foliage. As well as upright specimens we can also get prostrate forms that make excellent groundcover. Flowers are generally insignificant, although some such as the pines eventually produce attractive cones which are the seed-bearing structures. However, some make huge forest, timber or parkland trees and you should be careful when selecting conifers to check the ultimate height.

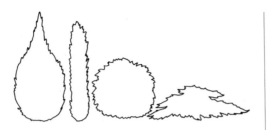

Conifers can be anything between very narrow and upright down to those that are totally prostrate.

Colourful conifers

Thuya plicata 'Atrovirens' – upright dark green conifer, screening or specimen

Juniperus virginiana 'Skyrocket' – upright, blue-grey foliage, small specimen

Chamaecyparis nootkatensis 'Pendula' – upright, lovely drooping branchlets

Ginkgo biloba – maidenhair tree, deciduous, an elegant curiosity

Cryptomeria japonica 'Elegans' – upright, lovely bronze winter tints

THE LEYLANDII ISSUE

In recent years, conifers have gained a bad reputation particularly because of the over use of Leyland's cypress, *X Cupressocyparis leylandii*. This is a very fast growing hybrid evergreen that once established, will grow about 1 m (3 ft 2 in) a year. In a private garden situation this means a hedge will require a great deal of trimming each year or it rapidly grows enormous. Such tall hedges cause great dispute between neighbours and in the UK legislation has been introduced to authorise local authorities to reduce hedges where a dispute is registered. Think very carefully before planting this monster!

Juniperus media 'Old Gold' – spreading and gold, good groundcover

Juniperus virginiana 'Grey Owl' – very flat with grey foliage, groundcover again

Pinus mugo – compact pine tree growing to about 1 m (3 ft 2 in), good on rock gardens

Thuya occidentalis 'Rheingold' – upright, gold foliage and slow growing

Chamaecyparis lawsoniana 'Ellwoodii' – small upright green conifer, rock gardens or container specimen

Even some of the larger growing species such as *Cedrus atlantica Glauca*, *Ginkgo biloba* or *Taxodium distichum* the blue atlas cedar, are fairly slow growing and therefore can be enjoyed for many years before they become too big.

Specimen conifers should be treated as trees when planting, giving them a well prepared site. As most conifers are evergreens, they will usually be supplied either pot-grown or as rootballed specimens. This means that they will have been dug up carefully from the nursery with a generous ball of soil containing roots. This will be wrapped in plastic or sacking. When planting, carefully remove the covering but do not disturb the rootball. Stake and tie as for other trees.

Care and attention for mature trees

Householders with large existing trees are sometimes concerned for their safety. In general, trees are immensely strong structures and you should never be tempted or persuaded to prune mature trees unless there is a valid reason to do so. Any pruning cut opens a wound and is likely to cause more future problems than if left alone.

Nevertheless you should keep an eye on any mature trees in your property just the same as you would check your roof, gutters or fences for problems.

Tree pruning

The pruning of mature trees is a job for the professional. The amateur, however practical, should never try to use chainsaws, climb trees, prune large limbs or fell trees. There are many safety issues involved and many risks. A properly qualified tree surgeon will have had much training and will be competent to prune your tree skilfully and safely. Equally, never be tempted by attractive offers from those who offer a cheap deal to 'lop your trees'. The traditional method of pollarding trees, whereby all the top growth is butchered back to a stump is no longer recommended. Such trees regrow at a phenomenal rate and there is always a point of weakness where they were previously pruned.

A good professional tree surgeon will use a number of techniques. If a mature tree is casting too much shade it is usually possible to 'lift the head', which involves removal of a number of the lower branches. Where a tree has genuinely become too tall, the tree surgeon may suggest 'crown reduction'. This means that a proportion of the upper branches of the tree will be pruned back to side branches. When this is done skilfully the natural shape of the tree is retained. Where a defect has been discovered, it is often possible to remove the damaged limbs or to reduce the crown and still leave the tree safe for future years. Only when there is a severe risk, will a tree surgeon recommend complete felling.

TREE DEFECTS

- Tree surgery is always best left to the professional but the observant amateur can always look for the early signs of defects.
- Fungal growths – often appearing in autumn at base of tree or higher up
- Cavities or hollow trunks – weakens tree
- Cracks in limbs – makes tree unstable and opens to rot
- Weeping – signs that water is running out of the trunk
- Weak fork – V-shaped crotches are structurally weak
- Hanging branches – partially severed limbs that are hooked up
- Lightning damage – bark destroyed on one side of tree
- Loose bark – may indicate rot underneath
- Crown die-back – small weak foliage

Hooked branch

Hanging branch

Snag

High level cavity

Weeping

Lightning damage

Fungus

Low level cavity

Tree defects

Any of these are indications that the tree may have a defect and should be referred to a tree surgeon who will do a climbing survey. He will report on the health of the tree and recommend any essential tree surgery.

Tree Preservation Orders

Some special trees have Tree Preservation Orders placed on them, which makes it an offence to cut down, top, lop, uproot or wilfully damage or destroy the tree, or permit these actions, without first seeking legal consent to do so. TPO's as they are known for short, are administered by the local planning authorities. Contravening a TPO may lead to a serious fine.

If you are the owner of a tree with a TPO and you wish to prune it, you will need to obtain permission. The local Tree Officer will probably pay a visit to discuss what work you wish to do and will, if agreed, grant very precise conditions. If a tree is dead, it is no longer covered by the TPO. If you merely regard it as dying or dangerous, you should still approach the planners for authority to do the work needed.

Should you be concerned for the future of a nearby tree, it is a relatively easy process to apply for a TPO. The tree and its location will be considered and if the tree is thought to be valuable or at risk, a TPO will be served. The owner can object but not directly stop the procedure. In most cases the tree is immediately protected when the process is initiated, although the matter will be discussed by the local planning committee before it is formally confirmed.

GROUNDCOVER PLANTS

The use of groundcover plants is all part of low maintenance gardening. By covering the ground with a thick carpet of foliage, seedling weeds are prevented from developing. In order for this to be successful, it is essential that the site is initially free of perennial weeds and that the young plants are kept weed free until the foliage meets and creates the blanket effect. A mulch combined with hand weeding will achieve this. Plants with big broad leaves such as *Bergenia* (elephant's ears) are most effective. Shrubs and particularly evergreens will be the most efficient plants.

A few well-behaved groundcover plants

Bergenia 'Ballawley' – large leaves, red winter tints, pink flowers in spring

Euonymus fortunei 'Sunspot' – evergreen, shiny golden centres to leaves

Lonicera pileata 'Lemon Spreader' – evergreen, tiny yellow variegated leaves

Hebe pinguifolia 'Pagei' – low mat of silver foliage plus white flowers

Juniperus virginiana 'Grey Owl' – silvery grey carpet of evergreen foliage

Viburnum davidii – leathery dark green leaves, turquoise berries

Potentilla fruticosa 'Goldstar' – deciduous, yellow flowers through summer

Stephanandra incisa 'Crispa' – delicate light green foliage and white flowers

Cistus x pulverulentus 'Sunset' – vivid pink flowers, steely grey foliage

Artemesis arborescens 'Powis Castle' – feathery silver foliage

All these plants are attractive in their own right and have a valid place in the garden as well as being good weed smotherers. Groundcover plants associate well with both winter and summer bulbs, which can be planted through them.

HERBACEOUS PERENNIALS

THESE ARE PLANTS THAT LIVE for a number of years but die back to the ground in the winter. Amongst this group of plants are many colourful and easy subjects that are quite fast growing and will quickly give a display. Traditionally they were displayed in a herbaceous border, which would have been a long border, often backed by a hedge, packed full of serried ranks of herbaceous plants. Although splendid, this style is not very practical for our modern small gardens and so other styles of display have developed.

DISPLAY STYLES

Island beds are areas of planting cut out of a lawn so that they can be viewed from all sides. This gives added interest. The all round sunlight also means that plants grow stocky and sturdy and are less likely to need staking. These are usually informal shapes but can be geometric, if appropriate to the garden. Such borders need careful planning to ensure they look good from all directions.

Whilst traditional borders can look spectacular in the summer, they are totally devoid of colour and interest in the winter, so perennials are now often grouped with shrubs, roses, bulbs and other plants in mixed plantings. These can be very successful and spread interest throughout the year. Perennials can be particularly useful as fillers between newly planted shrubs, giving quick impact whilst slower growing shrubs are establishing and filling out. Such mixed displays offer great opportunity for creativity.

PLANTING HERBACEOUS PLANTS

Most herbaceous perennials are greedy plants, so respond well to good, thorough preparation by digging with generous amounts of organic matter added to the soil. Most herbaceous perennials need an open sunny site but there are those such as *Hostas* and *Euphorbias* that grow well in shade or woodland conditions.

Generally a fuller effect will be achieved with a larger quantity of smaller plants. If you buy larger plants with a number of obvious shoots, these can be divided before you plant them by gently pulling or cutting apart into smaller divisions. Generally, most perennials need to be planted between 30–60 cm (12 in–2 ft) apart depending on their vigour. Usually the smaller edging plants will need the closer spacing and the more vigorous plants for the centre of the bed the extra space.

Herbaceous perennials should be planted in groups for the best effect.

Planting can take place in autumn or spring or throughout the summer if using container-grown plants. Most herbaceous perennials are container grown, although they may sometimes be available as small open ground divisions or you may have divided plants of your own. Never let such plants dry out. Plant carefully using a trowel for the smaller plants and a spade for larger clumps, firming them in with the boots and finishing off with a good watering if the soil is dry.

The taller herbaceous perennials will need staking to stop them flopping over. This is best done at an early stage before they start to droop. The traditional way is by using bushy brushwood, inserted in and around the clump so that the plants push through and support themselves as they grow. You can also obtain wire frames on legs that are placed over the plants, again so that they grow through. Plants with just a few stems, such as delphiniums, can be supported with individual bamboo canes, tying in each stem as it grows with soft garden string.

Some hand-picked herbaceous perennials
Alchemilla mollis – low growing, lemon yellow hazy flowers, early summer
Anchusa azurea 'Loddon Royalist' – spires of rich blue flowers, mid summer
Coreopsis verticillata – masses of small yellow flowers, long season of display
Geranium 'Johnson's Blue' – soft pale blue flowers, attracts bees
Hemerocallis 'Stafford' – vivid red day lilies, narrow foliage
Heuchera micrantha 'Palace Purple' – low growing, plush purple foliage
Kniphofia 'Little Maid' – dwarf red hot poker, but this one lemon yellow
Polygonum bistorta 'Superbum' – delicate wands of pale pink flowers
Sedum spectabile 'Autumn Joy' – late summer, soft red flowers, attracts bees
Astrantia major 'Hadspen Blood' – early summer, elegant ruby red flowers

When the display has faded in the autumn, it is useful to cut down herbaceous perennials, back almost to the ground before winter, quite simply to leave a tidy effect. A few perennials such as ornamental grasses and *Sedum spectabile* (the Ice Plant) look good as brown winter skeletons, so should be left until spring. A few others such as *Bergenia* and *Euphorbia* are evergreen and should not be cut back.

ORNAMENTAL GRASSES
In recent years ornamental grasses and related plants such as rushes and sedges have become very popular. As well as infinite variety in foliage, many have lovely graceful plumes of flowers that gently move in the breeze. Most like open sunny situations but there are grasses for shade, moist and dry soils. They are all types of herbaceous perennial so should be treated as above. They do prefer to be divided and planted in the spring months.

A few graceful grasses
Acorus gramineus 'Ogon' - golden variegated evergreen grass. Low growing
Miscanthus sinensis 'Cosmopolitan' – huge white variegated grass
Imperata cylindrica 'Rubra' – blood grass, rich red foliage, likes a damp spot

Cortaderia selloana 'Aureolineata' – golden foliage version of pampas grass
Pennisetum setaceum 'Purpureum' – purple fountain grass, lovely but tender
Stipa gigantea AGM – golden oats, lovely seed heads, tall

PLANTS FOR CUT FLOWERS

Many herbaceous perennials and also annuals make good cut flowers for use in the home. The following are easy to grow.

Perennials

Scabiosa caucasica 'Clive Greaves' – single, pale blue flowers, early summer
Gypsophila paniculata 'Bristol Fairy' – clouds of tiny white flowers, early summer
Helenium 'Moerheim Beauty' – orange with dark centres, mid summer
Rudbeckia 'Goldsturm' – yellow daisies with darker centres, late summer
Solidago 'Goldenmosa' – soft yellow plumes, mid summer

Annuals

Zinnia – single flowers in luminous colours
Antirrhinum (snapdragon) – tall spires of flowers in many colours
Callistephus (aster) – shaggy single or double blooms in late summer
Lathyrus (sweet pea) – delicate flowers with beautiful scent
Limonium sinuatum (statice) – (can be dried) various pastel shades
Mollucella laevis – (can be dried) lime green curiously shaped flowers

Try to collect cut flowers early in the morning or the evening when it is cool and condition them in a deep bucket of water before arranging.

ALPINES

Alpine plants include a whole host of diminutive plants that generally come from mountainous regions and would normally be grown in a rock garden. Most alpine plants like a well drained soil, so make up a mixture of John Innes Potting Compost with extra grit. Place a layer of broken bricks or small rubble in the bottom, fill with the gritty compost and then plant your alpines.

Ten easy alpines

Aubretia deltoidea – many cultivars, pinks and lavender shades
Diascia 'Ruby Fields' – close mat with pink flowers, free-flowering
Sempervivum 'Commander Hay' – succulent with bronze foliage, evergreen
Phlox subulata – many cultivars, pinks, whites, pale blues
Euphorbia myrsinites – silver foliage, yellow flowers
Dianthus alpinus – alpine 'pinks', early summer, silver foliage
Sedum spathulifolium 'Purpureum' – silver foliage, purple hue, yellow flowers
Gypsophila repens – tiny white flowers
Sisyrinchium 'E. K. Balls' – spikey leaves, blue flowers, yellow centres
Rhodohypoxis baurii – tiny pink flowers

After planting, water well and finish off the surface off the trough with a dressing of pea gravel, which will keep the roots cool and moist.

An alpine sink with a selection of plants,
spaced out ready for planting.

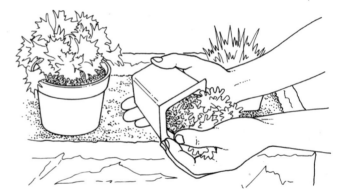

Knock the plants out carefully to preserve
the roots at planting.

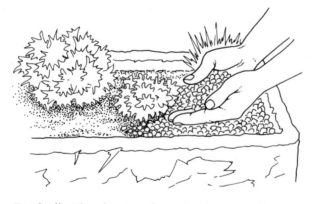

Finish off with a dressing of pea shingle to keep the
roots cool and moist.

FERNS

Amongst the plants known as ferns are both tender and hardy plants for many situations, although by far the majority of ferns like moist, shady conditions. Most are lush leafy plants with green foliage, which add an exotic atmosphere to a planting scheme. Species such as *Matteuccia struthiopteris*, the shuttlecock fern, *Cyrtomium falcatum*, the holly fern and *Asplenium scolopendrium*, the hart's tongue, are all easy to grow. *Osmunda regalis*, the royal fern is a good waterside plant.

They are a group of plants all on their own in that they are not flowering plants and do not perpetuate by seed. They actually reproduce naturally by spores, although many can also be divided. Most hardy ferns are tough and like a shady site with a humus-rich moist soil. They are usually available from garden centres in the spring as small, pot-grown plants.

SEASONAL PLANTS

MANY NEW GARDENERS START OFF by planting a few bedding plants or bulbs and then move on to discover the whole world of gardening and the wealth of the plant world. Such seasonal planting is fast in its response and gives a good reward to novice gardeners in a short space of time.

BEDDING PLANTS

Bedding is sometimes criticised for being vulgar and brash and indeed any style of garden can be distasteful if badly conceived and executed. Amongst the world of bedding plants there is a whole range of plant material in both bright colours and pastel shades. There are flowers, foliage and scent; most of it is easy to grow and will provide a display within a few weeks of planting. Although often planted on their own, they can be very successfully mixed with other permanent plants such as shrubs, roses and herbaceous plants. They are the ideal plants for new gardeners. Bedding plants are normally planted twice a year, in early summer for summer display and in the autumn for flowering the next spring.

Summer bedding

Most summer bedding plants are not hardy and should not be planted out before all danger of frost is past. In many areas this will be early summer. Sadly many garden centres and nurseries offer bedding plants far too early each year. They are of course quite happy if your plants die and you have to return to buy more! Even if they survive,

TOP TEN BEDDING PLANTS

Begonia 'Non Stop' range – wide colour range, long season of flower
Impatiens 'Accent Range' – very floriferous, sun or shade
Marigolds (French or African) – long season of display, drought tolerant
Petunia 'Lavender Storm' – huge lavender flowers, likes it hot and dry
Cineraria 'Silverdust' – silver foliage, compact and goes with anything
Cosmos 'Sonata White' – useful taller plant, flowers until the frosts
Ageratum 'White Hawai' – white version of this old favourite
Antirhinums (snapdragons) – good for early season colour
Dahlia 'Redskin Mixed' – dark foliage and brightly coloured flowers, dwarf
Rudbeckia 'Indian summer' – enormous pale yellow daisies with dark centres

when planted in cold soil, they will struggle and take many weeks to recover. Plants that are planted out at the right time, in warm soil without a cold check, grow away far more quickly and will easily beat those planted out too early.

The best bedding schemes are those that have been carefully thought out and have a colour scheme, linking the different plants together. It is not necessary to provide an edging, such as lobelia, unless you trying to create a Victorian style planting but it is useful to add taller plants, often called dot plants, such as Cordyline, to give height and interest to the scheme. Foliage plants such as *Cineraria* 'Silverdust' or coleus are very useful to provide a softer foil and you could add plants such as heliotrope or nicotiana for scent.

The soil for bedding plants should be dug and raked down to a fine tilth. Organic matter can be added but is not essential although it is worth adding a balanced fertiliser such as Growmore at 60 g/m^2 (2 oz/yd^2). Plants are planted with a trowel, generally 15–20 cm (6–8 in) apart, firming in lightly with the fingers or the back of the trowel. Freshly planted bedding plants should be kept watered for two or three weeks until established but after that they will tend generally not to need much water unless conditions are very dry. If slugs are likely to be a problem, use some sort of slug control (see pages 62) as bedding plants can be decimated by slugs.

During the summer, little other attention is needed. The display will need to be kept weeded either by hand or with a hoe. If you have the patience to remove the dead flower heads as they fade, then the display will look tidier and this will also promote more flowers to follow but it is not essential.

CONTAINER GARDENING

Window boxes, planters and hanging baskets provide an extra point of interest in a garden and the opportunity to create a floral focal point. For some people, such displays will be little 'mini' flowerbeds on their own and

Bedding plants should be spaced quite close for an instant effect.

therefore require plants that will be particularly showy and long lasting.

There are many containers available, from simple terracotta pots to timber and stainless steel. Plastic look-alikes can be very convincing and are usually cheap to purchase and light to move. In general choose the largest containers that the site will accommodate or that you can afford. Grouping together, maybe three similar style containers in different sizes can be very effective.

All containers should have drainage holes in the base to avoid them becoming waterlogged. If they don't have, carefully drill a number of holes so that excess water can drain away. Traditionally the base of such containers would have a layer of crocks, pieces of broken flower pot to further aid drainage. As it is unlikely that many gardeners will have these, use stones, broken bricks or gravel. The container should then be filled with a good potting compost. Although any

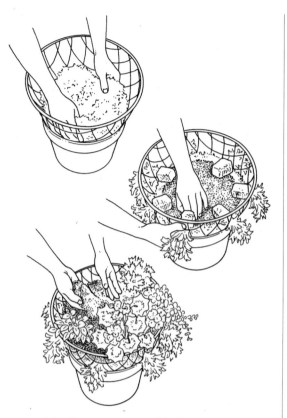

After lining, you can add plants to the side of a hanging basket before filling up and planting the top layer.

good potting compost can be used, I prefer to use a soil-based compost such as John Innes 3 for outdoor containers. This will be quite heavy and so avoid plants being blown over when they are fully grown. However because of this it is best to site your pots before filling. Don't fill quite to the top, as the soil displaced when you add your plants will raise the level considerably.

Any sort of container should be planted generously and we can pack plants quite tight together. The effect when fully grown, should be a container that is absolutely bursting with colour. Depending on the situation, choose a mixture of plants, some that will trail, some to give height and some to generally fill in. A mixture of flower and foliage is usually effective. Many of the best plants for containers are tender perennials that will have been grown from cuttings, so their price will be slightly more than bedding plants but the display they produce will be worth it. In theory they can be kept from year to year but as they are not hardy you will need to take cuttings and keep them frost-free over winter. It is best to treat them as single season plants.

Top ten container plants

Surfinia Petunias – huge flowers and trailing plants, floriferous

Begonia 'Illumination' range – trailing, free flowering, many colours

Fuchsia – trailing and bush types, delicate flowers, keep moist

Cordyline australis – spikey upright dot plant, also coloured leaved forms

Argyranthemums – bushy dot plants, masses of coloured or white daisies

Coleus cultivars – brilliant leaved foliage plants

Verbena 'Sissinghurst' – brilliant pink, trailing, long season of flower

New Guinea *Impatiens* – large flowered form of 'busy lizzie'

Helichryssum petiolare – trailing silver foliage

Begonia 'Dragon Wing Red' – floriferous and long season, outstanding!

HANGING BASKETS

These are merely a variation on container growing. Generally all the plants we choose will be trailing and we must be aware that a

TEN USEFUL SPRING BEDDING PLANTS

Bellis 'Habanera Blush' – cultivated form of lawn daisy with huge double heads

Myosotis 'Royal Blue' (forget-me-nots) – in blue, pink and white

Polyanthus 'Crescendo' – mixed and individual colours available

Pansy Universal range – many colours available, winter flowering

Cheiranthus cvs (wallflowers) – wonderful scent as well as many colours

Primula denticulata – the drumstick primula, lavender and white

Viola 'Blue Moon' – tiny very free flowering blue pansies

Primrose 'Husky' – a tough outdoor range with many colours

Lunaria biennis – honesty, purple and white forms available

Ornamental cabbages – good for autumn but tend to fade by spring

Use a loamless compost to fill the basket to keep the weight as light as possible and add both a slow release fertiliser and some water retaining crystals. The latter is a useful product that swells up when wet and stores moisture for use by the plants. You can add some plants to the sides of the basket as it is filled and then finish off with the main plants in the top. Just as with any other container, a colour scheme is advisable and fill the basket as full as possible.

It can be useful to plant up a hanging basket in a greenhouse of conservatory if you have one and let it establish before moving outside, when all danger of frost is past. Be sure to use a strong bracket, well fixed to whatever surface and remember that a wet basket is heavy when hanging it up.

Care of containers and baskets

Frequent watering is essential, often every other day or even daily in a hot summer. Regular feeding with a liquid feed is essential, although the use of a slow release fertiliser will reduce this. Dead-heading flowering plants will help to prolong the display. Watch for any pests and diseases such as whitefly or greenfly. A well tended container should go on giving interest until the autumn frosts.

SPRING BEDDING PLANTS

When the summer flowers fade in the autumn, it is time to think about a follow on display. Most spring bedding is planted in the autumn but does not give its main show until the spring months. Some of the modern strains such as the Universal pansies and Crescendo polyanthus will however give

hanging basket is exposed to drying from all sides so adequate provision must be made to keep it moist.

Most hanging baskets are made of wire, although some plastic or even ones made of natural twigs are available. Initially the basket must be lined with something suitable. Traditionally this was moss, but for environmental reasons this is less than acceptable and it is better to use a pre-formed liner made of a fabric of some kind. It is then a good practice to put a small circle of polythene or an old saucer in the base to act as a small water reservoir.

some colour throughout the winter if the weather is kind. Spring bedding plants are often associated with bulbs such as tulips.

Usually sometime around mid autumn, the summer flowers will be looking rather tired and a decision can be made to clear them. Dig over the beds and at this time of the year, it is good to add some organic matter such as compost but no fertiliser. If wallflowers or tulips are going to be planted, a dressing of lime may be needed to keep the soil alkaline. This discourages the diseases, tulip fire and clubroot on wallflowers. If a mixture of plants and bulbs are to be used, then use the plants first then add the bulbs.

BULBS, CORMS, TUBERS AND SO ON

There are many good bulbous plants that we can use in the garden. Botanically some will be corms, others tubers or rhizomes but generally for cultivation purposes they are often grouped together as 'bulbs'. Although the majority flower in the spring, there are others that give their display throughout the year. Tulips and hyacinths associate well with spring bedding plants such as pansies and *narcissus* (daffodils) and crocus naturalise well in grass areas. There are many others that can be used

Planting and caring for bulbs

Spring bulbs are hardy and can be planted directly outside. Most will require a well drained sunny location, although there are a few woodland species, such as bluebell, that prefer light shade. In a bedding scheme, you should plant bulbs evenly spaced throughout

TOP TEN SPRING BULBS

Tulip **'Heart's Delight'** – red edged rosy white, very early
Tulip **'Arabian Mystery'** – purple edged white, late spring
Tulip **'Big Chief'** – classic big red tulip, late spring
Narcissus **'Ice Follies'** – creamy white trumpet daffodils, early spring
Narcissus **'Spellbinder'** – sulphur yellow trumpet daffodils, early spring
Narcissus cyclamineus **'February Gold'** – miniature yellow daffodil, late winter
Crocus **'Zwanenburg Orange'** – golden yellow with bronze exterior, late winter
Hyacinth **'Woodstock'** – reddish purple, scented, early spring
Muscari **'Blue Spike'** - large blue grape hyacinth, mid spring
Iris reticulata – tiny bright blue irises, late winter

the other plants but in most other settings they will look best in informal groups of ten or more. You can plant bulbs almost as close as you want and indeed the best effects are from generous plantings.

Planting is simple. Take out a hole, three times the depth of the bulb, making sure the base is flat. Place the bulb firmly on the base and return the soil. With groups of bulbs this can be done with a spade.

Many bulbs such as daffodils and crocus establish well in grass and the effect is natural. These can be planted individually with a little tool called a bulb planter that takes out a core of soil. However, this is slow

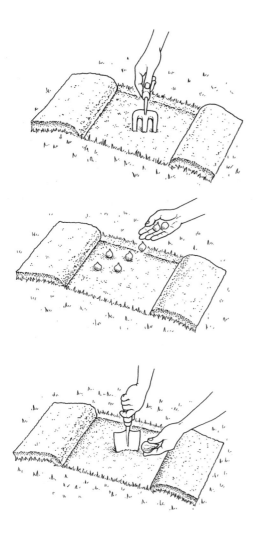

Loosen the soil before planting bulbs under turf and remember to make a deeper hole for the larger bulbs.

and tedious. In grass it is easier to gently lift a square of turf with a spade, loosen the underlying soil and then plant a group of bulbs. The turf is replaced, watered if dry and soon settles back in.

Bulbs really need very little ongoing care and can reward you for many years with their display. After flowering, do not be in a rush to cut them down and don't tie up the foliage as some gardeners do. It is beneficial to remove the dead heads and prevent them forming seeds but in general the foliage must be left to feed the bulb until it dies down naturally. With any bulbs growing in grass, the grass and bulbs must be left uncut, until the foliage has started to yellow in early summer. Tulips in formal bedding displays can be carefully lifted and then heeled into a temporary trench to finish their annual cycle. They can then be cleaned up and re-used the next autumn. If you want to feed bulbs, the critical time is between flowering and when they die down as this is when they are forming the flower buds for next year.

Bulbs for summer display

These are not quite as commonly grown, although many are easy and well worth trying. Many lilies are relatively easy to grow and give spectacular flower heads. *Cannas* are also stunning plants with bold foliage as well as brilliant flowers, although you must be careful to avoid stock infected with virus. *Eucomis*, the pineapple plant, produces fascinating pale green flower heads with pineapple-like tufts at the top. *Gladiolus* are well known by most people as a cut flower, although there are also many charming smaller garden forms.

ANNUALS AND BIENNIALS

Hardy annuals are a neglected group of plants that can be grown from seed to full display in a single season. As well as familiar plants such as cornflower and calendula, there are scented plants such as mignonette

GROWING LILIES

Easy lilies include *Lilium regale*, 'Connecticut King', 'Enchantment' and 'Fire King'. Lily bulbs can dry out quite quickly, so examine carefully before buying to make sure they are plump and not shrivelled. Lilies should be planted in mid autumn before the soil gets too cold. Most lilies like lightly shaded situations with a damp but not wet, well-prepared, organic rich soil. Scoop out a hole three times the depth of the bulb and line with a shallow layer of sharp sand to aid drainage. Place the bulb firmly in the base and cover over with soil. When growth starts in the spring use a slug control if this pest is likely. Keep moist during dry conditions and stake with a slender cane if the stem starts to sway. Lilies also do well in pots or containers. Watch out for lily beetle, a scarlet beetle that eats holes in the leaves and leaves unpleasant droppings. The simplest control is to hand pick them.

annuals can be sown from early to mid spring and will usually germinate in a couple of weeks. Annuals look good in big irregular patches but it is easier to manage them and weed if they are sown in rows across the patches.

When they germinate they must be kept weed free and then thinned to leave single plants about every 15 cm (6 in). With plenty of space, the remaining plants grow away strongly. They will be in flower by mid summer but their life cycle is completed at the end of the summer and they must be thrown away.

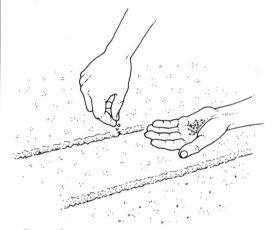

Even when growing annuals in patches, it is useful to make short, straight drills for sowing.

Biennials also complete their life cycle in less than twelve months but spread over two seasons. They will normally be sown in summer one year, grow and flower the next spring or early summer. The foxglove is probably one of the most familiar biennials but there are others such as sweet William and *Myosotis*, the forget-me-not. There are also some plants such as wallflower and hollyhock which are truly perennial but we

and climbers including canary creeper and the cup and saucer vine. Many will flower for several weeks and some are good cut flowers. The annual border is an easy feature to produce in a new garden with minimum cost. As all are hardy, they can be sown direct in the border soil without the need for protection.

The soil for an annual border should be prepared by digging and raked out level. A balanced fertiliser such as Growmore should be applied at 60 g/m² (2 oz/yd²). It is a good idea to prepare the border a few weeks before sowing so that weed seeds can germinate and be hoed off in advance. Hardy

TEN TOP HARDY ANNUALS

Iberis **'Fairy Mixed'** (Candytuft) – low growing, many colours, very hardy

Calendula **'Fiesta Gitana'** (pot marigold) – bright orange flowers

Clarkia elegans **"Pretty Polly Mix'** – delicate pastel shades

Larkspur **' Little Rocket Mixed'** – pastel shades, spires like small delphiniums

Amaranthus caudatus (Love-Lies-Bleeding) – dark red trailing tassels

Tropaelum **'Jewel Mix'** (Nasturtium) – hot colours, dwarf plants, fast growing

Matthiola bicornis (Night Scented stock) – insignificant flowers but rich perfume

Godetia **'Azalea Flowered'** – pastel shades, very hardy

Centaurea cyanus **'Polka Dot Mix'** (Cornflower) – pastel shades, hardy and easy

Eschscholtzia **'Tropical Punch Mix'** (Californian Poppy) – hot colours, short

grow them as biennials and throw away after flowering as they are easy to grow and are best when young.

SPECIALIST PLANTS

There are a few plants that seem to be particularly attractive to amateur gardeners and many will grow them to perfection and sometimes go on to exhibit them. As such, many amateur gardeners have become experts in these plants.

Sweet peas

A climbing hardy annual that is generally grown as a cut flower, it doesn't last particularly long in water but its sweet perfume makes it highly desirable. It responds very well to detailed culture and superb specimens can be grown with concerted effort.

Sweet pea seed is hard and needs to be gently chipped with a knife before sowing. Although they can be sown directly outside, they are best sown with a little protection, such as a cold frame or unheated greenhouse. Sow one, two or three seeds in small pots of potting compost or special deep containers called sweet pea tubes. They can either be sown in mid autumn or early spring. Pinch out the tips when they have about five leaves. If plants are being grown for general garden decoration all the resulting shoots can be left to grow. If exhibition blooms are required, then thin the shoots, removing all but the strongest one.

Sweet peas thrive in an open sunny site in a rich, well-drained soil. It is worth double digging the ground for sweet peas and filling the trench with rich organic matter such as farmyard manure. A pre-planting balanced fertiliser such as Growmore can also be applied at 60 g/m^2 (2 oz/yd^2).

Being climbing plants, sweet peas will need a support. A wigwam of bamboos can be used, a bundle of twiggy pea sticks, a plastic mesh or for exhibition blooms individual canes in a row. Plants are usually planted out in mid to late spring, spacing them about 20 cm (8 in) apart and alongside their supports.

Bush sweet peas for ordinary garden display will grow away naturally but may

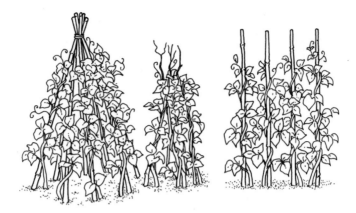

Sweet peas can be grown up wigwams of bamboos, bundles of pea sticks or more formally as cordons on canes.

require some initial help to encourage the climbing tendrils to find the supports. Cordon sweet peas for exhibition will require far more precise attention. The single stem has its own cane and as it starts to grow, the plant is looped in to its cane with metal plant rings. All sideshoots and tendrils are removed to encourage the plant to concentrate on flowering. In this way the best stems with five or more flowers are produced. Keep them well fed with liquid feeds and pick the flowers regularly to promote continuous flowering.

Dahlias

These are tender plants that originate from Mexico and were introduced to the UK in the late 18th century. Over the years many thousands of cultivars have been produced. The flowers have many petals and come in several forms leading to a complex classification system for the different types. They make good cut flowers but are also extensively grown for exhibiting. Many cultivars produce huge, brightly coloured flowers that are not for the faint hearted!

Dahlias are tuberous plants and can be bought in spring as dry dormant tubers or in early summer as green plants. Dormant tubers can be planted directly into the soil in late spring, although they are better potted and started into growth in a frost free greenhouse. When the young shoots are growing, they can be divided making sure that each plant has a shoot and a part of the tuber and root system. You can also propagate them by using the young shoots as softwood cuttings. They must be taken when no more than

When dividing dahlias, make sure there is a shoot on each portion.

about 5 cm (2 in) long as older stems become hollow and will not root. Plants from cuttings can be pinched to get a bushy plant with several stems. Plants produced from either starting tubers or from rooted cuttings must not be planted out until all danger of frost is passed, usually in early summer.

The site for growing dahlias should be in full sun with a rich well drained soil. The site should be prepared by single digging, incorporating generous quantities of organic matter and finishing off with a dressing of a general fertiliser such as Growmore at 60 g/m² (2 oz/yd²). Plants need generous spacing, allowing 60 cm (2 ft) for the smallest types and up to 90 cm (3 ft) for the tallest most vigorous types. Dahlias tend to be floppy plants and so require a small stake or a triangle of sturdy bamboo canes. They will need tying in as they grow. Dahlias are very attractive to slugs, so some protection is needed as soon as they are planted.

Dahlias are greedy plants and require generous supplies of water and feed during the season. As flower buds develop, use a liquid feed with high potassium. Behind each flower bud will be found two or more smaller buds. To produce high quality blooms, remove all but the central bud on each stem. This process is called disbudding. For general garden display, leave all the buds and you will get a larger quantity of smaller flowers.

Dahlias are at their best through the late summer and autumn months. Enjoy them until the first frost arrives. This will blacken the foliage. They should then be cut down to about 15 cm (6 in), labelled and carefully dug up. Shake or wash all the loose soil off the tubers and stand them upside down in a frost-free place for a couple of weeks to dry. When dry, they can be packed into trays of bark or old potting compost to store for the winter. They must be kept frost free and checked occasionally for mould or excess drying out. They should not be allowed to shrivel so may need occasional damping over.

Chrysanthemums

These are another group of hobby plants that has been highly developed over the years. Chrysanthemums originated from China and Japan and have been widely grown for many years as cut flowers and also for exhibition purposes. There are many different types. Early chrysanthemums are grown outdoors in the border and flower in August and September. There are those that produce large flower heads for cut flowers and also shorter bushy types for general border display.

Late chrysanthemums do not flower until November and so are usually grown in pots and finished off in a greenhouse. There are many different forms to the flowers and there is a complex classification system. As well as those with large heads grown for exhibition and cut flowers, there are also bushy types called Charm Chrysanthemums, which produce hundreds of tiny, often single flowers. A variation on these are the cascades that are very lax growing and can be trained to produce huge trailing specimens or indeed other fancy shapes.

Commercially, chrysanthemums can be produced to flower at any time of the year by altering the day length in greenhouses to trigger the plants' flowering responses.

SELECTED CHRYSANTHEMUMS

'Martin Riley' – incurved, yellow, early outdoor type

'Tracey Waller' – reflexed pink, early outdoor type

'Cricket' – white, intermediate outdoor type

'Peggy Steven' – yellow large single flowers, greenhouse

'Fairie' – compact pink pompom type, outdoors

'Yellow Rayonette' – yellow spider flowers, greenhouse

'Red Charm' – compact, tiny single red flowers, greenhouse

'Pink Cascade' – trails of single pink flowers, greenhouse

A well grown chrysanthemum plant, neatly tied in to a stout bamboo cane.

Chrysanthemums grown as pot plants are also often treated with growth retardant to produce a dwarf plant. Plants purchased from florists and then grown on for a second year can often be disappointing as they will not produce the same quality of display, when grown without the commercial techniques.

Garden chrysanthemums

The growing of a crop of outdoor chrysanthemums is quite straightforward and some very acceptable cut flowers can be produced. Plants will be available from garden centres and nurseries in late spring. They are generally hardy but should be carefully hardened off before planting outside.

Chrysanthemums like an open sunny site with a well prepared, fairly rich soil, finished off with a dressing of a general fertiliser such as Growmore at 60 g/m^2 (2 oz/yd^2). Space plants about 45 cm (18 in) apart and tie each plant closely to a 1.2-m (4-ft) bamboo cane. Soon after planting pinch the tip of the plant to encourage side shoots. If you are growing for exhibition, you can use the time of pinching to schedule the predicted flowering time. As the shoots grow they must be loosely looped in to the cane for support. Aim to finish three to five stems per plant for good quality blooms.

Water and feed regularly with a balanced liquid feed. When the flower buds appear, they should be disbudded. Those grown for large flower heads should have all but the central bud removed. Some are grown for sprays of flowers and with these, you should remove the central bud and leave all the others.

After flowering, the plants can be cut back and the roots, often called 'stools' lifted and boxed up in potting compost. They should be overwintered in a cold greenhouse. As conditions improve in the spring new shoots will be produced and these can be rooted as softwood cuttings and the whole process started again.

THE LAWN

GRASS IN SOME FORM OR OTHER is a component of most but not all gardens. A lawn affords a simple green foil for all the other more colourful and bolder garden features. It also provides a practical surface for walking on, relaxing or playing. It is quite simply a living carpet and in quality, it can be anything from Axminster to shag-pile! For many, the perfection of a close-cropped and striped emerald sward will be a constant goal. Others may prefer something more natural and some gardeners like to allow at least part of their lawns to grow long so that native meadow plants can grow, flower and seed. Such areas provide valuable wildlife havens.

GROWING A LAWN FROM SEED

This is undoubtedly the cheapest way of producing a lawn. The end result is likely to be a very high quality lawn but much effort is required and it will be many months before the lawn is ready for any wear.

Preparing the site

The site for a new lawn needs to be well prepared and ideally well in advance of sowing. Initially as many weeds as possible should be eradicated in particular perennial weeds. A couple of sprays with a translocated herbicide containing glyphosate will eradicate most perennial weeds. Techniques for doing this are described in more detail on pages 59–60. The soil should then be thoroughly cultivated by either single digging or with the use of a rotary cultivator. Should drainage be needed, it should be installed at this stage. Minor improvements to drainage can be made by the addition of sharp sand to the soil during cultivations.

Although it is not necessary for a lawn to be precisely level, this will be the time to smooth out any humps or hollows by raking the soil or possibly even barrowing some across the site. The final level of a lawn should, whenever possible, be just above the level of any adjacent paths, so adjust where necessary. This allows for easy mowing when the lawn is grown.

The final preparations of the tilth for seed sowing will be made by alternately treading the soil to firm any soft spots and raking. Ideally leave the surface for two or three weeks to allow any weeds to germinate. These can then be hoed off before the grass seed is sown. Raking should be used to break up any clods of soil, to create an even surface and to rake off any stones or other unwanted debris. Just before the final raking, a pre-seeding fertiliser should be used. This will have high phosphate and low nitrogen levels.

Grass seed mixes

There are many different blends of grass seed available for lawns. Seed used for lawns in temperate areas will generally be divided into those with or without perennial rye grass. PRG as it is sometimes known, is a tough hard-wearing grass but is not as fine as some of the other grasses available. If you want a general purpose lawn for a family garden, you should choose a mix with PRG. For a show lawn, maybe in a front garden or which will not get much wear, choose a mix without PRG. It will contain bents, fescues and meadow grasses. Such fine mixes will, however, require more attention.

Like any other plants grasses have been specially bred to give certain characteristics. Choose a good seed mix, as a cheap one will be unlikely to contain the latest and most suitable cultivars. There are also special mixes for particular conditions such as shade or soil types. Lawns for areas with a warmer climate will require totally different seed mixes, usually known as warm season grasses.

Lawn seed should ideally be sown in mid spring or early autumn, although it is possible to attempt this at any time when the soil is warm and moist. Seed should be sown evenly and carefully. Rates of sowing will generally be about 25–30 g/m^2 for a non rye grass mix and 35–40 g/m^2 for a rye grass mix. These are quite small quantities and it is not advisable to exceed them.

When sowing by hand, it is worth devising a small measure that will contain the correct quantity. The area should be marked out into strips 1 m (3 ft 2 in) wide to help gauge the correct application rate. The seed is then sown with half the quantity from one direction and half from the other to give a thorough and even coverage. Larger areas can be sown using a fertiliser spreader, which can be calibrated in advance by wheeling across a square metre (or yard) of paper or polythene and then altering the settings until the correct quantity is being applied. After sowing, the site is given one last very light rake to mix the seed in with the soil.

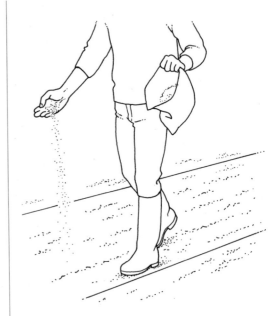

Mark out a new lawn into metre-wide strips to make seed sowing easier.

Given moist conditions, the very first green shoots should be seen in about 14 days. If watering is necessary, use a very fine sprinkler. At this stage it is very easy for heavy water droplets to disturb the surface or wash the seed into uneven patches, so water with care.

Caring for a young lawn

When the young grasses are about 2.5 cm (1 in) tall, the area can be lightly firmed with a light roller. This helps the grasses to 'tiller', which means to produce side shoots and bush out. If you don't have a roller but do have a mower with a roller use this but do not let the blades cut the grass at this stage by setting the blades very high. When the grass is about 5 cm (2 in) tall, you should give the lawn its first cut using a sharp mower, which will cleanly cut the grass and not pull it. The height of cut should be set no less than 2.5 cm (1 in) so that just the tops of the grasses are removed. Rake up or remove all the clippings to avoid them smothering the young growth. Mowing can then take place when needed but be very careful not to lower the cut until the lawn is thick and well established.

Creating a lawn from turf

Using turf to create a lawn has the advantage of creating an instant lawn that can be used in a relatively short time. It requires a little less effort but is generally considerably more expensive. Most turf nowadays is produced from seed mixes grown on a turf nursery and so you will again be able to choose between with or without rye grass and the same principles apply with turf as with seed. In the past, meadow turf was often offered for lawns. This is most unsuitable as it will usually originate from an agricultural situation and the grasses will be coarse and never thicken up to a good lawn. The results will always be disappointing.

Turf usually comes in rolls that cover a square metre, although smaller sized rolls may be available. You should time the delivery of turf to make sure preparation is complete and the turf can be laid without delay. Turf does not like to be stored for much more than 24 hours or it will turn yellow and deteriorate quickly. If the job has to be delayed and there is a suitable space, turf can be temporarily unrolled and kept watered but this is a tedious job.

Preparation for turfing is similar to that for seeding as described on page 117. The final preparation need not be quite as precise, although the turf will still follow any humps and hollows that are not corrected and any large stones left on the surface will project through the turf. A pre-seeding fertiliser is desirable but perhaps not essential for turf.

Laying turf

Start the job from the side of the lawn nearest to the stack of delivered turf. Ideally lay the first row from a footpath if there is one or use a straight edge to start the process. The second and subsequent rows are laid working from a plank placed on the previous row. Not only does this protect the new turf but working from the plank helps to firm the turf in place. If you are barrowing turf onto the site you will need a network of planks leading to the laying area. Lay each subsequent row so that the joins alternate like brickwork. And be sure to tightly butt each turf against its neighbour.

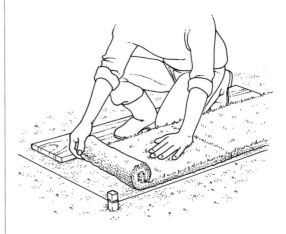

Butt each turf firmly against the next when laying new lawns.

Avoid finishing a row with a small sliver of turf, which will dry out quickly and be likely to be misplaced. Use full turves at the ends and bed small fillers in between full turves. When the lawn is finished, straight edges can be cut using a half-moon edging iron alongside a plank. Curves are best cut using a rope or hose pipe laid out to the desired shape. It is easier to lay the lawn beyond the desired shape and cut this out a week or so later when the turf has started to root in to the soil.

Freshly laid turf must never be allowed to dry until it is properly rooted and established. On warm sunny days this will mean watering the turf at one end of the lawn while you are still working at the other. This is quite critical and if neglected, the turf will rapidly dry, go straw yellow and shrink within a few hours. It is then almost impossible to recover such a situation. Always keep newly laid turf watered, when conditions are dry.

A turfed lawn can be mown as soon as it needs it but like its seeded counterpart, avoid cutting too close until well established.

Caring for the lawn

If lawns are to retain their attractive appearance, they will need regular maintenance and this means more than just mowing. In particular lawns benefit from an annual autumn maintenance procedure. Nearly all the tasks perfomed on lawns are quite heavy and laborious but fortunately most can be mechanised and many of the machines can be hired if only required for a short span of time.

Mowing

Regular cutting of grass is essential if we want a lawn that is easy to walk or play on and has the manicured look that many gardeners desire. In temperate climates we normally need to mow lawns once or twice week. This will vary with the time of year, growing conditions and vigour of the lawn. It is always best to cut more frequently, removing small amounts than to cut less regularly and drastically. This shocks the grasses, which struggle to recover. Traditionally we used to mow from mid spring to mid autumn but with our changing climates and seasons, this mowing period is much longer and it may be necessary to mow during a mild winter if grass has continued to grow.

Setting the mower to cut at the correct height is quite important. Many good lawns are often ruined by cutting too low, so if in doubt keep the height of cut up. General purpose lawns should be cut to about 2.5 cm (1 in) in summer but very fine lawns without rye grass could be cut lower to about 1 cm ($1/2$ in). In both cases the height of cut should be increased for the winter, leaving more grass. The height of cut should also be raised in hot dry weather.

Many people like to see a striped lawn but achieving this effect is only possible if you have a mower with a rear roller. With fine lawns it is best to use a mower with a grass box that collects the trimmings. On general-purpose lawns this is less important and the mowings can be allowed to 'fly'. Under most conditions they will soon disappear back into the sward, although when the grass is long and conditions are wet, they may stay on the surface as wet lumps, causing the grass to deteriorate. The final finish is given to a lawn by trimming the edges with edging shears or a strimmer.

Watering

Most grass will tolerate water shortage for some time although it will eventually suffer, scorch and die out. You may wish to water fine lawns in key locations to keep them looking fresh and green. Ideally water early in the day or in the evening to minimise evaporation. Use a sprinkler and provide sufficient water to ensure that the soil becomes thoroughly moist.

Fertilising

To keep a lawn looking pristine, it will need regular feeding. This is particularly so with lawns where the clippings are removed, as this processes will slowly but steadily replenish the soil. Two applications of fertiliser per year are normal, although a number of smaller applications are sometimes used. In the spring you should use a fertiliser high in nitrogen. Ideally use a slow release fertiliser, which will slowly feed the lawn over a period of time or split the application into two smaller doses. This avoids a big surge of growth.

An autumn fertiliser will have low nitrogen and high levels of potassium and phosphate. It may also contain iron which helps toughen the grass and protect it from diseases. Some turf experts suggest that autumn feeds are not essential as most soils contain adequate phosphates and potassium. An autumn feed should be applied after scarification and spiking.

All fertilisers should be applied very carefully to turf areas. A fertiliser spreader should be accurately calibrated to ensure that it spreads at the correct rate. The area should then be carefully marked out to ensure that the fertiliser is applied evenly and that there are no overlaps or missed areas. Overlaps will mean a double dose, which can cause scorch or death of the grass and a very patchy finish. If there is no rain within 24 hours, it is advisable to irrigate the lawn to wash the fertiliser off the grass blades and into the soil.

Autumn lawn maintenance

Once a year it is beneficial to give quality lawns some major attention. None of the following jobs are essential but when carried out, they will make a major difference to the lawn in the following season.

The first job is scarification, sometimes called thatch removal. This involves removing as much as possible of the dead grass, moss and other debris that has accumulated in the surface around the base of the grass plants. It can be done by hand using a spring-tined rake. It is hard work but amazing how much rubbish can be pulled out of the surface of a lawn. When done by hand it should be

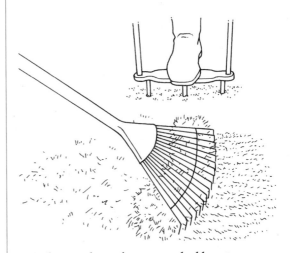

Spiking and scarifying are valuable autumn jobs if you want a top quality lawn.

followed by mowing to cut back any long stringy grass stems and to gather up the loose debris in the grass box. Fortunately there are also machines for this job, which scarify and collect the debris in a box. These can be hired.

This is followed by spiking which allows air into the soil and improves surface drainage. The simplest way of doing this is with a garden fork but again this is laborious and hard work. There are purpose made tools and machines which will do this far more effectively. If the lawn has serious compaction or drainage problems, you can opt to use a hollow tiner, which actually removes thin cores of soil down to about 10 cm (4 in). These must be gathered up and removed.

The final stage is top dressing. This is done with a light sandy soil mixture. Such mixes can be bought or it can be made from sieved garden compost. It is applied at about 1 kg/m² (30 oz/yd²) or more if the lawn has been hollow tined. It is usually spread evenly with a shovel and then gently worked into the surface with a birch besom or the back of a rake. If there are any particular hollows, the opportunity can be taken to work the soil into them and improve the levels. Any bare patches can be reseeded.

Renovating a neglected lawn

You may be faced with a neglected lawn, possibly with a new house that you have purchased. Generally with good attention an old lawn can be brought back into good shape. Firstly assess what it contains. Providing the majority of it is fine grasses without too much weed and moss, then renovation should be possible.

If it hasn't been cut for a long time, the first job is to mow, setting the mower at its highest setting but no lower than 5 cm (2 in) and removing all the clippings. Mow on a weekly basis slowly reducing the height of cut until the desired height is reached. Depending on the time of year, apply a suitable feed and water in if conditions are dry.

Scarification, spiking and top dressing are all valuable techniques to use on a neglected lawn and can be carried out at almost any time of the year although it would be best to avoid mid summer or the depths of winter. Scarifying a neglected lawn will usually pull out a great deal of thatch and may leave the lawn very patchy so after top dressing you can overseed, concentrating on bare areas. If the edges are damaged, cut out a square of turf containing the damaged part and turn this round so that the damaged piece faces into the lawn. The resulting hole can easily be filled with soil and seeded.

Controlling lawn weeds and mosses

Quite a number of broad-leaved weeds will survive in a lawn despite regular mowing and may spread at the expense of the grasses, which are smothered out. In an average quality lawn, some of these, such as daisies and clover, may be regarded as acceptable or even desirable. However, in a very fine lawn, the aim will be for a perfect grass sward and weeds will need to be controlled. Large weeds such as plantains can be removed by hand with a sharp knife, although this is a slow job. Generally it is quickest to use a selective lawn herbicide which will kill lawn weeds and not harm the grass. This can be applied with a watering can or sprayer, making sure that the chemical does not drift onto other plants, which will be damaged. If there are just a few weeds you need not spray the whole lawn but just spot treat with a small sprayer of herbicide. You can also obtain small 'stick' of herbicide for dabbing on individual weeds. Another easy way is to use a 'weed and feed' fertiliser in the spring, which is a fertiliser with added herbicide.

Moss can be a major problem in lawns. Basically moss grows where conditions are suitable and this means poor drainage, poor light and damp conditions. The autumn renovation procedure will do much to eradicate moss and deter its return. Where moss is a big problem, you can use lawn sand or a specific moss treatment, but the likelihood is that if underlying conditions are conducive to moss growth, it will always be a problem.

ALTERNATIVES TO GRASS

Where the area allocated to lawn is very small, it may be appropriate to use something other than grass. Both camomile and thyme make very effective green carpets with the benefit of aromatic foliage and some flowers. Camomile has a special form called 'Treneague' which is non-flowering but very compact and good for lawns. Both camomile and thyme will take some pedestrian wear, although not heavy usage.

It is essential that the site for establishing these is as free from weeds as possible. It should be prepared well in advance and all emerging weeds treated. Plants should be spaced about 20 cm (8 in) apart. As quite a large number of plants may be required it can be more economical to buy some plants in advance and then bulk these up by dividing or by rooting cuttings.

Both thyme and camomile require occasional trimming and it is most important to regularly weed until the surface is colonised by the planted species.

Meadow gardening and wildflowers

Some people favour the more natural approach to grass and like to see longer grass with wild flowers. This is called meadow gardening and requires totally different techniques to making a lawn. To encourage wildflowers rather than grasses, you will need a very poor soil with a low nutrient level so fertilisers should never be used. Ideally the topsoil should be stripped off or replaced with a poor soil but this is rarely practical.

There are several specialist firms offering wildflower seed mixes for the many different situations that occur. Be sure to purchase a seed mix that matches the conditions you have in your garden. Preparation is the same for a lawn but weed freedom is particularly important and no fertiliser should be used. Wildflower mixes are applied at very low rates and it may be easier to bulk them up with sand to make sowing easier. For those who are more impatient, small plants or plugs of wildflowers are readily available that will give a head start.

Bulbs of all sorts mix well with wild flower meadows, although this will be taking the style a little away from the natural. Narcissus, crocus and even tulips can be naturalised in grassland and will regrow and flower each year.

Wildflower meadows should generally be cut only once or twice a year. The main cut will be around July–August. This will follow the main spring and early summer display of wild flowers and bulbs and also allow for many of the life cycles of creatures living in the meadow to complete. The cut grass should always be raked off and removed. This avoids the sward being smothered and also continues to denude the soil of nutrients. A second cut can take place in autumn purely for tidiness. The actual timing of cuts should take into account the species in the mix.

Poppy field mixes

Many will have admired the typical cornfield annuals such as poppy, cornflower, corncockle, corn marigold and corn camomile and would like to recreate the effect in the garden. These seeds are all annuals and will only germinate on freshly cultivated soil so although it is easy to create this effect it will not last into future seasons unless cultivation and reseeding takes place every year. This is easily done by waiting until the plants have shed their seeds, then mow the tops off and rotavate the ground lightly to mix the seeds into the loose soil.

GARDENING UNDER COVER

THE WHOLE CONCEPT OF GARDENING away from the onslaught of chillier climates is attractive to many gardeners and for centuries various structures such as greenhouses, conservatories and more recently polythene tunnels have held great fascination.

PROTECTED CROPPING

Greenhouses and polythene tunnels tend to be productive areas, used for growing crops of various types. Conservatories are usually linked to the house and as such treated as a sort of inside/outside room, usually with furniture as well as plants – a place where the garden meets the house.

Such structures enable earlier crops, the raising of your own bedding and vegetable plants and the means to propagate all sorts of other garden plants. You can also achieve valuable crops of tender vegetables such as tomatoes, cucumbers and peppers and produce your own pot plants and cut flowers. There is also the sheer joy of being able to continue gardening in comfort when the weather outside is awful!

All of these structures should be sited in a sunny area of the garden. A greenhouse that does not receive full sunshine will be of little use during the winter and spring months. Avoid a wind tunnel and position it so that the long side faces south. Siting near to the house will be of value, particularly if you intend to make electricity and water connections. If really close to the house, you may extend the central heating system to provide winter heating at an economical rate.

GREENHOUSES

Greenhouses are relatively inexpensive and much more useful and substantial than polythene tunnels. They will last many years and give good protection against the elements. Buy as large a greenhouse as you can afford and fit into your garden. Controlling the temperature is easier and you are bound to need the space as your interest develops. The smallest viable size is 1.8 x 2.4 m (6 x 8 ft). Smaller ones are really impractical. Most greenhouses are manufactured from aluminium, which is tough and durable. Some are powder coated, often green. Timber greenhouses are available, often made from hardwood, and look very elegant but there will be a need for periodic treatment of the timber. As well as traditional shaped greenhouses, octagonal ones are available and also those that fix against a wall, called lean-to greenhouses.

In the past glasshouses were glazed with horticultural glass, which was cheap but fragile. For domestic purposes, particularly where there are children, it is worth getting toughened glass, which will withstand the onslaught of footballs and not be a major hazard. Acrylic sheets are also possible but do not allow as much light through, particularly as they age.

A good greenhouse will have enough height to stand up in, without the risk of banging your head. The door should be wide enough for access with a wheelbarrow and it should be well braced at the ends and corners to withstand wind. In particular it

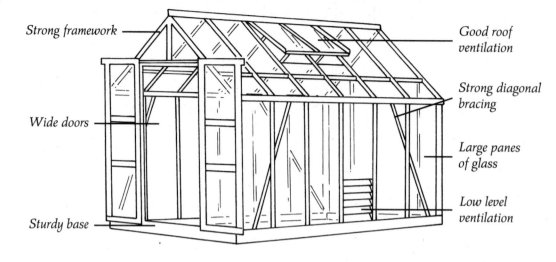

Strong framework

Good roof
ventilation

Strong diagonal
bracing

Wide doors

Large panes
of glass

Low level
ventilation

Sturdy base

Look for these characteristics when choosing a greenhouse to ensure it will be a good investment.

should have adequate ventilation with opening vents on both sides of the roof and on the side walls. Autovent openers are simple devices that will open the vents automatically on a warm day and are well worth the extra cost.

Some greenhouses have prefabricated or integral bases and do not require a permanent foundation. They must still be placed on a firm level base. Ideally a concrete and brick foundation is by far the best and will avoid the structure shifting at a later stage. Most domestic greenhouses are relatively easy to construct although most suppliers will offer an erection service as well. When handling glass always use stout leather gloves.

Heating a greenhouse

An unheated greenhouse does have some value in that it will enable you to provide a little basic protection to plants and start crops a bit earlier but not much. The real

advantage comes if you install a simple heating system that enables you to keep your greenhouse or polythene tunnel frost free. This may not be for the whole year but at least for the spring months, when you are raising young plants.

Electric greenhouse heaters are possible and have the advantage of thermostatic control. Remember that all electrical installations should be done by a competent electrician particularly in a situation such as a greenhouse where there will be water in close proximity to electrical equipment. Paraffin heaters are cheap but they have no control and must be refuelled frequently. They can also release noxious fumes. Heaters run from bottled gas are an excellent option and will have some thermostatic control. You can even get a changeover valve, which operates with two bottles of gas so that when one runs out, the supply transfers to the second. In certain circumstances where say a lean-to greenhouse is attached to the dwelling, it may be possible to extend the central heating system.

You can reduce heating bills and help to maintain a more even temperature by lining a greenhouse in winter with bubble wrap. You can also reduce the heated area with a partition made from polythene or by stretching polythene or bubble wrap across the greenhouse just above head height. Don't forget though that this will have the disadvantage of reducing winter light, which is valuable, so plants may become more leggy.

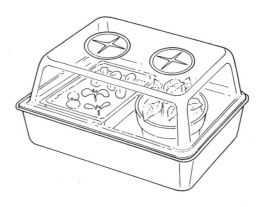

Many different types of cutting can be easily rooted in a simple plastic propagator like this.

Greenhouse equipment

Some benching is always useful in a greenhouse as it brings smaller plants closer to working height. Watering and tending of them is much easier. Also the ground is always the coldest, so young plants are better off the ground. A potting bench where you can keep composts and pots is essential, although this may not be in the greenhouse but possibly in a nearby shed. Some gardeners make a small three-sided tray, which can be used for potting and then stored away when not needed.

A propagating area is valuable. For cuttings, this will need to be an enclosed box of some sort with a glass top. You can fabricate such a structure or buy various sized plastic propagators, which work very well. For both seeds and cuttings, ideally you need a source of bottom heat. Small electric propagators are available with a simple heating element in the bottom. For those that do not have electricity in the greenhouse, it will be simpler to site such a propagator on a windowsill in the house and then transfer seedlings and rooted cuttings to the greenhouse when established.

A clean watering can will be needed, although where lots of plants are grown, it will be quicker to use a hose pipe with a rose. Under no circumstances should you use water from a static tank or water butt. This is almost always contaminated with various plant diseases. It is a fallacy that rainwater is always better! Pots, trays, composts, plant labels, a small dibber and a garden sieve are the other basic requirements.

Greenhouse management

Looking after a greenhouse is fairly straightforward but it does require more determination and regular care than the garden outside. Most gardens can be left for a few days or even weeks without major problems but greenhouses require daily attention, throughout most of the year. Certain automatic features are possible but even they require monitoring and checking. Managing a greenhouse is all about creating the ideal environment for the plants you are growing. This involves managing the heat, light, ventilation and humidity.

Firstly the temperature should be controlled as evenly as possible. Wildly fluctuating temperatures between day and night will stress plants. This means making sure that heaters operate efficiently at night time and that ventilators are opened early on warm days. A closed greenhouse can get very hot very quickly early on a summer's day and a Sunday lie-in is not advised! Ventilating a greenhouse also provides a fresh source of air for plants, which need carbon dioxide to grow and this can be quickly depleted in a greenhouse that is closed up tight. In winter it is beneficial to provide a crack of ventilation whenever the weather allows, particularly to avoid a build up of humidity, which often results in diseases such as botrytis.

Unheated greenhouses need particularly careful attention. The very construction of a greenhouse traps the sun's heat so it is prudent to close the ventilators on an unheated greenhouse in late afternoon or early evening to trap a little of the sun's warmth.

In summer it is useful to shade a greenhouse to reduce excessively high temperatures. This can be done with purpose-made blinds, plastic mesh or with a coating of a special greenhouse shading paint that can be washed off in the winter. Never use emulsion paint for this job as it remains permanently!

Humidity is also of importance and will depend on the crop you are growing. For example, cucumbers like to grow in a much damper atmosphere than tomatoes.

Humidity is easily increased by damping down the floors of the greenhouse with a hose. Damping down is also a useful means of cooling the greenhouse in very hot weather, in that evaporating water produces a cooling effect. By contrast, in the winter we would normally aim for a drier atmosphere to avoid disease, unless you are running a very well heated greenhouse filled with tropical plants.

Light is a vital consideration for plants and without adequate levels, plants cannot grow. So even if you heat a greenhouse in winter, plants will not grow unless there is enough light. This means that it is important to keep the greenhouse glass clean in winter to allow the maximum amount of winter sunshine to reach your plants. If you have electricity in your greenhouse and wish to grow plants over winter, it may be worth investing in special grow lights. These are particularly valuable set above propagating areas, where you may be growing new seedlings and young fragile plants.

Giving plants adequate water for growth, without drowning them is also especially important in the greenhouse. In general far more plants are killed by overwatering than underwatering. With potted plants, you should always wait until the compost is looking or feeling dry, then give each pot a thorough soaking. This may need to be daily in mid summer but less than once a week in winter. Hard and fast rules for watering cannot be given and you must check each plant to assess its water requirements. Feeding of potted plants is important as the roots are restricted and the nutrients in the compost are soon exhausted.

Hygiene is very important in a greenhouse. Any pests or diseases spread rapidly in the enclosed atmosphere. Make sure all pots, trays and equipment are thoroughly clean. Avoid storing things under the benches as this inevitably becomes untidy and a hiding place for pests. Once a year, it is a good practice to thoroughly wash down the greenhouse inside and out, ideally using a horticultural disinfectant. If green algae have collected between the overlaps of the glass, clean them out with a thin strip of rigid plastic. Keep it clean and tidy!

POLYTUNNELS

These are undoubtedly a cheaper means of providing protection. They are made from hoops of galvanised steel, linked together to make a semi-circular tunnel shape. A large sheet of polythene is stretched over the whole structure and anchored in a trench in the ground. Always cover a polytunnel on a warm day as the polythene will be soft and stretch tight across the frame. There are usually simple doors at one or both ends, which also act as ventilation.

Polythene tunnels provide a low-cost means of plant protection particularly useful for vegetables and growing bedding plants.

Polytunnels are useful for providing limited protection for vegetable crops such as tomatoes or for producing bedding plants or cut flowers. They lose heat quickly in the winter and heat up excessively in the summer. The polythene will usually last for two to three seasons but will then need replacing. There is always the risk of tears which easily happen and then a freak gust of wind can rip the whole structure and remove the protection in a few minutes.

CONSERVATORIES

These are somewhat different to glasshouses in style and management. Usually they are built by specialist contractors, very much as an extension to the house. Much of their construction is based on aesthetics rather than practicalities and they are likely to have an ornamental floor and such items as domestic light fittings and furniture. Nevertheless make sure you get one with adequate ventilation and some means of shading or it is not going to be comfortable for either you or plants.

Conservatory plants are likely to be ornamental specimens in pots or large tubs, although there is no reason why you cannot leave an area of open soil so that you can plant suitable exotics to add to the ambience. All those points of heating, ventilating and shading are just as important, although it may be a little more difficult in a conservatory. For example you may not wish to splash water around in areas where there are soft furnishings. As an alternative you can try standing pots in large dishes of pebbles, which can be kept damp to raise the humidity.

the kitchen garden

GROWING FRUIT AND VEGETABLES

MOST GARDENERS TRY THEIR HAND at producing crops of fruit and vegetables at some stage. Sadly few of our small modern gardens really have enough space to make production properly viable. However, growing, cooking and eating your own produce can be extremely satisfying. Not only can it be economical, but there are all the advantages of freshness, freedom from unknown pesticides, flavour, not to mention the extra health benefits of working a kitchen garden. That said, it can be hard work!

At one end of the spectrum there is no reason why anyone with a small garden cannot grow a few pots or tubs of salads, choice vegetables or fruit. At the far extreme will be those who will want to take on a full allotment and end up producing enough to feed not only their own families but half the street! Eventually some growers go on to try to attain perfection and grow for showing, producing enormous specimens out of all proportion to any cooking pot!

Another of the advantages of vegetable production is the ability to grow and eat a crop that is not available in the shops. For example, golden beet, white French beans, purple sprouts or yellow tomatoes. These and many other vegetables provide not only novelty value but often totally different or superior flavours.

Vegetables are quick-growing crops and usually produce results within a single season, often in just a few weeks. By contrast, fruit are permanent crops on woody bushes and trees and will take several seasons to grow, settle down and start cropping.

For those who do not have enough space in their own gardens to grow vegetables, there are allotment gardens in many areas. Rental of such a space is low and most allotment associations will allow you to share or rent a half size allotment if you think a full size too demanding. Check out the plots and sites available. Some may be very overgrown and derelict although the advantage of this is that uncropped time may have allowed pests and diseases in the soil to diminish.

Sites vary in the facilities they offer. Most are owned by the local authority but some will be managed by an allotment society. Some will have a water supply and may also have storage space and even a small trading post selling low-cost seed and fertilisers to members. A good allotment site will probably have a waiting list and may take several years for your name to reach the top and a plot to become available.

Whether you grow on a large scale on an allotment or on a smaller scale in a few tubs, the provision of home-grown vegetables is a very healthy pursuit. We all know the values of vegetables in our diets and when we grow our own, we are also adding the benefit of the good, steady exercise taken to produce them. A double success!

VEGETABLE PRODUCTION

BEFORE WE START TO TALK ABOUT the individual crops in our vegetable garden, it is worth outlining some of the basic techniques that are common to all vegetable production. Understanding these will go a long way towards achieving a good crop.

SUCCESSION

This is all important and quite simply means producing crops over a period of time so that we can continue to harvest and use them for many weeks, maybe the whole summer. The classic mistake is to grow too much of one thing so that, for example, you may have a whole row of thirty lettuces all maturing at the same time. No one likes that much salad! With many crops this will mean making a number of sowings at different stages so that the crops mature at different intervals.

With some crops we will also need to use early-, mid- and late-season cultivars that mature at different times. Sometimes the very act of harvesting a crop, such as with runner beans, means that they will continue to produce, giving a longer harvesting season.

Succession also involves the continued use of the space in a vegetable garden. So, for example, when a crop of spring cabbage has been harvested in late spring, the ground can be cleared and cultivated ready to take a row of celery that will mature later in the summer.

CROP ROTATION

Using a crop rotation is a very traditional way of managing a vegetable plot or allotment. In tiny vegetable plots it may be difficult to follow this slavishly but in understanding the principles of rotation you can help to avoid some problems. With crop rotation we group together some basic vegetable types in order to give them the conditions they like for growth and to avoid a build-up of pests and diseases. The three main groups are brassicas, including cabbages, cauliflowers, and Brussels sprouts; secondly root crops, including carrots, parsnips, beetroot and potatoes; and thirdly legumes: the whole range of peas and beans. Some gardeners would make a fourth group with tender vegetables such as courgettes, sweet corn, celery and tomatoes.

We then divide up our vegetable garden into three or four areas and move the grouped crops around over a three or four year period. In this way we can hope to avoid the build up of pests and diseases that can occur when crops are always grown on the same land. You should also try to treat the soil in the ideal way for each crop. Peas and beans are rich feeders so we would try to add manure or organic matter before these crops. Brassicas need a high pH so we would aim to lime before these crops. Root crops do not like lumpy organic matter in the soil as the roots will be misshapen so if we aim to grow these the third year after manuring, this will be well absorbed into the soil. In a tiny

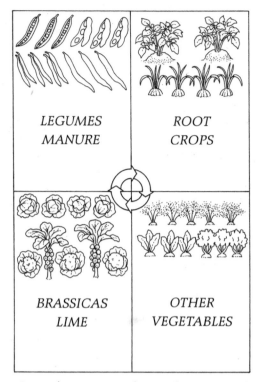

| LEGUMES MANURE | ROOT CROPS |

| BRASSICAS LIME | OTHER VEGETABLES |

Over a four-year period, move these crops and their cultural requirements round the four areas.

vegetable plot it may not be practical to slavishly follow this, although observing the basic principles is valuable.

Salads are not particularly fussy and can be squeezed in wherever there is a gap. Onions can be put with root vegetables although some growers like to build up a specialist onion bed with high fertility. Some vegetables such as asparagus and rhubarb will need a permanent site.

INTERCROPPING

This is quite simply making the best of limited space by juggling one crop between another. So for example sweet corn, which is slow growing and will not be mature until

the end of summer would be planted at least 45 cm (18 in) apart. It is quite possible to grow a crop of lettuce between the corn, which is finished by mid summer. Sometimes this will mean planting or sowing the quick crop first leaving space for the later 'main' crop, which is planted in between. When planning intercrops, it is important to avoid planting too close and spoiling either crop.

COMPANION PLANTING

This is a technique of pest control, whereby we plant different crops together. Sometimes the scent of one plant will mask the other and so deter the pest. Growing spring onions amongst carrots will deter carrot root fly. Garlic is also said to deter pests. Nasturtiums can be used to mask the smell of brassicas and deter cabbage white butterflies. Alternatively we can use a plant that will attract a predator, which will naturally control the pest. French Marigolds attract beneficial hover flies, which feed on aphids so these are useful next to crops such as beans, which are liable to be attacked by aphids.

SEEDS

Most vegetable crops are raised annually from seed, which is not a cheap commodity nowadays. A good seed catalogue will show an amazing range of different seeds. Do not be tempted to buy the cheapest. Many of the best cultivars are F1 hybrids and because of their special breeding, will be more expensive. They are nevertheless worth the extra premium because of their added characteristics such as vigour, heavier cropping and disease resistance.

As well as 'ordinary' natural seed, some

Sweetcorn, maturing late summer, interplanted with lettuce for a quick early crop.

vegetable seeds may be available in special forms. Some seeds may come pre-treated with a fungicide to protect against diseases. Other tiny seeds such as lettuce are available as pellets, which consist of a seed coated with an inert material making them bigger and easier to handle.

All seed should last a full twelve months but many will last several years if stored carefully. Generally, the larger seeds such as peas and beans store the longest, while smaller seeds such as papery parsnips and carrots have a shorter storage span. If you have used part of a packet, seal the packet again and store in a cool, dry place. This is useful for crops where you may want just a few plants or a short row each year. Seeds such as peas and beans, which have been stored for a couple of years can be helped in their germination by soaking in warm water for 24 hours before sowing.

Seed bed preparation and sowing

The ground for growing vegetables, should have been well prepared by digging in advance (see pages 26–27). In the spring, as the soil starts to dry, finish the seed bed by breaking down the surface into a fine crumbly tilth using a rake. If the soil is not sticky, it can be useful to tread the soil at this stage, which breaks the clods and gently firms the surface. A general balanced fertiliser such as Growmore at 60 g/m² (2 oz/yd²) is applied before a final raking. Remove excess stones, remaining clods and any weeds. The surface should be fine and crumbly but not dusty.

Most seeds are sown in a drill, which is a narrow V-shaped shallow channel. Traditionally this is drawn out with a draw hoe running alongside a tightly stretched garden line. Some gardeners find it easier to use a straight edge such as a plank and to scratch out a drill using a stick or bamboo cane. The depth of the drill is very important and you should remember that seeds should be sown at a depth of no more than twice their diameter, which is very shallow for small seeds, often less than 1 cm ($^1/_2$ in).

Sow the seeds very thinly bearing mind the eventual spacing required. For example, lettuces will be thinned to about 30 cm (12 in) and parsnips to about 15 cm (6 in). If the seeds are large enough, we can individually sow at the final spacing, allowing a couple of seeds at each station. If both grow, one will be removed later. After sowing, the soil is gently raked back into the drill to cover the seed. If conditions are dry, you can run water along the drill before sowing but it is not good to water after sowing as this can pan the soil down too hard and inhibit germination.

GROWING IN MODULES

Many gardeners like to start off seeds of all sorts of crops in containers, using the protection of a cool greenhouse or a cold frame. This enables an earlier start and also a greater control over germination conditions. Special trays with forty or more individual cells can be used. A tiny pinch of seed is sown in each unit and the resulting seedlings thinned to one per unit on germination. When established these can be hardened off and then planted out at their final spacing. Although one would not normally grow root vegetables in containers, beetroot and stump-rooted carrots can be grown this way, providing they are planted out whilst very young.

FEEDING VEGETABLE CROPS

Most vegetables will crop adequately from residual nutrients in the soil from organic matter and the base dressing of general fertiliser applied at sowing. Some slow growing crops, such as winter brassicas, will benefit from a further top dressing of fertiliser. This should be sprinkled around them, hoed in lightly and then watered in. Crops such as courgettes or runner beans that we want to go on producing over an extended period of time respond well to regular liquid feeding. In general do not feed in the autumn as any overwintering vegetables do not want soft lush growth that would be damaged by the winter cold.

BRASSICAS

This large group of vegetables includes cabbages, Brussel sprouts and curly kale, all grown for their edible leaves, cauliflower and broccoli for their flower heads, and swedes and turnips for their roots. All are members of the same family, despite their disparate appearance. There are many different types that can be grown for cropping throughout the year. Sometimes turnips and swedes are grouped with root vegetables, although they should be treated as brassicas as they suffer from the same pests and diseases. Brassicas tend to have a high nitrogen requirement and need heavy feeding. They also need a soil with a high pH.

As well as the standard types, there is also red cabbage, ideal for pickling, a novelty red Brussels sprout and a purple form of cauliflower, which has a delicate flavour. Sadly these coloured forms do not always retain their colour when cooked, which rather negates the point!

Early summer cabbages, cauliflowers and calabrese

These should be sown under glass in early spring, sowing the seeds in modules to give small plants to plant out in mid spring for cropping early summer onwards. Cauliflowers in particular must not suffer a check to growth so it is best to raise plants in 9-cm (3.5-in) pots. In the garden, cabbages are spaced at about 45 cm (18 in) apart and cauliflowers at 60 cm (2 ft). Calabrese, often called broccoli, can be grown in the same way. Space calabrese much closer at about 30 cm (12 in) apart both ways. Calabrese will produce an initial green head like a small cauliflower. After harvesting that, the plant will regrow and produce several pickings of smaller very useful spears.

Selected summer brassicas

Cabbage 'Hispi' AGM– fast maturing, early summer, pointed cabbage

Cabbage 'Derby Day' AGM – a round, early summer cabbage

Cauliflower 'Aviso F1' AGM – vigorous, good flavour, very white curd

Cauliflower 'All the Year Round' – traditional cultivar for successional sowing

Cauliflower 'Romanesco' – pointed pale green spiral florets with a distinct flavour

Cauliflower 'Graffiti' – another novelty with rich violet colouring, good flavour

Calabrese 'Green Magic' – early cultivar with large heads

Calabrese 'Hydra' F1 AGM – good for producing successional shoots

Winter brassicas

These include Brussels sprouts, Savoy cabbages and winter cauliflower which are all sown in late spring. They can be sown in modules or alternatively sown in a seed bed in the garden, subsequently lifting and transplanting the seedlings when they have three or four leaves. Plant them all at about 60 cm (12 in) apart. Although very basic vegetables, they will need careful attention in order to produce valuable quality crops for winter use. There is also curly kale, which is a brassica from which you can continuously pick leaves. It is strongly flavoured and inclined to be tough but easy to grow and hardy.

Selected winter brassicas

Cabbage 'Celtic' AGM – a round Dutch white type, hardy and reliable

Cabbage 'Traviata' – Savoy style cabbage with crinkled leaves, hardy

Cabbage 'January King 3' – tried and tested, very hardy

Cabbage 'Red Drumhead' – solid dark red heads for pickling or cooking

Brussels sprouts 'Peer Gynt' – best known early, good crop, short plants

Brussels sprouts 'Silverline' – late, medium-sized sprouts with good flavour

Brussels sprouts 'Red Delicious' – late cropping, red sprouts, cooks red, too

Cauliflower 'Deakin' – matures late autumn–winter, medium sized

Cauliflower 'Galleon' – hardy, overwinters and matures late spring

Spring cabbage and sprouting broccoli

Sprouting broccoli is a biennial that produces a crop of small broccoli spears in either white or purple in late spring. Many would say the flavour is better than calabrese. It is sown in late spring and has a long growing season, not being ready for use until almost a year later. The plants are tall and may require staking. Spring cabbage is grown in a similar way, sowing in late summer and transplanting before winter. Both should be given an early spring feed of a nitrogenous fertiliser to boost their growth after the winter. There are also spring greens, which are grown like spring cabbage but do not make a firm heart.

Selected spring brassicas

Cabbage 'April' – compact pointed heads, hardy
Cabbage 'Spring Hero' – early ballhead type

Broccoli 'Purple Sprouting' AGM – hardy and reliable cropper
Broccoli 'White Sprouting' – similar but white in colour
Broccoli 'Claret' AGM – modern F1 hybrid, high yield purple spears

Pests and diseases

Brassicas suffer from caterpillar damage from cabbage white butterflies, from a particular whitefly and from cabbage root fly. The latter can be deterred by putting a small collar around young plants, which discourages the pest from laying its eggs around the plant. There is also a disease called club root which

Various brassica crops. Clockwise from left: Brussels sprouts, pointed cabbage, cauliflower, Romanesco broccoli, curly kale, turnip, calabrese and round cabbage.

can be devastating. It survives in the soil for many years so old vegetable gardens and allotments are often infected. It can be deterred by ensuring a high soil pH and by raising good strong healthy plants in containers, which get a good head start. Brassicas are also often attacked by birds, particularly pigeons and it may be necessary to net the crop to protect them. Seedlings also suffer from flea beetle damage.

Turnips and swedes are also members of the brassica family but are often considered as root vegetables, although they do get the same pests and diseases as other brassicas.

LEGUMES

This is the family of podded vegetables that we more generally refer to as peas and beans. Sometimes we eat the whole pod as in runner beans or sugar peas and with others such as broad beans or peas, we eat the seed itself and dispose of the pod.

This family of plants are said to be 'nitrogen fixing' as they have the ability to take nitrogen from the air and use for growth. This is done by means of lumpy nodules, which can be seen on the roots. When clearing pea and bean crops at the end of the season, it is useful to dig in the roots as the remaining fixed nitrogen will remain in the soil for the next crop.

Runner beans

These are a valuable summer crop, particularly because they will go on producing for many weeks. They are climbing plants, so must be provided with a support of some sort. Bamboo canes, 2.4 m (8 ft) in length can be used to make either wigwams or a crossed double row. Alternatively, if available, tall brushwood can be used to make a thick 'hedge', up which the beans can climb. Plastic nets are also available but will need a basic support of poles and wire. Whatever you use, remember that in full growth the plants will be heavy and structures, if too flimsy, will collapse or blow down in autumn gales.

Runner beans are tender plants and will not withstand frost so they should not be sown outside until late spring. They are large seeds and so can be individually sown putting two seeds at the base of each cane or piece of brushwood. They are planted with a dibber or small trowel, placing them about 2.5 cm (1 in) deep. Alternatively, they can be sown in modules or small pots under cover and planted out in early summer as soon as all danger of frost is past. They must be planted as quite young plants as they soon start to shoot up and become very leggy.

As soon as the stems start to elongate, they should be tucked in and encouraged to climb. Once started they will climb on their own. Runner beans are very sensitive to water, especially when flowering. If they are dry when flowering the young pods will fall off, so it is essential to keep them well watered. They should start to crop in mid summer and if you feed them regularly with a liquid feed, they will continue to produce a valuable crop until mid autumn.

An early crop of runner beans can be produced by growing as a single row and pinching the growing points, when the plant is about 30 cm (12 in). They do not need support. The side shoots will produce flowers and beans early but the beans will tend to

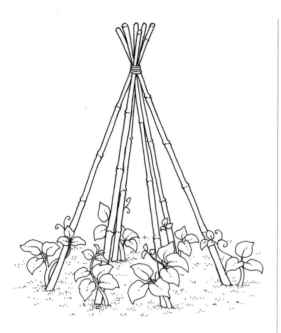

Tuck in the young shoots to encourage runner beans to grow up a bamboo wigwam.

lay on the ground and be curly rather than the straight ones produced from climbing plants.

Selected runner beans

'Enorma' AGM – huge bean, a good show bean

'Scarlet Emperor' – traditional cultivar, reliable, early and heavy cropping

'Painted Lady' – heavy cropper but also ornamental with red/white flowers

'White Apollo' – white flowered, excellent flavour, sets easily, heavy crop

'Polestar' – stringless type, early and heavy cropping

Pests and diseases

Runner beans tend to suffer from aphids and slugs. Halo blight may occur, which causes brown spots with yellow surrounds and anthracnose will cause brown patches on the beans. Infected plants of both should be destroyed.

French beans

These are less commonly grown than runner beans but when harvested young make a wonderful tender and succulent vegetable. French beans generally have a bush habit, although there are a few climbing versions. They tend to have a shorter cropping life so it is worth making two or three sowings in a season to give succession and continuity. They are also a tender plant, so sowing should not start until mid spring but can continue until early summer. Cropping will usually be from mid summer to mid autumn.

They should be sown in a single row, placing the seeds about 10 cm (4 in) apart and the rows about 45 cm (18 in) apart. These can also be sown slightly earlier under glass, using modules or small pots and planting out in early summer. A general balanced fertiliser such as Growmore applied at 60 g/m² (2 oz/yd²) before sowing should provide adequate nutrition for the crop. Keep well watered during dry conditions. They suffer from slugs and aphids but are otherwise generally trouble free.

Selected French beans

'The Prince' AGM – heavy crop and good continuity

'Purple Queen' – purple pods, heavy yield, excellent flavour, green on cooking

'Orinoco Golden Bean' – high yield, strong yellow colour, compact plant

'Borlotto' – novelty with red mottled pods, can also mature and dry beans

'Cobra' – a climbing French bean, grown like runner beans, long cropping season

Broad beans

These are a hardy crop and can actually be sown in mid autumn or early spring. An autumn sowing will only grow very slowly during the winter but will usually crop by late spring, giving a useful early crop. Sowings made in spring will crop by early summer, providing valuable succession.

Broad beans are usually sown in a double row about 20 cm (8 in) apart, also placing the seeds about 20 cm (8 in) apart. Multiple rows can be placed 60 cm (2 ft) from the next. The seeds are usually sown direct in the ground, about 5 cm (2 in) deep, although they too can be raised in small pots or modules and planted out. They are generally self-supporting but can sometimes flop so it is a useful precaution to surround the double rows with a ring of string, stretched between short posts.

Water if conditions are dry during flowering and pod formation. As soon as the first pods start to show, remove the tip of the plants as this concentrates the plant's energies into the crop. It also helps to discourage blackfly, which are attracted to the soft tips.

Selected broad beans

'The Sutton' AGM – a dwarf type, ideal for small gardens, good cropper

'Aquadulce Claudia' AGM – early crop, good for autumn sowing

'Masterpiece Green Longpod' AGM – reliable and high yielding

Pests and diseases

Blackfly is a major and serious pest of broad beans and can decimate the crop. It is worth spraying as soon as it appears to keep it under control. Harvest as soon as the beans start to show as raised bumps through the pods.

PEAS

Although frozen peas are very good and provide an easy way of sourcing a vegetable that is fiddly to grow, there is nothing quite like freshly picked green peas. Peas are nevertheless a demanding crop and require a great deal of space for a relatively small crop but it is worth growing the real thing at least once.

Peas are generally hardy, although some are tougher than others. There are lots of different types, which are initially divided into round (smooth) and wrinkled seeded varieties. The round seeded cultivars are the toughest and the earliest to crop. The wrinkled types are larger, sweeter and heavier cropping, although less hardy so cannot be sown as early.

Peas are also divided into early, second early and maincrop cultivars. By using a range of cultivars, you can produce crops of peas from late spring through until mid autumn. Peas are climbing plants, which cling by means of tendrils so they will need some support, which is usually best provided as short brushwood or netting stretched between wooden stakes. The shorter cultivars need less support but do not yield as heavy a crop as the tall ones.

Generally the first sowings take place in early spring, although in sheltered areas it is possible to make a late autumn sowing. Early sowings should use a round seeded early cultivar, moving on through the categories to maincrop wrinkled seeded types, which can be sown from late spring through to early or mid summer. With a careful choice of cultivars and a number of sowings, fresh peas can be available right through from early summer to autumn.

Peas are sown as a wide row in a flat bottomed drill about 15 cm (6 in) wide. Individual peas are scattered or spaced about 7.5 cm (3 in) apart. The spacing between the rows should be about the same as the expected height of the crop so dwarf early cultivars will be much closer than tall maincrops. Freshly sown peas are very attractive to both birds and mice. Protect from birds with black cotton tightly stretched between short canes or with wire netting guards. Traps can be set for mice.

As soon as the seedlings emerge, support from brushwood or a plastic netting needs to be erected. Keep the plants well watered in any dry spells. If they become too dry, the crop will not set or develop and powdery mildew is also likely to appear. Peas tend to

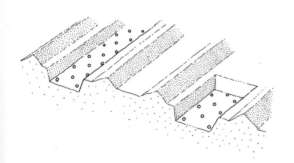

Pea seeds carefully spaced in a flat-bottomed drill.

OTHER PEAS

As well as the familiar garden peas, there are also 'mange tout' and 'sugar snap' peas, which are eaten complete with the tender pods. Both are useful for stir fries. Mange touts are eaten when the pods are flat, whereas sugar snap types are eaten when the peas within the pod have started to flesh out. There are also 'petit pois' types, which produce tiny very sweet peas, which are shelled, cooked and eaten like normal peas.

'Oregon Sugar Pod' – Mange tout type, gather and cook young

'Delikata' AGM – sugar snap type

'Waverex' – very sweet and tender

have one main flush of pods but healthy well grown plants will produce some extra pods for a short while.

Selected pea cultivars
1ST EARLIES – sow October/November or February/March
'Feltham First' – dwarf, very early and hardy
'Early Onward' AGM – heavy cropper

2ND EARLIES – sow March to June
'Kelvedon Wonder' AGM – heavy yielding and fine flavour, resistant to mildew
'Hurst Greenshaft' AGM – resistant to downy mildew and verticillium wilt

MAINCROP – sow March to June
'Onward' AGM – heavy crop, resistant to Fusarium wilt, good for exhibition
'Ambassador' AGM – tasty, long cropping period, resistant to powdery mildew

Pests and diseases

Various pests and diseases can trouble peas but the most likely is pea moth, which causes maggoty peas. This is prevented by spraying with a suitable pesticide seven to ten days after flowering. Powdery mildew may occur on the foliage and silvery patches on pods may be caused by thrips. The pea and bean weevil chops notches out of the leaves. Older plants are not severely damaged but if it appears early at seedling stage, it can be devastating. Damping off and wilt problems can also sometimes occur. Rotation helps to avoid these.

ROOT VEGETABLES

These are easily grouped together not because they are related but simply because we eat the swollen roots of all of them and their culture is similar. Some are eaten whilst very young and tender such as baby carrots but many will also produce mature hardy roots that will supply the kitchen throughout the winter.

Carrots

This vegetable can be harvested both whilst very young or allowed to mature into bigger roots that can be stored in various ways. Cook and serve with butter or great for using in soups. Most carrots are long and slender, although there are shorter stump rooted types such as 'Parmex'. In recent years, several novelty types have been developed and it is now possible to get carrots that are yellow, white, wine red or purple. Some of these hybrids have very good flavours.

Carrots grow best in light, sandy but moisture-retentive soils. They appreciate organic matter but any lumps or stones in the soil will cause the roots to fork and distort.

Carrots must generally be sown direct in the ground outside where they are to mature as they will not tolerate transplanting. They can be sown from early spring through to early summer to produce a crop from early summer through until the winter. Sow in shallow, 1 cm ($^1/_2$ in) drills about 15 cm (6 in apart). Sow the seed very thinly to avoid the need for excess thinning and disturbance, which attracts the carrot root fly.

If tiny tender young carrots are wanted, these can be harvested early without any thinning. For bigger carrots and those you wish to mature for winter use, thin to about 5–7.5 cm (2–3 in) apart and water in after thinning to minimise disturbance. They need regular watering to keep tender and succulent but they do not have a high fertiliser requirement.

Selected carrots

'Amsterdam Forcing 3' – fast early, baby carrot, top of the taste tests

'Early Nantes' – cylindrical but blunt rooted, good for successional sowings

'Parmex' AGM – early globe rooted carrot. Can be grown in containers

'Autumn King 2' AGM – maincrop, good size, stands and keeps well

'Flyaway' AGM – sweet and tasty maincrop, resistant to carrot root fly

'Purple Haze' – one of the novelties, purple skin, red core, great taste

Parsnips

This strongly flavoured root vegetable is either a firm favourite or equally detested.

CARROT ROOT FLY

This is a serious problem with carrot growing and even if the crop is not killed, the carrots can be rendered unusable. The adult carrot fly lays eggs at the base of the carrot plants. The resulting young maggots feed on the roots of the carrots. Young seedlings will be killed completely. Older plants will show a reddish discolouration of the foliage and the roots will be mined with tunnels and black rotting areas making them unpalatable.

Chemical protection is possible but there are several alternative cultural controls. Most of these are based on the fact that the adult carrot root fly is attracted by the smell of carrots.

Companion planting with alternate rows of onions helps to mask the effect or by mixing spring onion seeds in with the carrot seed at sowing stage. Avoiding thinning or other disturbance to the crop also helps. Delaying sowing maincrop varieties until June helps as this avoids the peak season of attack. Finally, covering the rows with a horticultural mesh or surrounding them with clear plastic also seems to deter the fly.

Wonderful roasted or cooked and mashed with leeks and crème fraiche. It is however quite easy to grow. Parsnips like a long growing season so sow in early spring for harvesting the following autumn and winter. Some would say that the best flavour does not develop until the crop has had a frost.

They have a low fertiliser requirement. Sow thinly in rows 30 cm (12 in apart) and thin seedlings to 15 cm (6 in) apart. Apart from keeping weed free and well watered, they need little attention.

Selected parsnips

'Tender and True' AGM – traditional and reliable cultivar, good flavour, good crop
'Gladiator' AGM – delicious flavour and canker resistant also good for exhibition
'Countess' AGM – very sweet flavour and canker resistance

Pests and diseases

They are relatively free of pests and diseases, although can occasionally attract carrot root fly or lettuce root aphids.

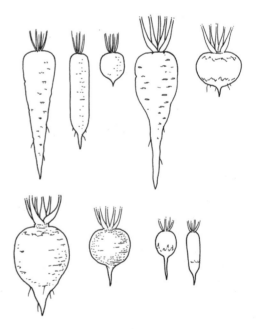

A selection of root vegetables. Clockwise from left: three types of carrot, parsnip, turnip, two types of radish, beetroot and swede.

144

TURNIPS

This humble vegetable is often much maligned. As well as white roots, both golden and pink skinned types are available. If harvested whilst young and tender and cooked carefully, the flavour can be superb. If left to get old and mature the flavour is stronger and they need then to be kept for stews and similar dishes.

Sow thinly about 1 cm ($1/2$ in) deep, in rows 30 cm (12 in) apart from early spring through to early summer. Thin to about 10 cm (4 in) and keep weed free and well watered. Harvesting can take place from late spring through to autumn. Successional sowings may be made throughout the summer, although some cultivars bolt in hot weather.

Selected turnips

'Golden Ball' – hardy but best eaten young
'Atlantic' AGM – very early, purple-topped roots, bolt-resistance
'Tokyo Cross' AGM – fast growing, pure white, well flavoured roots

Pests and diseases

They are relatively free from pests and diseases, although seedlings may attract flea beetles and they can also be prone to club-root.

BEETROOT

Most people are familiar with the strongly coloured red root vegetable, often pickled and served with salads. Fewer people know the easily grown and quite delicious golden form. When baked and served with butter it is a delicious vegetable. The leaves can also be used as a salad.

Beetroot are slightly tender and so should not be sown until soil temperatures are a little warmer than for other root vegetables. This is normally mid spring through to early summer, for cropping mid summer to early autumn. Sow thinly about 2.5 cm (1 in) deep in rows about 30 cm (12 in) apart and thin seedlings to 10 cm (4 in) apart. Despite being a root crop, beetroot can be sown under cover in modules, providing they are planted out whilst young. Water and keep weed free.

Selected beetroot

'Red Ace' AGM – high quality, stands well, good to eat and on the show bench
'Boltardy' AGM – good for early sowing, bolt resistance, good flavour
'Cylindica' – long cylindrical roots, good disease resistance
'Burpees Golden' – golden yellow roots with excellent flavour
'Albino' – a curiosity with white roots, attractive but short shelf life

Pests and diseases

Beetroot tend to be generally free from common pests and diseases. Occasionally you may see mangold fly damage, which is a type of leaf miner. Black fly may be troublesome. Beetroot are also sensitive to trace element deficiencies, which may cause strange foliage symptoms.

SWEDE

These are another winter root vegetable and are grown very much as we would grow parsnips. They are a good winter stand-by for stews and roasting. They are tough and hardy and so may be left in the ground during the winter and harvested as needed. Swedes are sown mid to late spring but are not harvested until late autumn or winter. They are totally hardy. Sow 1 cm ($1/2$ in) deep, in rows 30 cm (12 in) apart and thin to 20 cm (8 in) apart.

Selected swedes

'Ruby' AGM – sweet flesh, hardy and mildew resistant

'Marian' – purple skin, good flavour and clubroot resistant

Pests and diseases

Swedes tend to suffer from mildew, although some modern cultivars are resistant.

POTATOES

This vegetable needs no introduction! Potatoes are so readily available that many gardeners would not consider growing them. They also take up a great deal of space so are really only feasible if you have a large garden or allotment. However, young, freshly dug new potatoes have a flavour that is second to none and virtually always lost in those bought in shops. For this reason it is worth trying to grow a few early potatoes if nothing else.

The potato is a tuber and the plant that grows from it is tender, so we need to be careful not to plant too early or to allow them to be subjected to frost. Always buy good quality seed potatoes as these will be virus free. Home saved potatoes may be harbouring all sorts of pests and diseases and should not be used. In early spring set the potatoes out in seed trays with the 'eyes' uppermost and place in a light frost-free position to sprout. This can be a well lit

windowsill or a cool greenhouse but avoid anywhere too warm. This process is called 'chitting' and is essential for early crops and preferable for the later maincrops.

The ground for potatoes should be well prepared by deep digging, incorporating a generous supply of organic matter. Knock down the soil surface to provide a rough but not too fine tilth. Apply a base dressing of a suitable balanced granular fertiliser such as Growmore and work into the surface.

Early potatoes are planted in rows 60 cm (24 in) apart with the individual potatoes 30 cm (12 in) apart. Planting depth should be about 12.5 cm (5 in), so although you can take out a drill, it is usually easier to plant them individually with a trowel. Maincrop potatoes need more space with rows 75 cm (30 in) and individual plants 40 cm (16 in) apart. Do not remove any of the shoots, which are essential for a sturdy plant and eventually a heavy crop. Planting can take place from mid spring onwards.

The new shoots are likely to emerge from the soil quite quickly and possibly before the danger of frost is past. If this is so, start gently earthing up the plants, drawing a little soil over the shoots for protection. Alternatively, with the forecast of a sudden frost, simple protection such as a plastic flower pot over each plant, just overnight, will help to avoid damage.

When the plants are growing strongly and about 25 cm (10 in) high it is time to earth them up properly. Loosen the soil between the rows lightly with a fork or hoe and, using a draw hoe, drag soil across each row making a ridge about 15 cm (6 in) high. You can add another dressing of fertiliser at this stage,

Use a draw hoe to gently draw the soil around potatoes and exclude the light.

hoeing it into the soil before forming the ridges. The new crop of potatoes forms very near the surface and earthing up keeps the light away from them and prevents them going green. Alternatively, crops can be grown under black polythene to avoid the need for earthing up but in this situation slugs can be particularly troublesome. Harvesting potatoes simply involves peeling the polythene back.

Potatoes should be kept well watered throughout the growing cycle. Early crops are ready for harvesting as soon as the flowers start to open. Carefully insert a fork to the side of the row and lever underneath pulling on the top of the plant at the same time. Most of the potatoes will come out still attached to the plant but the soil should be carefully forked through for other loose ones. They should be roughly the size of hen's eggs. If required a few very early potatoes can be harvested without digging up the crop by

gently digging alongside the plants and picking off a few small select tubers, leaving the rest to grow on.

Maincrops will be harvested at the end of the season when the stems (haulm) goes yellow and dies down. Dig in the same way as earlies. If storage is intended, carefully wash and dry the crop and store in a cool, dark, frost-free environment.

Selected potatoes
First earlies
'Foremost' – high yields, oval, white flesh and good flavour
'Maris Bard' – very early, heavy crops, scab and virus resistance
'Red Duke of York' – an older type, delicious flavour
'Accent' – newish cultivar, very early, good flavour, eelworm and scab resistant

Second earlies
'Maris Peer' – white flesh, good yields, scab and blight resistance, needs irrigation
'Estima' – oval, pale yellow flesh, heavy cropper
'Edzell Blue' – beautiful rich purple skins, white flesh and good flavour

Maincrops
'Maris Piper' – excellent yields and a good cooking potato, prone to slugs and scab
'Desirée' – pink skin, waxy yellow flesh, heavy cropper, drought resistant
'King Edward' – familiar old cultivar, excellent cooking quality, yields average

Salad potatoes
'Pink Fir Apple' – peculiar knobbly tubers,

POTATO TRICKS

A small crop of potatoes can be grown in a large pot or tub. Use one at least 40 cm (16 in) in diameter and start with about 20 cm (8 in) of good potting compost in the bottom. Plant the potatoes and keep well watered. As they grow, top up the compost in stages, no more than 7.5 cm (3 in) at a time. At harvest time, just tip out the whole potfull and separate the potatoes from the compost.

With a heated greenhouse or conservatory, you can grow a small crop of your own new potatoes for Christmas. Plant a few potatoes in large pots in late summer and grow on slowly outside. Seed potatoes will not be available at this time so you should choose some small potatoes of a suitable type. Top up the pots as above and in late September move them under the cover of a frost-free greenhouse. Growth will slow in the dull autumn days but if you can keep them growing until Christmas you will have a small crop to harvest and show off to the neighbours!

wonderful flavour, hot or cold

'Anya' – modern version of 'Pink Fir Apple' perhaps not quite as tasty

'**Charlotte**' – early maturing, small waxy potatoes, use hot or cold

Potatoes are sometimes described as good 'cleaning' crops for a weedy vegetable plot. The truth of this is that in growing potatoes we carry out a number of cultivations each of which, will help in destroying weeds; the initial digging, one or two earthing up exercises and then in harvesting the crop we once again dig through the soil.

Pests and diseases

Potatoes do suffer from a bewildering range of pests and diseases, of which two are particularly prevalent and destructive. Potato blight causes brown patches on the leaves with mouldy edges. It spreads rapidly in damp conditions and will cause the total death of the crop. It is well worth while doing a preventative spray for this in mid summer.

Slugs are also particularly attracted to potatoes and can render the crop totally unusable. They are worse in wet seasons and on heavy soils. Use slug control measures in mid summer and lift maincrops as soon as possible in the autumn.

ONIONS

Probably one of the most useful vegetables in the kitchen, used in many different ways and a host of different dishes. The most widely used onions are the bulb onions. Red cultivars, which have a mild flavour are available as well as the familiar white ones. Onions can be grown from seeds or from sets, which are small immature bulbs, which are easy to grow. Some suppliers offer heat treated versions of some sets that have been specially prepared to reduce bolting. Shallots are also planted as bulbs and make a cluster of mild flavoured small bulbs. There are also salad or spring onions that are harvested and eaten green.

Onions like a good, rich, well-drained soil that has been prepared by digging in generous amounts of organic matter. A reasonably fine tilth should be produced and a base dressing of a balanced fertiliser applied and raked in.

Onion sets are planted in early spring with

rows 25 cm (10 in) apart and the individual sets 10 cm (4 in) apart. Birds are inclined to tug them out by the little whiskery tops so it is worth trimming these short before planting. Plant with a trowel or small dibber so that just the top is showing. Shallots are planted in a similar fashion.

Growing onions from seed is a little more difficult. Prepare a fine tilth and sow the seed in drills about 1 cm ($^{1}/_{2}$ in) deep at the same row spacings as sets. Seed can be sown in early spring. Thin to 10 cm (4 in) apart when the seedlings are about 5 cm (2 in) tall. Seed can also be sown earlier in modules in a cool greenhouse and planted out in mid spring to the same spacings.

Keep onion crops well watered and weed free. Any plants that show a flower spike (called bolting), should have this removed.

Onion crops are usually ready for harvesting around mid to late summer when the foliage will start to yellow and topple. This can be encouraged by gently folding over the top growth just above the bulb. When the foliage has totally withered, gently loosen the bulbs and lift with a fork. The bulbs should be laid out in a dry airy position to continue ripening for about two to three weeks. They can then be stored in a cool frost-free shed for most of the winter. Any soft, bolted or oddly shaped bulbs should be eaten first. Over the storage months, check the crop and remove any that show signs of rotting.

Selected Onions
Onion sets
'Sturon' AGM – flavoursome, medium sized and good keeping qualities

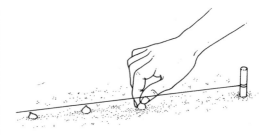

Onion sets are planted by just gently pressing into the soil surface in straight rows.

'Orion' – heavy yields and long storing potential
'Red Baron' – bright red skin, good flavour, stores well

Onion seeds
'Ailsa Craig' – traditional, large bulbs, good for exhibition, limited storage
'Napoleon' – F1 hybrid type with high yields and good storage capabilities
'Brunswick' – red skinned cultivar, mild flavour, excellent keeper

Other onions
Spring onions are also grown from seed but the rows can be much closer, say 15 cm (6 in) and the crop does not need thinning. The onions are just pulled young and succulent as needed. 'White Lisbon' is a good white variety and there are those such as 'North Holland Blood Red' with red skins. Pickling onions are produced from a small bulbing variety such as 'Paris Silverskin'. Garlic can also be grown by splitting up the bulbs into the individual scales, which are treated like onion sets. It should be planted in the autumn to give a long growing season so may not be successful in cold areas or on wet soils.

Pests and diseases

Onions suffer from onion fly, which causes yellow drooping leaves. The roots and bulbs will be infested with maggots. Sets are less prone to damage. Eelworm causes twisted distorted growth for which there is no cure. Grow the crop on fresh soil. White rot causes the bulbs to rot in the soil. It is a serious disease and again the only answer is crop rotation.

LEEKS

These are another member of the onion family, grown for their long white 'stems' that are produced by either earthing up the crop or by deep planting. They need a long growing season.

Sow leeks in a seed bed outside in early spring. They should be planted in their final positions in early summer. The young plants are carefully lifted from the seedbed with a fork and sorted, discarding any weak plants. The tops and roots are lightly trimmed. Mark out rows about 20 cm (8 in) apart and make holes with a dibber about 15 cm (6 in) deep. Drop the seedlings in and water to settle the roots. No filling or firming is needed. Plants can also be raised in modules under glass.

Keep the crop weeded and well watered. As they grow the crop can be further earthed up to give a greater length of blanched stem but care must be taken to ensure that soil does not go down between the leaves or the crop will be dirty and gritty when eaten.

Selected leeks

'Carlton' – a recent cultivar, rapid growth, good flavour, tight stems, so clean
'Musselburgh' – traditional, very hardy, tasty, reliable, thick stems

'Lyon Prizetaker' – mild, long thick white stems, good exhibition cultivar

Pests and diseases

Leeks suffer from onion flies and eelworm so crop rotation is recommended.

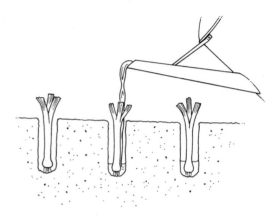

Leek transplants are planted deep and watered in, leaving space for the stem to develop.

SPINACH AND CHARD

True spinach is a fast growing annual vegetable with an acquired flavour which can be strong. It is very nutritious and can be cooked in various ways. Steamed when very young, adding crème fraîche and topped with cheese it is quite delicious. The secret is picking it when tender and young.

As this is a leafy crop, the soil should be well prepared with generous amounts of organic matter and a base dressing of balanced fertiliser. Sow from early spring onwards for cropping from early summer. It does not perform well in hot, dry summers as it tends to run to seed too quickly. Space rows about 30 cm (12 in) apart, sow sparingly in 2.5 cm (1 in) drills and thin seedlings to 7.5 cm (3 in) apart. Keep the crop adequately watered. Harvest when young, either picking individual leaves or cutting the whole plant to a stump, which will often re-sprout with a second flush of growth.

For those that find annual spinach difficult to grow, you can try perpetual spinach, also known as leaf beet, which is similar but does not run to seed and will grow on through the season and into the winter. It is not so tender or delicate flavoured. There are also the coloured chards or leaf beets, such as 'Ruby Chard' which are very ornamental and are grown and cooked in a similar way.

Selected spinach

'Scenic' AGM – high yielding and full flavoured, downy mildew resistant

'Cezanne' – an F1 hybrid, slow to bolt and resistant to downy mildew

'Perpetual Spinach' AGM (Leaf Beet) – hardy, good for a winter crop

Chard 'Bright Lights' – multicoloured leaf stems and mild flavour

Pests and diseases

Spinach plants tend to be relatively free from pests and diseases, although bolting in hot, dry weather is a common problem. Yellow leaves can indicate either a manganese deficiency or downy mildew. With the latter, there will be a grey mould on the underside of the leaves. Bolting occurs if the plants are stressed at any point by high temperatures, lack of water or low nutrition.

SALADS

The most traditional ingredient of salads is, of course, lettuce although there are many others such as endive, chicory, corn salad and mustard and cress. Others are available and they may nowadays be sold as packets of mixed seed that can be grown for cutting at a young stage as tender leaves.

Lettuce

These are a relatively easy crop to grow but the trick is maintaining a continuity and variety of this valuable salad. By choosing the right types and using some basic protection, lettuce can be produced throughout the year.

The commonest, although probably least attractive lettuce are the butterhead or round-head types which form a round soft heart. Crisphead lettuces are similar but have a crisp centre. Cos lettuces have long leaves and are usually fairly crisp. Loose-leaf lettuces are much softer in texture, and useful for just picking a few leaves. There are various fancy leaves types with frilly or oak-leaved foliage and they also come with red leaves as well as green. Some of the latter types are attractive as a garnish but are tough and tasteless.

Lettuce need a well cultivated soil with an alkaline pH and a high level of organic matter. Apply a general balanced fertiliser before sowing or planting.

A very early crop of lettuce can be produced by sowing seeds in a cool greenhouse in modules in early spring and planting out in mid spring. Even so, the protection of cloches, a polythene tunnel or cold frame will ensure an early crop. The first outdoor sowings can be made in mid spring as the soil is starting to warm up. Sow the seed 1 cm (1/2 in) deep in rows 30 cm (12 in) apart. Sow thinly or use pelleted seed to space the seed evenly. When large enough

Types of lettuce. Left to right: loose-leaf, butterhead, crisphead and cos.

to handle, thin to 20–30 cm (8–12 in) according to the cultivar and water gently.

Continue to sow lettuce in small quantities throughout the season at two-week intervals to maintain a succession. Sowing a packet of mixed lettuce seed gives not only variety but also succession as the different types mature at various rates. There are some tough winter varieties that can be sown in late summer for cropping outside up to Christmas. To produce lettuce through the winter, you will need a frost-free greenhouse and you must grow very carefully to avoid problems such as damping off.

Selected lettuce
Butterhead types
'Clarion' AGM – good for early sowing, mildew resistance
'Sangria' AGM – blush red heart, stands well and good mildew resistance
'Tom Thumb' – early, tiny solid heads, few outer leaves, individual portion size

Crisphead types
'Webb's Wonderful' – traditional favourite, slow to bolt

'Lakeland' AGM – good in cooler climates
'Set' AGM – very reliable, mildew resistant, slow to bolt

Cos types
'Lobjoits Green Cos' AGM – traditional cultivar, firm and crisp, good flavour
'Rusty' AGM – a bronze leaved cos type
'Little Gem' AGM – another tiny lettuce, sweet, resistant to root aphid

Loose leaf types
'Catalogna' AGM – tender leaves, good flavour
'Lolla Rossa' AGM – red frilly leaves tough but lovely garnish
'Delicato' AGM – very dark purple, oak leaved lettuce, stands well

Other types
'Winter Density' – hardy lettuce for autumn sowing outdoors
'Rosetta' – a winter lettuce for growing in a greenhouse, good flavour

Pests and diseases
Lettuce are badly attacked by slugs and birds, both of which can decimate the crop. They can also be attacked by ordinary aphid and also lettuce root aphid, which live on the roots but cause the tops to go yellow and wilt. Tipburn shows as brown edged leaves and is caused by sun scorch. Under glass and particularly during the winter, lettuce are likely to suffer from botrytis and downy mildew. Good ventilation is vital to discourage this.

MEDITERRANEAN VEGETABLES

A few vegetables are totally tender and must be raised as young plants under glass before planting outside after all danger of frost is past. Outside, the soil temperature is rarely high enough in the early part of the year to germinate and in order to get a reasonable crop you need a head start with part grown plants.

COURGETTES

These are like small marrows and in fact the techniques for growing are the same as they are for pumpkins and squashes. Normally courgettes form quite tight bushy plants, whereas the rest are trailing plants that take up a great deal of space.

Sow the seeds in a warm greenhouse in mid to late spring. Plants grow fast so do not sow too early. Use 9-cm (3½-in) pots filled with a good potting compost. Sow two seeds in each pot, pushing them gently into the compost about 2 cm (¾ in) deep. If both germinate reduce to one seedling and grow on in a warm, sunny, frost-free situation. Harden off before planting out in early summer.

Courgettes need an open sunny situation and respond to a deeply cultivated, very rich soil. You should prepare a small pit partly filled with compost and topped off with topsoil for each plant. Finish off with a base fertiliser and a saucer-like depression around the plant to make watering easy later on. Bush courgettes should be spaced at least 60 cm (24 in) apart and trailing marrows and squashes need 1.2 m (4 ft) apart.

Courgettes and marrows all produce separate male and female flowers and you can see the females as they have tiny embryonic fruits behind the flower. These are normally pollinated by insects but if the season is cold it can be helpful to hand pollinate, transferring pollen from the male flower to the female.

Keep well watered at all times and feed regularly with a high potash liquid feed such as a tomato feed. Courgettes must be picked very frequently when the fruits are about 10 cm (4 in) long. If missed, they will rapidly grow into marrows and production slows down. Some people find the prickly leaves an irritant so you may wish to harvest wearing gloves and a long sleeved shirt.

Selected courgettes, marrows and squashes

'Green Bush' – traditional courgette, early, abundant small fruits

'Defender' AGM – early, compact, heavy cropping courgette, resistant to virus

'Orielia' – golden yellow courgette, heavy cropping

'Sunburst' – golden patty pan style squash to eat small, great taste

'Tiger Cross' AGM – grow for either courgettes or marrows, virus resistant

'Hundredweight' – traditional Halloween style pumpkin, trailing

Pests and diseases

They are very prone to slug damage so use protection as soon as planted. In a warm summer they may suffer from whitefly and viruses sometimes appear which check growth of the crop.

SWEET CORN

This tall growing annual grass is a relative of the maize grown as a farm fodder crop and has been bred for its high flavour and sugar content. It does need warm summers to perform at its best but some of the more recent F1 hybrids have been bred to respond better to cooler climates.

Sow the seed in mid to late spring in 9 cm (3 1/2 in) pots of good potting compost, placing two seeds about 2 cm (3/4 in) deep and lightly covering. Germinate in a warm greenhouse and then grow on in good light. Remove the weaker of the two seedlings if both germinate. Harden off before planting out after all danger of frost is past in early summer.

Sweet corn also has separate male and female flowers but is wind pollinated. The male flowers are large decorative tassels at the top of the plants and the female flowers that will lead to the cobs are lower down on the plant. Sweet corn is best grown in a block to encourage pollination, rather than individual rows.

The site should be warm and sunny with a well-drained soil. Prepare in the normal way by digging and incorporating organic matter, finishing off with a base fertiliser dressing. Space the plants about 45 cm (18 in) square watering in well after planting. Keep free of weeds and water in dry weather.

Each plant will produce two to three cobs which normally ripen in late summer and early autumn. The remains of the female flowers are called 'silks' and as they turn brown, it is an indication that the crop is ripening. Gently peel back the green outer sheath and press into a kernal with a fingernail. If the fluid appears milky rather than clear then the cob is ripe and ready to harvest.

Succulent sweet corn

'Swift' AGM – very early, vigorous, sugar enhanced, good on cold soils

'Sundance' AGM – early, reliable, long cobs, good in cooler summers

'Minipop' – produces baby corn, harvest at early stage

Pests and diseases

They are relatively free from pests and diseases but may suffer from slug damage.

Two sweet corn seeds are sown in each pot and if both grow, the weakest is removed.

CELERY

Traditionally celery was a very tedious vegetable to produce, requiring growing in a trench and then earthing up the plants to create tender white stems. Modern self-blanching types do away with the need for this but the taste is possibly inferior and they are not hardy so must be harvested before the autumn frosts.

Sow the seed under heated glass in early spring and prick off seedlings into trays or small modules. Grow cool and harden off before planting out in late spring. Prepare the site in the normal way by digging, incorporating organic matter and a base fertiliser. The site should be open and sunny. Plant the seedlings 23 cm (9 in) apart in blocks as the close proximity of neighbouring plants will assist the blanching process. Keep well watered and weed-free and they should be ready for harvesting from late summer.

Selected celery

'Giant Pascal' – traditional green trench celery

'Golden Self-blanching' – very early, compact crisp heads from August

'Loretta' – self-blanching, excellent flavour, white sticks

Pests and diseases

Celery may be attacked by slugs and also by celery fly, which is a type of leaf miner causing brown blisters on the leaves.

TOMATOES

These are probably one of the most common vegetables grown by amateur gardeners, although of course they are a fruit! Home grown tomatoes seem to have far more flavour than those bought from shops and are always welcome. Tomatoes can be grown both outside in summer or in a greenhouse for a slightly earlier and heavier crop. There is a huge range of cultivars available and as well as the familiar red tomatoes, you can get yellow and purple types and in various sizes from tiny currant-sized fruits, through to whopping slicing fruits.

Greenhouse tomatoes

Generally tomato plants can be obtained from any garden centre in the spring and early summer. If you have a heated greenhouse, you can grow your own from seed. It is then easy to choose exactly which types you want to grow. Sowing can take place anytime from mid winter onwards but you must be sure that adequate temperatures can be maintained.

Seed should be sown in a warm propagator at about 21° C (70° F) Prick out the seedlings as soon as the seed leaves have expanded, putting one seedling in a 9–10 cm ($3^1/2$–4 in) pot in a good potting compost. Keep the plants in a light area at a temperature of about 16° C (60° F) as they grow, space out the pots to avoid overcrowding. Plants are ready to move on, when the first flowers are just starting to show. Plants will usually be about 20–30 cm (8–12 in) tall.

You can grow tomatoes in the border soil in the greenhouse if this has not happened previously but a build-up of pests and diseases rapidly occurs so in future years, this will not be so successful. The alternative is to use large pots of potting compost or gro-bags, which are large bags of special potting compost. These are laid flat and two or three holes are made in the top surface into which tomatoes are planted. Holes must also be punctured in the base of the bag to create drainage. These are reasonably successful but they will need very regular watering in hot weather and heavy feeding.

If you are growing tomatoes in an unheated greenhouse, do not plant before late spring. If you are buying in plants rather than growing your own, look for stocky, sturdy, smaller plants rather than tall, leggy ones. Space them out in the greenhouse to acclimatise for a few days before planting.

Most greenhouse tomatoes are tall plants and so will require support. Canes can be used in pots or border soil but these are more difficult in gro-bags. Alternatively, you can use strings tied to the greenhouse roof above the plants and dropped down the plant. The lower end of the string is tied loosely around the plant and as the plant grows it is gently twisted around the string.

Greenhouse tomatoes are also normally restricted to one stem, so all sideshoots are removed as they appear. It is good to damp the plants over daily with water or lightly shake the plants to encourage the dispersal of pollen and the pollination process. As soon as young tomatoes have formed, commence feeding regularly with a proprietary tomato feed, which should be high in potassium. As the fruit starts to ripen, traditionally the lower leaves are removed to allow light to the ripening fruit. This should only be done in moderation as the leaves are vital for the plant's growth.

It is essential with tomatoes to water and feed regularly. Water shortage will cause the young fruits to drop off or the development of blossom end rot, which is a physiological disorder showing as brown corky patches on the fruits. The ideal temperature for growing tomatoes is around 16° C (60° F). Ventilate the greenhouse as necessary on warm days to avoid a build up of high temperatures.

Tasty greenhouse tomatoes

'Shirley' AGM – an established cultivar, heavy crops, good in a cold greenhouse
'Alicante' AGM – another reliable old cultivar, medium size, fine flavoured fruit
'Vanessa' AGM – vine-ripening style, fruit remains firm, sweet and juicy
'Sweet Million' AGM – heavy cropping cherry-sized fruit, long season
'Golden Sunrise' AGM – golden yellow fruits with a very sweet flavour
'Snapper' – a midi-plum shaped fruit, early, tasty and prolific

Pests and diseases

Tomatoes suffer from a bewildering range of pests and diseases, although most fortunately do not often occur. Whitefly is the greatest pest of tomatoes in a greenhouse. The best method of control is by means of the predator Encarsia. You may have to introduce this more than once in the season as it is sometimes so successful that it eradicates all whitefly and then dies itself. Some people also have success with marigolds planted around their tomatoes, which are strong smelling and discourage the whitefly. If you decide to use chemical pesticides, you will need to spray frequently and there is always then the problem of the safe period between spraying and being able to eat the fruit.

Tomatoes also suffer from potato blight. If you are also growing potatoes, it is worth spraying the tomatoes at the same time as the potatoes as a preventative. Virus sometimes shows as mottled, distorted leaves. Destroy plants before it spreads to others. In wet seasons, botrytis may appear on leaves, stems or fruit, particularly where there is any wound, such as where a sideshoot has been removed. Good ventilation will help to reduce this. Yellowing between the leaves is a sign of magnesium deficiency, which often occurs with tomatoes. Use a dilute solution of Epsom salts 210 g in 10 litres (7 oz in 2 gallons) of water and water round the roots.

Outdoor tomatoes

These are a bit of a gamble in cooler climates although given a sheltered spot and a reasonable summer some useful later fruit can be grown. Prepare a patch of well-drained soil with generous dressings of organic matter. Just prior to planting rake in a balanced fertiliser such as Growmore.

Outdoor cultivars of tomatoes should be specifically selected. Most of the best ones are bush types and will not need staking, although there are some of the taller cordon types for outdoor growing. Plants should be raised as for glasshouse types but delaying sowing until early to mid spring. Prior to planting harden off carefully. Both types are planted 45 cm (18 in) apart with rows 90 cm (3 ft) apart. Use a 1.5 m (5 ft) cane for the cordon types and tie in loosely.

Keep weed free and water regularly in dry weather. Feed at regular intervals, at least weekly with a proprietary tomato liquid feed. Bush types do not need pinching or staking. As the fruit develops it is advisable to spread a mulch of straw to keep the fruit off the ground. Also apply slug pellets.

All the sideshoots are removed from cordon tomatoes to concentrate the energy into fruit production.

The cordon cultivars should have the side-shoots removed as you would greenhouse tomatoes and be tied to the cane as they grow. You should remove the growing point after the fourth truss as this is likely to be all that the plant can ripen in a cool climate outdoors. Harvest the fruits as they ripen. At the end of the season, before the frost, pick all remaining fruit. These should be placed in an enclosed area such as a drawer with a ripe apple, which encourages ripening by means of the ethylene it produces.

Tough outdoor tomatoes

'Roma VF' – heavy cropping plum-shaped fruits, almost seedless, excellent
'Marmande' – huge beefsteak style tomato, very fleshy, excellent for slicing
'Tornado' AGM – early, compact, good for cool summer, sweet, heavy crop

Pests and diseases

Outdoor tomatoes suffer from similar pests and diseases but probably to a lesser extent. Potato blight is particularly troublesome if potatoes are growing nearby.

UNUSUAL VEGETABLES

As well as all the familiar crops described above, there is a host of other vegetables that are often not available in the shops and can provide interesting crops to grow and fresh flavours for the kitchen. Salsify, celeriac, kohl rabi and scorzonera are easy root vegetables. Globe artichoke makes a very attractive ornamental plant with gourmet seed heads. Chicory and endive are useful winter salads. Then there is the whole host of oriental brassicas such as Chinese cabbage, pak choi, mizuna greens and the oriental mustards. None is difficult to grow and seed is readily available of many exciting alternatives.

VEGETABLES IN POTS

Small quantities of vegetables can be grown in large pots or tubs in a tiny garden. Many vegetables are quite attractive and can easily double as ornamental plants or be mixed with other flowering and foliage plants. For example a wigwam of runner beans can be grown in a large tub and surrounded with a group of lettuce early in the season. The red flowers are attractive and a significant crop can be produced if they are well watered and regularly fed. Courgettes, tomatoes and French beans will all perform well in containers.

PROTECTED CROPPING

Earlier crops of all sorts of vegetables are possible with some protection. Small, low polythene tunnels are cheap to purchase and easy to construct. They enable the soil to warm up and seeds to be sown earlier resulting in an early crop. Salads respond very well to this as do tender crops such as French beans.

Small temporary protection can be provided for individual plants such as sweet corn by using the cut off bottoms of plastic soft drink bottles like tiny greenhouses. They should only be used as overnight protection as they will heat up too much in the daytime sun.

OTHER TENDER CROPS

It is also quite possible to grow cucumbers, melons, peppers and aubergines in a glasshouse. They do not all like the same conditions though. Peppers and aubergines will grow happily with tomatoes but cucumbers and melons like a higher temperature and damper atmosphere. All of them are more challenging than tomatoes but can be rewarding when successful. Ridge cucumbers are a tough outdoor cucumber that produces small chunky fruits with a good flavour. These do not require a greenhouse.

RHUBARB

This is a permanent crop that takes a few years to reach peak cropping and then with care will produce useful crops for five to ten years. It is worth buying good named varieties rather than seedlings to get a good crop.

Rhubarb should be planted in the winter using dormant crowns or in the spring with green pot-grown plants. Prepare the soil in the normal way and plant 90 cm (3 ft) apart both ways. The crop is the thick succulent leaf stalks but do not remove any of these in the first season. Water and feed regularly to build up a good strong plant for future years. Remove any stems that show signs of flowers.

Rhubarb can be left to grow normally for an early summer crop or you can cover crowns with an upturned bucket and pack round with straw to force for an early spring crop. Do not force newly planted crops or force the same plants two years running. When harvesting, never remove all the leaves and stop picking by mid July to allow the plants to build up strength for the next year. Remember the green leaves are poisonous, so only the red stems can be eaten.

Recommended rhubarb

'Champagne Early' – deep red stems, good for forcing
'Timperley Early' – good for forcing
'Victoria' – popular, reliable but late

Pests and diseases

Rhubarb is generally trouble free, although older crowns can suffer from crown rot. Dig out and destroy infected clumps.

ASPARAGUS

This is another perennial crop that can be productive for many years once it is established. The edible parts are the young stems as they are pushing through the ground in spring and early summer. These are called spears.

Buy one-year-old crowns, which will have been grown from seed. These are quite cumbersome plants with wide spreading thongy roots. Never let them dry out whilst waiting to plant. As the crop will be in place for many years, make particular effort to thoroughly prepare the soil, ideally by double digging, incorporating generous amounts of organic matter. Plant in winter whilst the roots are still dormant.

Take out a trench that is about 15 cm (6 in) deep and 30 cm (12 in) wide, leaving a slight mound in the centre. Spread the roots out carefully and cover with about 5 cm (2 in) of fine topsoil. Space the crowns about 40 cm (15 in) apart. During the first season, keep the area carefully weeded and regularly watered. As the asparagus 'fern' grows, gently replace the remaining soil back into the trench, around the asparagus plants until it is level by autumn. When the foliage yellows in the autumn cut down to about 5 cm (2 in).

During subsequent years, apply a general fertiliser in early spring and rake or hoe into the surface. Earth up each plant lightly using a draw hoe. This will increase the length of the white spear.

Harvesting can take place from the second year onwards. Cut the spears when they are about 10–12.5 cm, (4–5 in) above ground. Use a serrated bladed knife to sever them about 7.5 cm (3 in) below ground. Stop cutting by early summer to let the foliage grow and the plant to build up its strength for the next season. The foliage on asparagus in late summer is very delicate and attractive so you can grow a few plants in a flower border and enjoy it for both eating and as an ornamental.

Asparagus is planted on a shallow mound in a trench and slowly earthed up as it grows.

Some succulent asparagus

'Connovers Colossal' – early, good quality, reliable, readily available

'Cito' – all male variety, early, heavy cropping

'Franklin' – thick spears and heavy cropping

Pests and diseases

Asparagus suffers from slugs, which eat the young spears. Later in the season asparagus beetles, which have distinctive black and orange bodies with white blotches feed on the foliage. They can be controlled by spraying.

HERBS

Herbs are plants that can easily fall into either the kitchen garden criteria or the ornamental garden. Many are very attractive plants in their own right and have the bonus of aromatic foliage. Equally they are invaluable plants for their culinary uses. Remember that the coloured leaved forms of herbs are edible just the same as the green leaved types although the strength of flavour may vary.

Some herbs are perennials such as the shrubby rosemary, sage and bay or herbaceous such as chives, sorrel, fennel or mint and will come up from year to year. Many others, however, are annuals and will have to be raised from seed afresh each year. These include parsley, basil, dill, coriander, chervil and borage. They are all easy to raise and can be germinated from seed sown in small modules in a cool glasshouse in the spring.

Mint is a very invasive herb and spreads rapidly. It is best grown in a container such as an old bucket or flower pot with its base removed, sunk in the ground. This will keep it from straying too far. Basil can often be disappointing in this country as our summers are usually too cool. If you try it, plant it in a very warm sunny position. Parsley can be notoriously slow to germinate so it may be preferable to buy a tray of seedlings from a nursery in the spring. The curled parsley is the most attractive, but the flat-leaved the best flavoured. Remember that parsley also suffers from carrot root fly, which shows as a reddening of the foliage.

A bouquet of herbs

Parsley 'Moss Curled' AGM – annual, the most common type, best for a garnish

Parsley 'Plain Leaved' – annual, less attractive but stronger flavour

Chives – hardy perennial, clump forming, attractive pink flowers

Dill – annual, delicate foliage, runs to seed quickly

Angelica – biennial, tall, architectural plant

Tarragon – perennial but inclined to be tender

Borage – annual, use flowers as well as leaves

Coriander – annual, pungent flavour

Fennel – perennial but seeds freely, also bronze leaved form

Bay – shrub, often clipped as a pyramid, needs a sheltered spot

Mint – perennial, many different types, inclined to be invasive

Marjoram – perennial, easy, attractive pink flowers

Rosemary – shrub, keep trimmed to encourage young growths

Sage – perennial sub shrub, coloured leaf forms available

Thymes vulgaris – common thyme, good for cooking but plain

Basil – annual, very tender, grow in sheltered spot or in a greenhouse.

Herbs can be mixed in with other plants, grown as an edging in the vegetable garden or grown very successfully in tubs or pots.

To prevent it spreading, mint should be planted in a pot or bucket submerged in the ground.

FRUIT GROWING

MOST FRUITS ARE PERMANENT long-term crops and usually require quite a bit of space. A few are attractive garden plants in their own right and so can be mixed in with other plants. For example, pears bear lovely spring blossom and any fruit could be considered a bonus! Fruit is generally divided into top fruit and soft fruit. Top fruits are the tree fruits such as apple, pear, plum and cherry with the possible addition of apricots, peaches, nectarines and figs which are usually grown with the protection of a wall or under glass. Soft fruits include the bush fruits such as gooseberries, red, white and black currants, the cane fruits such as raspberry, blackberry and loganberry and of course strawberries. There are also other fruits such as the whole range of hybrid berries such as tayberries, blueberries which are becoming popular, and tender fruits such as kiwis and grapes.

TOP FRUIT

Consider the space available for growing tree fruits. A full size apple tree will take up a great deal of space and may not come into cropping for many years. Fortunately there are ways of producing small trees by grafting onto dwarfing rootstocks so always check on the rootstock when buying a fruit tree. Most fruit trees can also be grown in a number of shapes. Trained trees such as cordons take up very little space and when coupled with a dwarfing rootstock, enable a small quantity of fresh fruit to be produced in a small garden.

Fan, espalier or cordon trees are particularly useful if you have spare wall space to use. Bush and standard generally take up the most space and are really only used if you have space to grow a traditional orchard. Pyramids and cordons are very good for a small garden and take up little space. Spindlebush training is a modern technique that is very space efficient but requires quite a bit of pruning and fiddly training. The branches are tied down with cords to encourage early fruiting and this is not particularly attractive.

Fruit trees may be available container-grown in garden centres throughout the season, but it is preferable to plant during the winter dormant months. You can either buy a small 'maiden' tree, which will need training into the desired shape or you can obtain older partly trained trees, which have had some of the formative pruning and training carried out. Always prepare the site well for planting fruit trees (see also pages 95–97). Prepare a good size area of deeply cultivated soil, well enriched with organic matter. Plant like any other tree and secure to a substantial stake.

APPLES

Apples are divided into cooking and dessert (eating) apples and there is an extensive choice particularly of the latter. Some wonderfully flavoured apples are available to grow that you will never find in the greengrocers.

Apples are always grafted onto a

FRUIT TREE SHAPES

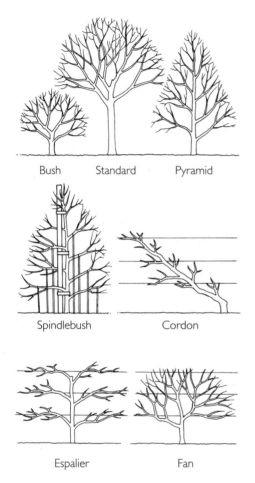

Bush   Standard   Pyramid

Spindlebush   Cordon

Espalier   Fan

So there are three initial decisions to make: the rootstock needed, the shape in which you are going to train your tree and, of course, the variety of fruit that you want.

When choosing fruit cultivars, it is also necessary to choose ones that will pollinate each other. Without pollination, fruit will not form and this means they need to flower at the same time. Reliable fruit catalogues will group together the cultivars according to their fruiting times and pollination needs.

A few dependable apples

(pollination groups after name)

'Discovery' B – one of the best and earliest dessert apples, doesn't keep

'Crispin' B – unusual yellow fruit, crisp and well flavoured

'Cox's Orange Pippin' B – well known but difficult to grow well

'Egremont Russet' A – rough skin, sweet nutty flesh, lovely old apple

'Katy' B – modern variety, good cropping, juicy and refreshing

'James Grieve' B – a good pollinator, early cooker or dessert apple when ripe

'Epicure' B – compact tree, easy to grow, juicy fruit

'Fiesta' B – good substitute for 'Cox', reliable, reasonable flavour

'Golden Delicious' C – not recommended in cold climates

'Bramley Seedling' B – the best of cooking apples but a huge spreading tree

'Rev W Wilks' A – a good compact cooking apple, but a biennial bearer

'Pixie' C – prolific cropping, disease resistant, small, crisp, juicy fruit

rootstock as they do not grow well on their own roots. The stock will govern the eventual size of the tree, the space it needs and the speed of cropping. It is very important to choose an apple on the right rootstock for your garden. Rootstocks also govern other things such as disease resistance. A good reliable nursery will always state the rootstock for fruit trees but cheap deals may be grafted on anything and this may not be declared or accurate.

Pruning apples

Young apple trees are pruned fairly hard for the first few years, removing a third to a half of the new growth and always back to a bud that is pointing in the direction we want the following years' growth to go. Pruning normally takes place during the winter dormant period from November through to February. Trees such as cordons that are being trained to a support, must be tied in, ideally as they are growing during the summer. By the time branches have ripened for the winter, they will be less pliable.

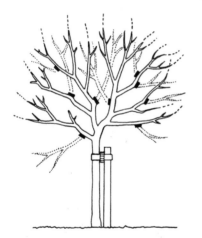

Mature apples are pruned to keep the centre open and encourage fruit spurs.

By the time an apple tree is approaching its fruiting phase, we alter the style of pruning to encourage fruit production rather than strong growth. Various techniques are possible but at its simplest we want to encourage fruiting spurs, which are short stubby growths that appear as sideshoots and bear a pronounced plump round bud that will be next year's flower and fruit. Pruning will tend to leave these alone and merely reduce the stronger non-fruiting shoots back to about five or six buds to encourage these to also become fruiting spurs. Shoots at the end of the main branches will also be pruned if you still want the tree to get bigger. Older apple trees may have very complex spurs, which will need shortening and simplifying to maintain fruit quality. You can also prune fruit trees in the summer, reducing back the sideshoots to three or four leaves to encourage these to become fruiting spurs.

During the first few years, fruit trees can be fed with an annual dressing of a balanced fertiliser such as Growmore at 60 g/m^2 (2 oz/yd^2). As the trees go into their fruiting cycle this can change to a feed with a higher potash level such as sulphate of potash.

TABLE OF ROOTSTOCKS AND THEIR EFFECTS

Rootstock	Description	Height	Cropping	Spacing
M27	Extremely dwarfing	1.5–1.8 m (5–6 ft)	2–3 years	0.9–1.2 m (3–4 ft)
M9	Very dwarfing	2.4–3.8 m (8–10 ft)	3–4 years	1.2–2.4 m (4–8 ft)
M26	Dwarfing	3–3.6 m (10–12 ft)	3–4 years	2.4–3.6 m (8–12 ft)
MM106	Vigorous	4.3–5.5 m (14–18 ft)	4–5 years	3.6–4.8 m (12–16 ft)
MM111 & M2	Very vigorous	5.5–7.6 m (18–25 ft)	6–7 years	4.3–7.6 m (14–18 ft)

APPLES FOR SMALL GARDENS

One possibility for very small gardens is the concept of a 'family' apple tree. Three or more cultivars grafted onto the same tree, grow and produce three types of fruit. It is essential with such a tree that the different types will pollinate each other and that they will grow at a similar rate to each other to keep the tree in balance. Vigorous cultivars such as Bramley will soon outgrow all the others so avoid these. You can also get pears grafted as family trees.

There are also 'Ballerina' trees, which make very narrow upright single stemmed pillars with fruit on tight spurs. There are six different types with varying fruits but of limited value.

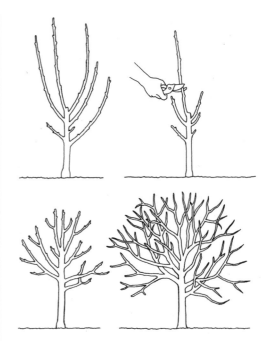

Young fruit trees are pruned quite hard, encouraging the development of a strong framework.

POLLINATION AND FRUIT THINNING

Flowering time is a very critical season for fruit crops and a late frost can destroy all the blossom or tiny fruits and result in a partial or total crop failure. If a frost is predicted smaller trees can be protected sufficiently with a layer of horticultural fleece or old net curtains.

If pollination and fruit set is successful, you can sometimes have an excess of fruit that will never mature properly. A natural drop occurs during June so wait until after that and then thin the young fruitlets to one per cluster.

ONGOING CARE

Keep the area around fruit trees free from weeds and water in dry spells, particularly as the fruit is swelling through the summer. A mulch will help to retain soil moisture.

Pests and diseases

Apples suffer from a bewildering range of pests and diseases. Various caterpillars and sawflies eat the foliage and flowers, and some burrow into the fruit causing the typical maggoty fruit. Mildew and scab diseases affect the foliage and weaken growth. For good quality fruit, it is necessary to spray repeatedly throughout the season using a mixture of a fungicide and an insecticide for caterpillars. Spray about every two weeks from leaf burst through until mid summer, avoiding blossom time.

If you do not like the idea of spraying regularly, don't spray at all but allow the natural balance of predators and parasites to develop. Fruit will not be prefect but some crop should be possible.

Harvesting and storage
Fruit is ripe when you gently lift a fruit and the stem parts easily without force. Some types of apple will store well into the winter in a cool, dark shed or garage. Wrapping in greaseproof paper or in perforated polythene bags will help to avoid shrinkage.

PEARS
The culture of pears is very similar to that of apples. As well as being valuable fruit trees, the blossom is early and attractive and they tend to have rich autumn tints. They can all be trained in a range of shapes and the general planting, formative pruning and routine culture is the same. In general pears like a warmer location than apples and prefer a heavier soil, although good drainage is essential.

The choice of rootstocks for pears is much simpler with Quince A, which makes a medium sized tree and Quince C, which makes a dwarf tree. Pears also require a compatible pollinator and this can be complicated as there are some that are totally incompatible, even though they may flower at the same time.

Routine pruning is similar to that of apples, although they will tolerate harder pruning. Pears tend to produce copious spurs and so spur thinning on older trees is essential to maintain fruit quality and vigour.

Selected pears
(pollination groups after name)
'William's Bon Chretien' – B - good early cropper, disease resistant, will not store
'Conference' – B – easy, partly self-fertile, hardy but susceptible to scab

'Doyenne du Comice' – C – exquisite fruit, but difficult and irregular cropper
'Concorde' – C – recent introduction, reliable, heavy cropping, good flavour
'Beth' – B – another new one, regular and heavy cropping, superb texture and flavour
'Winter Nelis' – C – heavy cropping, hardy and stores well right into January

Pests and diseases
Pears are affected by similar pests and diseases to apples plus the pear midge, which causes fruitlets to go black and drop off. Always destroy any fallen fruitlets before the maggots enter the soil and pupate. You can also spray for this pest.

Harvesting and storage
Early pears must be picked and eaten as soon as they are ripe. Watch for a slight lightening of the skin colour and check to see if the stalk parts easily from the tree. If left too long the fruit loses its delicate flavour and the flesh becomes brown and mushy, described as 'sleepy'. Late pears are best harvested and ripened in store. Bring the fruit into a warm room for a couple of days before eating to allow the full flavours to develop.

PLUMS
These are classed as stone fruits and provide some of the most succulent fruit available in temperate gardens. Gages and Damsons also come within this group. Plum trees are not particularly fussy but succeed best on a warm, sheltered site with a well drained moisture retentive soil. Recommendations for soil preparation and planting are the same as for apples or planting any other tree. Plums are

most often grown as bushes, half standards and sometimes as fan trained trees.

Rootstocks

There are four regularly used rootstocks with plums. Pixie makes very dwarf trees that have a mature height of around 3 m (10 ft) and is therefore ideal for small gardens. 'St Julien A' is a very common semi-dwarfing stock that makes a mature tree a bit bigger and is a better choice than Pixie if conditions are not ideal. 'Brompton' and 'Myrobalan B' make huge spreading plum trees that are far too big for most gardens. Not only do they take up too much space but the fruit is difficult to reach for picking.

Pruning plum trees

Young plum trees are pruned to encourage three to five strong main branches. Plum trees produce fruit on spurs, on two-year-old wood and sometimes at the base of one-year wood so pruning is similar to that of apples and pears but less complicated. Generally remove dead, diseased or damaged wood and generally keep the tree open, avoiding overcrowding. The most critical thing to remember is that you should always prune plums during the summer. This is because plums are very susceptible to silver leaf disease, which is more readily transmitted in the winter. Any major pruning cuts should also be treated with an arboricultural paint to seal them.

Routine care

Mulch annually and feed with a balanced general fertiliser in early spring. Plums flower quite early and the blossom can be damaged by frost. If trees are small enough, protect blossom or your fruitlets with fleece or old net curtains if frost is forecasted. Keep well watered when the fruit is developing.

Selected plums

'Victoria' – B - best known plum, reliable and heavy cropping, but prone to disease
'Marjorie's Seedling' – C – late plum for cooking and eating
'Opal' – B – newish variety, easy to grow and good flavour
'Oullin's Golden Gage' – C – an exquisite golden plum, reasonably healthy
'Cambridge Gage' – C – a traditional green gage, juicy, good flavour, reliable

Pests and diseases

Silver leaf disease is the main problem. Leaves on affected plants appear silvery white and almost translucent. It is a fungus and will spread throughout the tree. It passes from tree to tree via open wounds and pruning cuts and then spreads within the tree. If just a small part of the tree appears to be infected cut those branches out, cutting at least 12 cm (5 in) beyond where the symptoms are showing. Bacterial canker shows as cankers on the stems that ooze. Aphids and winter moth caterpillars may also attack plums. When the fruit is ripening wasps can be a major problem, feeding on the fruit and becoming a hazard to pickers.

CHERRIES

These are not a widely grown crop in private gardens, as the trees tend to be large. The newer dwarfing rootstock 'Colt' does make cherry growing more feasible although they are still large trees for a relatively small crop. The variety 'Stella' is a good one for the private garden as it is self-fertile and produces .sweet juicy fruits. 'Morello' is a good self-fertile cooking cherry that grows well as a fan-trained tree. Pruned similar to plums. Cherries also suffer from silver leaf disease so prune these in the summer too.

SOFT FRUIT

This is a wide group of fruits, generally so named because of their soft skins and includes bushes, cane fruiting types and strawberries, which are a herbaceous perennial. Generally they are all relatively low growing and can be looked after and harvested from ground level. Because they are a wide group, there are many variations in their culture. Soft fruit is not difficult to grow but will not perform well if neglected so be prepared to make an investment of time in order to reap a good crop.

STRAWBERRIES

Growing your own strawberries also gives you the opportunity to grow some of the better flavoured cultivars that are often not sold in the shops. This wonderful fruit gives worthwhile crops for three years maximum, after which they should be discarded. Many people find strawberry growing disappointing, because they keep old plants which have become worn out, overcrowded and diseased and then are surprised when the crop and quality is poor. If you have room for three rows of strawberries replant one row each year. If you have little space, grow them in tubs, pots or even hanging baskets. It is a very rewarding crop giving the biggest

BUYING HEALTHY STOCK

All soft fruits, and particularly strawberries, suffer from many pests and diseases, especially viruses. Specialist producers grow stock that is certified as totally healthy. You should always buy good certified stock from a reputable nursery. If your own plants appear to be healthy and crop well you can propagate these, although it is wise to buy in new fresh stock every few years. Do not be tempted to buy or accept stocks from an unknown source.

fruit and best quality fruit in the year after planting. The heavier yield is in the second year, tailing off in the third.

Planting strawberries

Strawberries like an open sunny site, with some shelter. They will grow on most soils, provided they are well drained but prefer a slightly acid soil. Prepare the site by digging and incorporating organic matter. Apply a balanced base fertiliser dressing just before planting and rake in.

The best time to plant strawberries is in mid to late summer, which will result in a welcome crop the following year. If you plant in spring, the flowers must be removed to avoid cropping the same season. Don't be tempted to leave them on! Plant strawberries shallowly, 45 cm (18 in) apart in rows 75 cm (30 in) apart. Finish off by firming in and watering. During the rest of the season of planting, keep watered and weed free. The plants may produce runners, which are long waving shoots that the plant uses to replicate itself. At this stage remove these.

Routine care

During the following spring, apply a high potash fertiliser and rake or hoe into the surface. At the same time, it is valuable to tidy up the plants removing any of last year's leaves that have died. As the weather warms up, the plants will burst into fresh growth and by mid to late spring, flowers will appear. At this stage it is important to mulch the plants. With this crop, this is particularly aimed at keeping the developing fruit off the soil to keep it clean. Straw is often used or special fibre strawberry mats are available, which slip around the plants. Water frequently as the fruit develops and ripens.

PROPAGATING STRAWBERRIES

If strawberry plants are healthy, they are very easy to propagate. In early summer watch out for healthy strong runners and pin these down into small pots of potting compost plunged alongside the mother plants. Keep the pots moist and in about four or five weeks the runners will have rooted and can be severed from the mother plant.

Remove any extension runner that may also be present on the new plants so that it can concentrate its energies on building up a strong crown for next year. These can be planted out almost straightaway in mid to late summer.

Harvest when fully ripe and pick daily during the cropping season. The fruit is picked by gently cupping in the palm and pinching the stalk so that the fruit is harvested with its stalk. Handle very gently at all times. Pick all ripe fruits and discard any damaged ones. Damaged fruit left on the plant will encourage disease. When cropping has finished, the plants can be trimmed back, removing old foliage, runners and the straw. Apply a general fertiliser and water well to start back into fresh growth and build up the plants ready for the next year.

Sumptuous strawberries

'Elsanta' –wonderful flavour and high yields but prone to disease

'Hapil' – good flavour, high yields, does well in light soils and dry seasons

'Pantagruella' – very early but otherwise poor

'Tenira' – excellent flavour, vigorous and disease resistant but average yield

'Gento' – a perpetual fruiting type with good flavour

'Elvira' – early, good for cropping under tunnels, flavour good but mildew prone

'Royal Sovereign' – an old variety with a reputation for taste, now superseded

'Cambridge Favourite' – a reliable high cropper but tasteless fruit – avoid!

Pests and diseases

Strawberry fruit is very prone to damage by birds and slugs as it ripens. Netting must be used to keep birds away and some form of slug protection is essential. Without protection from these two, the crop can be rendered useless. Strawberries are prone to attack by aphids, which transmit viruses and occasionally by red spider mite. In damp seasons, the fruit may be attacked by grey mould and rot. Remove and burn any affected fruit as soon as it is seen. Red core is a serious soil borne disease that causes the plant to collapse. Destroy the plants and grow strawberries on a fresh site.

RASPBERRIES

This fruit grows better in cool conditions and as it flowers later, is less likely to be damaged by frost. The fruit is borne on a woody stem that is called a cane. Each cane lasts two years making most of its growth from the ground in the first season and then fruiting in the second before dying.

Planting raspberries

After planting, a row of canes can be expected to last and remain productive for at least five years, so good thorough preparation with plenty of organic matter is advisable. Raspberries are not self-supporting, so need some sort of framework to tie them to. The simplest is an arrangement of posts and wire. 2.4-m (8-ft) tree stakes are ideal and should be driven in the ground at each end of the row. If the row is longer than 3 m (10 ft), add intermediate posts. Stretch three galvanised wires between the posts at 75 cm (30 in), 1.2 m (4 ft) and 1.6 m (5 ft 6 in) above the ground. These will not be needed until growth is strong but it is easiest to construct before planting.

Raspberry canes are best planted when dormant in the winter, spacing them between 30 cm (12 in) to 45 cm (18 in) apart. The closer spacing will require more canes but achieve a bigger crop quicker. Further rows should be spaced 1.8 m (6 ft) apart. Plant them along the row, spreading out the fibrous roots, immediately under the wires. When you buy raspberry canes they will usually have already been shortened to about 30–45 cm (12–18 in). In early spring of the first year, further prune them back to about 15 cm (6 in). This will stimulate the production of a number of young vigorous shoots, which will be our fruiting canes for next year.

Routine care

During the first season keep the young canes weed free and well watered. A general fertiliser should be applied in early spring. As the canes grow they can be tied in to the wires, aiming for canes no closer than 10 cm (4 in) apart, although it is unlikely that we shall get that many canes in the first year. For this you can use string, looping this around the wire before the cane to avoid the cane slipping. Alternatively you can use short proprietary wire ties but be careful not to strangle the cane. Any canes that grow beyond the top wire should be tipped back at the end of the season.

AUTUMN FRUITING RASPBERRIES

Most raspberries fruit in early summer but there are some that crop in the autumn on the current year's canes. They are pruned hard in the spring and generally do not require support. Otherwise they need similar conditions. They produce a very worthwhile crop at a useful time of the year.

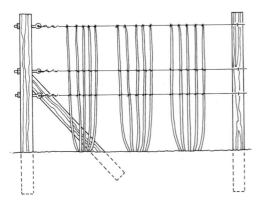

Raspberries need a strong framework of posts and wires to support the slender canes.

Repeat the general fertiliser and mulch at the beginning of the second and subsequent seasons. During the period between flowering and fruiting, keep the plants well watered to ensure that the fruit swells correctly.

Pruning and training the established crop

After cropping the first batch of canes will start to die and a further batch of new canes will be pushing up from ground level. Pruning can take place in late summer but most gardeners find it easier to wait until winter and prune during the dormant season. At this stage all the old fruited canes are pruned out to ground level together with any weak or distorted canes. The new canes are then tied in aiming for a spacing of 10 cm (4 in).

This time an easy way to do this is to use a running string, anchored at the end of the row, working along the bottom wire first. Select a suitable cane, position it against the wire and wrap the string around the cane, then loop around the wire and proceed on to the next cane. This is much quicker than individually tying each cane and also prevents the knots sliding along and the canes becoming bunched. Repeat the process for the middle and top wire. In a good plantation there will be surplus canes and all the remaining unwanted canes are then cut out to ground level. Alternatively, unwanted canes can be gently dug up as new stock for a fresh plantation.

Harvesting

Raspberries must be ripened on the plant so must be handled very carefully plucking the fruit and leaving the plug and stalk. Handle with great care at all times.

Recommended raspberries

'Malling Admiral' – good flavour, spine-free, free cropping

'Glen Clova' – very early, but low yields and average flavour

'Joy' – good flavour, high yield, aphid resistant and crops for six weeks

'Autumn Bliss' – good autumn variety, good flavour, heavy cropper

'Fallgold' – a golden fruited raspberry, a colourful novelty but not much more

Pests and diseases

Birds attack the fruit making it essential to net the crop. Raspberry beetle causes the typical maggoty fruit and must be controlled by spraying after flowering. In a wet season, the fruit may become infected with botrytis and start to rot. Spur blight and cane blight can cause die-back of the canes.

BLACKBERRIES AND HYBRID BERRIES

This includes loganberries, tayberries and a host of other less common fruits such as the boysenberry and Japanese Wineberry. They all produce fruit on canes, which live for only two years. Compared to raspberries, they have a more rampant and straggling habit with vicious thorns. So in the garden they need to be trained to wires or a support to make them manageable and for the fruit to be accessible.

A suitable support can be made from 2.4-m (8-ft) posts, driven into the ground with wires stretched across about 30 cm (1 ft) apart, starting about 90 cm (3 ft) above ground. The long whippy canes are tied to the wires as they grow. If there are more canes than wires, several canes can be tied at each level.

After fruiting the old fruited canes are cut out and the new young ones trained in. During the growing season the new canes can be loosely looped in to prevent damage and then finally trained in position after the previous year's canes are removed. Otherwise

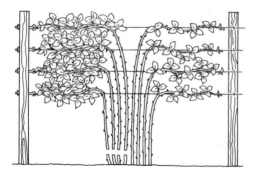

A blackberry with the new growth trained in one direction and the old growth being removed from the other side.

culture is similar to that of raspberries. These fruits also suffer from raspberry beetle, bird damage and botrytis.

Selected berries

'Ashton Cross' – good natural blackberry flavour, heavy crops

'Merton Thornless' – compact, thornless blackberry, tasty, moderate crop

'Loganberry LY59' – original hybrid berry, sharp taste, good for cooking

'Tayberry Medana' – better and sweeter than loganberry, crops well

'Japanese Wineberry' – more of an ornamental but with a red fruit, low yields

All the above berries can be propagated by layering shoots or more specifically by tip layering. This involves burying the tip of a growing shoot in summer. Roots will form and a new shoot will develop. When established, this can be severed from the parent plant and transplanted to a new location. Propagate only from healthy plants.

BLACKCURRANTS

This fruit is grown almost solely for cooking or preserving as the fruit is generally too sharp to be used fresh. Blackcurrants are nevertheless an easy and valuable crop to grow giving heavy yields.

Choose an open sunny sheltered site and prepare the ground in the normal way by digging and incorporating organic matter. Blackcurrants are best planted as dormant bushes in the winter. Use a pre-planting high phosphate fertiliser such as bonemeal before planting. Like some other fruits, you should look for healthy certified stock. One- or two-year-old bushes are usually available. Plant them 1.2–1.5 m (4–5 ft) apart, burying the roots about 5 cm (2 in) deeper than they were previously growing. You can usually see a soil mark on the stem to give an indication of this. After planting prune hard back to 2.5–5 cm (1–2 in) above ground level.

This will result in strong new growth. During the first season, keep weed free and watered during dry spells. A mulch will help to retain moisture. Additional feeding during early summer will encourage strong growth. At the end of the first season, little pruning is needed, although any weak shoots, crossed or damaged growths should be removed back to ground level. The first crop will come in the second season. Blackcurrants come in long clusters called 'strigs', which should be picked when the majority of the fruit is ripe.

Established blackcurrant bushes will need pruning every year. This can take place in late summer after the fruit has been picked or it can be left until winter when the structure of the bush is more easily discerned. Each year aim to cut out between 25 to 30% of the older fruited stems. Although individual stems will fruit for a number of years, the younger stems

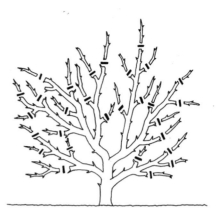

Redcurrants and gooseberries have a permanent framework but aim to keep the centre open.

give better quality and higher yields. Old wood can be recognised as it is darker, almost blackish-brown in colour. Removing old stems encourages a succession of young growths from ground level. You should also remove low growing, crossing, damaged or weak growths. The sideshooots on remaining stems should also be lightly thinned.

Selected blackcurrants
'Ben Lomond' – compact plant, heavy crop, later flowering and disease resistant
'Ben More' – similar cultivar, heavy cropping and disease resistant
'Baldwin' – good traditional cultivar but early flowering makes it prone to frost
'Wellington XXX' – said to have the best flavour, heavy crops, but a huge plant

Blackcurrants can be easily propagated by hardwood cuttings of one-year shoots taken in the autumn (see pages 46–47). These root very easily. You can even plant a group of three cuttings, where you want a new bush to grow and avoid the need for transplanting later.

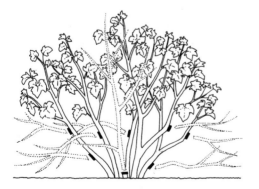

Aim to completely remove some old branches from blackcurrants every year.

Pests and diseases
Blackcurrants suffer from aphids, winter moth caterpillars and bird damage. They are also prey to big bud mite, which causes large round distorted buds that do not develop. This mite also spreads reversion disease, causing distorted leaves. Remove and burn infected branches and if necessary whole bushes.

RED AND WHITE CURRANTS
Although less commonly grown, these are a very pleasant and easily grown summer fruit. They are both sweeter than blackcurrants and so can be served fresh as well as used for cooking or preserving.

Although liking similar conditions to blackcurrants, they are pruned and trained in an entirely different manner. Whereas with blackcurrants, we are constantly pruning some branches hard to get new growth, red and white currants retain a framework of branches permanently throughout their lives. You can therefore train these as bushes or sometimes as cordons or standards.

There is no certification scheme but nevertheless aim to buy healthy stock from a good source. Plant during the dormant season, spacing the bushes 1.2–1.5 m (4–5 ft) apart. This time do not bury the plant but keep the root system at the same level as previously. Initial pruning should aim for an open, goblet-shaped bush with a clear stem at the base so you should remove any low branches. Remove about a third of the tips of the remaining shoots, leaving an outward facing bud at the top.

During future years, the process is similar, aiming to keep the centre of the bush open and new growth directed to the sides. Fruit is produced on small sideshoots called spurs. Sideshoots should be reduced to one or two buds to encourage spur formation. In later years, complex spurs will need thinning. Weed control, feeding, mulching and watering in dry weather are all routine matters, similar to other soft fruits.

Reliable red and white currants
'Red Lake' – reliable, moderately vigorous, heavy crops, good flavour
'Redstart' – newish introduction, high yields, late, acid flavour
'Laxton's No 1' – old cultivar, early, good flavour, heavy crops, spreading
'White Versailles' – traditional cultivar but still good, sweet and reliable
'White Grape' – excellent flavour, source from a specialist nursery

Pests and diseases
Currants suffer from aphids and birds, which in this instance eat the winter buds too. Fruit may develop botrytis in damp summers and shoots may be infected with coral spot disease, which is a pink fungus that appears on dead shoots but can spread to live tissues.

GOOSEBERRIES
This fruit is mainly used for cooking, although it can be quite succulent when fully ripe. Culture and pruning is very similar to that of redcurrants. It can be trained as a bush, standard or cordon. As the stems bear vicious spines it is particularly important to aim for an open shape when pruning to allow for easy access to the fruit when picking.

Great gooseberries

'Invicta' – relatively new, high yields and mildew resistant, mainly cooking use

'Golden Drop' – thin skins and excellent flavour, so good fresh, moderate yields

'Leveller' – good large dessert fruit, exceptional flavour and high yields

'Whinham's Industry' – another good dessert fruit, ruby red, good flavour

Birds can be particularly damaging to the buds in winter and mildew can devastate the foliage in summer. Sawfly larvae are like small caterpillars and will feed on the foliage until it is totally skeletonised if not controlled.

GRAPES

These are rather a specialist fruit that require particular study and skills to grow well. Fruit can be white (actually pale green) or black (more ruby red). Top quality dessert fruit must be grown in glasshouses in temperate climates but fruit suitable for modest wine making can be grown successfully outside in most seasons. Outdoors they will need a very warm sheltered south facing slope or a warm wall. Grapes are really for the expert gardener or those that want a new challenge!

UNUSUAL FRUITS

Various other fruits can possibly be grown purely for their curiosity value. Blueberries

MORE HYBRIDS

The Worcesterberry is like a small black gooseberry, although it is really a type of currant. Grow like a gooseberry. Another hybrid between blackberry and gooseberry is called the Jostaberry with fruit like double size blackcurrants. Grow this one like blackcurrants. Both are curiosities rather than heavy croppers and are spreading plants so leave plenty of space.

or cranberries are possible, although the latter needs boggy conditions and both need an acid soil. Figs are relatively easy and also highly ornamental wall shrubs. Tiny fruits are formed one year and remain on the bushes until the next year when they ripen. Kiwi fruits are possible with a sheltered wall in a warm location but the vines make huge plants. Cape gooseberry has become popular in recent years and is a half hardy annual that can be grown from seed and will fruit in the first year. It is more often used as a garnish than a main fruit.

Under glass it is possible to grow various citrus fruits and although it may be possible to mature the occasional fruit, you are unlikely to have a useful crop. Mangos, papayas and pineapples can also be tried but don't expect to sell surplus fruit!

GARDENING CALENDAR

Gardens need constant care all year round. The following calendar, with its helpful hints and tips for each month, will help you to plan ahead and make sure your plants, trees and crops are getting the care they require.

JANUARY

This is the time of year to plan ahead and prepare. Plants are not visibly growing but there is much that can be done in the garden. Snowdrops remind us that all is not dead!

1. Use a half-moon to recut crisp edges to your lawns.
2. Inspect stored dahlias, begonias and cannas for rot or shrivelling.
3. Plan new features and browse the catalogues.
4. Wash any flower pots and seed trays ready for use in the spring.
5. Dig over any vacant plots that have not been dug already.
6. If the ground is frozen, barrow compost onto plots for later use.
7. Prune apple and pear trees, also soft fruits such as currants and gooseberries.
8. Start forcing rhubarb by covering with an upturned bucket or straw.
9. Buy seeds for the vegetable garden and plan crop rotations.
10. Ventilate greenhouses and frames on sunny days.

FEBRUARY

Winter is still with us but there are glimmers of spring with witch hazel, aconites and early crocus. A frustrating time as most jobs are still preparatory. Longer days give a promise of spring.

1. Check and replace tree stakes and ties if needed.
2. Divide and replant snowdrops whilst 'in the green'.
3. Prune all types of roses.
4. Prune late summer shrubs such as *Buddleia, Caryopteris* and *Ceratostigma.*
5. Prune hardy evergreen hedges and renovate overgrown deciduous hedges.
6. Send mowers and other equipment for servicing and avoid the spring rush.
7. Make some early vegetable sowings under cover.
8. Lay out seed potatoes to chit.
9. Prune autumn fruiting raspberries.
10. Don't be tempted to sow seeds too early – a cold greenhouse is still cold!

MARCH

Almost spring with some sunny days and bulbs starting to flower. Drying winds should be making soil more manageable and greenhouses warming up a bit.

1. Use slug pellets around susceptible plants such as Hostas.
2. Plant summer-flowering bulbs including gladioli, alliums and lilies.
3. Lift and divide herbaceous perennials.
4. Complete planting any trees, roses or open ground shrubs.
5. Mow the lawn on dry days (if needed).
6. Hard prune dogwoods, rubus and coloured stemmed willows.
7. Check over fountain in pools, remove any accumulated leaves.
8. Apply a balanced fertiliser as a topdressing to roses and young shrubs.
9. Plant shallots, onion sets and early potatoes.
10. Start vegetable sowing outside as the weather allows.
11. Start sowing bedding plants in a warm greenhouse.

APRIL

Spring at last! A very busy season with everything including weeds starting to grow. Spring bulbs and flowers in full display. Many plants needing attention and lots of seeds to sow.

1. Weeds come back in to growth – deal with them before they get out of hand.
2. Sow hardy annuals outdoors.
3. Plant or divide ornamental grasses.
4. Increase the amount of water given to houseplants.
5. Apply a spring feed to established lawns.
6. Sow new lawns or re-seed bare patches.
7. Plant or transplant evergreens.
8. Use brushwood to stake herbaceous plants before they flop.
9. Divide or repot houseplants.
10. Many vegetables to be sown this month.
11. Apply mulches where appropriate before the soil dries out.

MAY

As the trees finally unfurl their fresh new leaves, summer seems to have arrived. Spring flowers fade and it's time to plant summer displays. The earliest vegetables and fruit are starting to mature.

1. Watch out for late frosts. Protect tender plants and fruit blossom.
2. Harden off bedding ready for planting out at the end of the month.
3. Water newly planted trees and other plants in dry spells.
4. Mow lawns regularly, gradually reducing the height of cut.
5. Divide or plant aquatic plants and water lilies.
6. Protect strawberries from slugs.
7. Sow winter brassicas and wallflowers in a nursery bed.
8. Earth up potatoes to protect from frost and keep tubers white.
9. Plant tomatoes in unheated greenhouses.
10. Apply shading and regularly ventilate greenhouses to keep them cool.

JUNE

Summer proper at last! Fruit vegetables and flowers everywhere in the garden. A month to enjoy the garden as well as work in it.

1. Check for nesting birds before trimming hedges.
2. Take softwood cuttings of deciduous shrubs.
3. Treat young growth on perennial weeds with a translocated herbicide.
4. Cut lawns at least once a week, removing mowings if possible.
5. Position hanging baskets outside and water regularly.
6. Ensure newly planted trees, shrubs and other plants do not dry out.
7. Plant out tender plants such as dahlias and cannas.
8. Keep ponds and water features topped up in hot weather.
9. Plant out tender vegetables such as courgettes, sweet corn and beans.
10. Keep up successional sowings of vegetables.

JULY

Lots of colour in the garden, although growth and weed problems tailing off particularly if the weather is dry. Keep harvesting crops to encourage succession.

1. Place conservatory plants outside, now that it is warm.
2. Liquid feed tubs and hanging baskets to keep the display going.
3. Dead-head roses, bedding plants and herbaceous perennials.
4. Clear algae, blanket weeds and debris from ponds, and keep them topped up.
5. Give lawns a second summer feed and water in if dry.
6. Use preservative on garden seats and other outdoor woodwork.
7. Prune spring and early summer flowering shrubs.
8. Harvest vegetables regularly to encourage continuity.
9. Spray potato crops to protect from blight.
10. Peg down strawberry runners from healthy plants.

AUGUST

Often hot and sometimes dry. The holiday season, so make plans to avoid your garden going wild if you are going away. Late summer colour and bedding displays at their peak.

1. Visit gardens and nurseries to get ideas for your own plot.
2. Make notes of successes and failures to help planning next year.
3. Order bulbs for autumn planting.
4. Sow pansies for spring bedding.
5. Prune raspberries and blackcurrants after fruiting.
6. Harvest sweet corn and other vegetables as they become ready.
7. Cut out old fruited canes on raspberries.
8. Lift and replant rooted strawberry runners.
9. Keep ponds and water features topped up.
10. Lift onions as they ripen and dry ready for storage.

SEPTEMBER

The weather is often great and late summer colour from plants such as dahlias and cannas is at its best, although the fresh 'greens' of early summer have gone. Shorter days and a chill in the evening remind us that winter is coming.

1. Net ponds before leaf fall gets underway.
2. Keep up with watering in the garden if conditions remain dry.
3. Start to reduce the frequency of houseplant watering.
4. Clean out greenhouses ready for use in the autumn.
5. Give evergreen hedges a final trim.
6. Sow grass seed for new lawns.
7. Propagate, fuchsias, pelargoniums and other tender perennials.
8. Plant prepared hyacinths for Christmas flowering.
9. Sow greenhouse lettuces for overwintering.
10. Harvest potatoes before slug damage spoils them.

OCTOBER

Still some nice days but the garden will be starting to look tired. Summer flowers will be fading and colour from berries and autumn leaves will be starting to show. Plenty of produce still available.

1. Start clearing autumn leaves as they fall.
2. Cut back fading herbaceous perennials.
3. Divide herbaceous perennials and rhubarb crowns.
4. Lift tender plants and return to the greenhouse for winter.
5. Plant spring bulbs such as narcissus, hyacinth and crocus.
6. Plant polyanthus, pansies and wallflowers for spring display.
7. Trim any hedges missed earlier in the season.
8. Carry out autumn lawn renovation and apply an autumn feed.
9. Plant out spring cabbages.
10. Harvest apples and pears as they ripen.

NOVEMBER

Not a favourite month for many of us! Usually cold, dull and wet, reminding us that winter is here! A time to wind down the garden and tuck it up for winter.

1. Continue leaf clearance, avoiding smothering lawns.
2. Plant tulip bulbs for a spring display next year.
3. Shorten roses to prevent winter wind-rock.
4. Start planting trees, roses and open ground shrubs.
5. Lift dahlias and cannas after the first frost and store under cover.
6. Create new lawns by laying turf.
7. Drain down and turn off any outdoor water supplies before frost.
8. Cover winter brassicas with netting if pigeons are a problem.
9. Apply grease bands to fruit trees to discourage winter moth damage.
10. Insulate the greenhouse with bubblewrap to reduce heat loss.

DECEMBER

Not exactly a resting month, but one of the quietest in the gardening calendar. Brightened up by a few winter flowering treasures such Mahonia, winter sweet and Viburnums.

1. Prepare hardwood cuttings of deciduous shrubs and soft fruits.
2. Rake over gravel paths and top up where needed.
3. Clear vegetable patches and herbaceous borders and compost the waste.
4. Start winter digging, especially clay soils which should be left rough.
5. Keep mice away from stored produce and bulbs.
6. Prune apples and pears.
7. Prune grape vines early to avoid bleeding.
8. Harvest leeks, parsnips, winter cabbage, sprouts and remaining root crops.
9. Order a load of farmyard manure and stack to mature.
10. Count the plants in bloom on Christmas day – can be surprising!

GLOSSARY

The following pages list all the gardening terms you will come across either in this book or in other gardening handbooks.

Acaricide: a pesticide for controlling mites such as red spider mite.

Acid soil: a soil or potting compost which contains little or no lime and has a pH of less than 6.5. Often referred to as 'sour' soil by gardeners.

Aeration: the loosening of soil by digging or other means to allow air to pass freely.

Aerial root: a root which grows out from the stem above ground level. Aerial roots are commonly seen on ivy plants and Monstera, the Swiss cheese plant.

Aerobic: describes favourable conditions in the soil or a compost heap, which contains oxygen and encourages beneficial bacteria. (Opposite Anaerobic.)

Air layering: a method of propagating leggy plants, such as Ficus elastica or climbers.

Alkaline soil: soil that has a pH level of about 7.0 or more. Also called chalky. Sometimes referred to as 'sweet' soil by gardeners.

Alpine: a plant that originates from mountainous regions.

Alternate: leaf arrangement, where the leaves are arranged singly at different heights on the stem. (Compare Opposite and Whorled.)

Anaerobic: describes organisms living or occurring when oxygen is absent. Usually term used when talking about compost heaps or waterlogged soils. (Opposite Aerobic.)

Annual: a plant that completes its life cycle within one year of germination. (Compare Biennial and Perennial.)

Anther: the male part of the flower, which produces pollen. It is the upper section of the stamen.

Apical bud: the bud at the tip of a branch.

Aquatic: any plant which grows partially or completely in water.

Asexual reproduction: vegetative reproduction, e.g. cuttings and division.

Auxins: natural chemicals within plants that control growth and development.

Axillary bud: a growth bud that occurs in a leaf axil.

Bare root: usually refers to deciduous shrubs, roses, trees and some other perennials, that are sold with all the soil removed from their roots.

Bark ringing: removal of part of the bark around a fruit tree to slow growth and encourage fruiting.

Bedding plants: seasonal plants used for floral display, often in formal beds.

Bicolour: a flower with petals which bear two distinctly different colours.

Biennial: a plant which completes its life cycle in two seasons. (Compare Annual and Perennial.)

Biological pest control: using living organisms such as beneficial insects or parasites to destroy garden pests.

Blanch: to exclude light and force a vegetable to produce white tissues.

Bleeding: the loss of sap from plant tissues which have been cut or damaged.

Blindness: a condition when a plant fails to produce a flower or the growing point dies.

Bloom: a natural mealy or waxy coating covering the leaves, flowers or fruit of some plants.

Bolt: to run to flower and seed prematurely, e.g. onions.

Bonsai: the ancient art of dwarfing trees by careful root and stem pruning, training and root restriction.

Botanic name: the Latin scientific name of a plant is its botanical name.

Bottom heat: heat provided in the soil or underneath a greenhouse bench by electric cables or hot water pipes.

Bract: a modified leaf, often highly coloured and sometimes mistaken for a petal. Examples of plants with showy bracts are Poinsettia and Bougainvillea.

Breaks: side shoots produced from axillary buds after removal of the growing point.

Budding: a method of propagation where a single bud is united with another plant.

Bulb: a storage organ, usually formed below ground level, used for propagation. A true bulb consists of fleshy scales surrounding the central bud, but the term is often loosely applied to corms, rhizomes and tubers.

Bulbil: an immature small bulb formed on the stem of a plant, e.g. Lily.

Bulblet: an immature small bulb formed at the base of a mature bulb, e.g. Hyacinth.

Calcifuge: a lime hating plant or plant that needs a low pH soil.

Callus: protective tissue that a plant forms in response to damage, i.e. at the base of a cutting.

Calyx: the outer ring of flower parts, usually green but sometimes coloured and also known as sepals.

Cambium: the layer of tissue under the bark of plants, that is capable of growth and allows the plant to increase in size. Also important in rooting and grafting.

Capillary action: the natural upward movement of water in confined areas, such as the spaces between soil particles.

Capping: the crust that forms on the surface of some soils after heavy rain.

Carnivorous plants: a group of plants, often tropical that nature has adapted to trap and consume insects for nutritional purposes, e.g. Venus Flytrap plant.

Carpet bedding: elaborate closely planted, low growing plants laid out to form a motif, crest or pattern.

Chlorophyll: the green matter in leaves, which is essential for photosynthesis and growth.

Chlorosis: an abnormal yellowing or blanching of the leaves due to lack of chlorophyll.

Clamp: a storage technique for root vegetables where they are made into a heap and covered with soil.

Cloche: a portable structure made of glass or polythene for covering early outdoor crops such as vegetables.

Clone: a group of genetically identical plants produced by vegetative propagation.

Cold frame: a glazed box providing some protection from the weather for vegetables and young plants.

Companion planting: mixing plants together that have a beneficial effect on each other such as deterring pests.

Compost: a manufactured potting mixture usually made from materials such as sterilised soil, peat and sand. Also used to refer to the material produced after decomposition of organic waste.

Compound: divided into a number of different parts, e.g. compound leaves divided into leaflets; rowan or compound flowers with many florets, e.g. Chrysanthemum.

Conifer: otherwise known as gymnosperms. One group of the plant kingdom with naked ovules borne in cones.

Contact action: usually referring to pesticides or herbicides which have an instant knock-down effect.

Coppicing: hard pruning of trees or shrubs to encourage a thicket of strong growth from the base, e.g. hazel.

Cordon: a trained plant restricted to one stem that is often grown at a 45° angle. Particularly used for growing certain fruits.

Corm: a storage organ comprised of swollen, underground stem bases, e.g. Crocus.

Corolla: the ring of separate or fused petals, which is nearly always responsible for the main floral display.

Cotyledon: the seed leaf, which is the first to emerge when a seed germinates. Most plants are dicotyledonous having two seed leaves, although some, such as grasses, are monocotyledonous.

Cristate: cockscomb-like growth of leaves, stems or flowers. Otherwise called crested.

Crock: a piece of broken pot used to help drainage in the bottom of large pots or planters. Almost always referring to clay or ceramic pieces.

Crop rotation: a system for managing a vegetable plot to avoid the build-up of pests and diseases and to make the best use of nutrients within the soil.

Cross pollination: the transfer of pollen from one flower to another.

Crown: the region where shoot and root join, usually at or very near ground level. Also used to refer to the head of a tree.

Cultivar: used when determining plant names. Indicates the variety originated in cultivation and not the wild. This portion of a plant's name is usually not Latin.

Cutting: a piece of a plant (leaf, stem or root) which can be induced to grow on its own and produce a new plant.

Cyme: a flat-topped or domed flower head in which the flowers at the centre open first.

Damping down: splashing water on the floor of a greenhouse on a hot day to increase the humidity and lower the temperature.

Damping off: decay of young seedlings at ground level following fungal attack. Often the result of soil-borne diseases and over watering.

Dead heading: the removal of faded heads of flowers.

Deciduous: plants that loose their leaves at the end of the growing season, e.g. beech, oak and horse chestnut.

Dehiscent: refers to seed capsules that split to release their seeds.

Dioecious: plants which have male and female flowers on separate plants. (Compare Monoecious).

Dibber: a piece of wood or plastic, pointed and shaped for making a hole for planting.

Digging: cultivating the soil with a spade which usually involves inverting each spadeful.

Disc: the flat central part of a compound flower. It is made up of short, tubular florets.

Disbudding: the removal of surplus flower buds on a plant to encourage the plant's energies into producing fewer but higher quality flowers or fruits.

Division: a method of propagating herbaceous plants by separating each one into two or more sections.

Dolomitic limestone: sometimes used when 'liming' soil that has a pH level that is too low. As it contains calcium and magnesium carbonate it should be used only with soils that are also deficient in magnesium as well. A useful source of magnesium.

Dormancy: the time when a plant has naturally stopped active growing and the leaves have fallen or the top growth has died down. The dormant period is usually, but not always, in winter.

Double flowers: this refers to flowers that have many petals present, such as roses. The Latin name for this is 'flore pleno'.

Drainage: the movement of excess water through the soil.

Drawn: excessively tall and weak growth, caused by plants being grown in too little light or too closely together.

Drill: a narrow, shallow trench for sowing seeds outside.

Earthing up: drawing up soil around a crop, such as potatoes or celery, to exclude the light.

Entire leaf: an undivided and unserrated leaf.

Epicormic shoots: growths that develop from the trunk of a tree – often called suckers.

Epiphyte: a plant that grows above ground attaching itself to trees or rocks. It obtains its moisture and nutrition from the air.

Ericaceous: plants belonging to the *Ericaceae* family or more generally used to refer to acid loving plants. Means the same as Calcifuge.

Espalier: a method of training plants, especially fruit trees having one main stem and several layers of parallel, horizontal branches trained along a wall or wires.

Evergreen: a plant that retains its leaves in a living state during the winter.

Everlasting: flowers with papery petals, which retain some or all of their colour when dried for winter decorations.

Exotic: strictly speaking, any plant which is not native to the area, but popularly used for any unusual or striking plant.

Eye: two unrelated meanings, an undeveloped growth bud such as we find on potatoes, or the centre of a flower.

F1 Hybrid: a first generation offspring of two pure bred strains. F1 hybrids are generally superior to ordinary hybrids.

Family: a category in plant classification, whereby we group together similar related plants.

Fastigiate: plants with a narrow erect habit of growth.

Feathered: refers to a young tree, usually with one stem and some small lateral branches, i.e. feathers.

Fertilise: means either to apply fertilisers or to the transfer of pollen from one flower to another to encourage seed or fruit formation.

Fertilisers: materials used to provide nutrition for plants and usually applied to the soil.

Fibrous roots: the many thin, feeding roots that make up the outer parts of a root system rather than the larger thong-like roots.

Flat: an American term for a shallow box or tray used to start cuttings or seedlings.

Floret: a small flower which is part

of a much larger compound flower head, e.g. *Cineraria*.

Flower head: a mass of smaller flowers growing together making up one large structure.

Formal: a garden style based on straight lines and geometric shapes.

Foliar feeding: applying a fertiliser in liquid form to a plant's foliage in a fine spray so that the plant can absorb the nutrients through its leaves.

Forcing: the process of making a plant grow or flower before its natural season, often by higher temperatures.

Formative pruning: pruning in the early years of a plant's life to encourage a specific shape and structure.

Friable: refers to soil that is crumbly, neither too wet nor too dry and will work easily to a good tilth.

Frond: refers to the leaves of a fern or palm.

Frost pocket: a depression where cold air collects and it becomes difficult to grow tender plants.

Fruit: the fertilised ripe ovary of a plant containing one or more seeds.

Fungicide: a chemical used to control plant diseases caused by fungi.

Fungus: a primitive form of plant life which is known to the gardener as the most common cause of diseases such as powdery mildew, botrytis and black spot. Mushrooms and toadstools are also fungi.

Genus: used when naming plants. Genus is the plant equivalent of our surnames. When followed by the 'species' name, you have its botanical name. Almost always in Latin.

Germination: the first stage in the development of a plant from seed.

Girdling: the removal of the bark from a tree by a wire, rope or other inflexible material, which often results in the plant's death.

Glabrous: plant surface which is smooth and hairless.

Glaucous: plant surface which is covered with a silvery bluish-grey bloom.

Grafting: a method of propagation which joins a stem or bud of one plant on to the stem of another.

Green manure: a crop, such as rye grass or clover that is grown and then dug into the soil to increase soil fertility and organic matter content.

Ground cover: plants used to provide a low-growing carpet between other plants and smother out weeds.

Growing point: the tip of a stem, which is responsible for extension growth. Correctly known as the meristem.

Growing medium: another term for a potting compost.

Half hardy: generally refers to plants which will not tolerate frost but can spend part of the year outside in the garden.

Half standard: a plant with a short clear stem before the head develops. Usually refers to roses or fruit trees.

Hardening off: gradual acclimatisation to colder conditions. Usually used when talking about moving of greenhouse plants or seedlings outside ready for planting in early summer.

Hardwood cuttings: stem cuttings taken of dormant wood from deciduous shrubs and soft fruits.

Hardy: refers to plants which can withstand year round climatic conditions in a given area. Often used to mean that plants are frost tolerant.

Haulm: the top growth of potatoes.

Heart: the central tightly packed area of a cabbage or lettuce.

Heavy: in the context of soils, this refers to clay soils as they are literally heavy work to cultivate.

Heel: a strip of bark and wood remaining at the base of a side shoot prepared as a cutting by pulling off a main shoot. Some cuttings root more readily if a heel is attached.

Herb: a plant grown for flavouring or medicinal purposes. Botanically it is short for herbaceous plant.

Herbaceous: a plant with a non-woody stem, that dies down to a crown each winter.

Herbicide: the correct term for a chemical used to kill weeds.

Honeydew: sticky, sugary secretion deposited on plants by insects such as aphid and whitefly.

Humidity: a measurement of the moisture in the air. Of particular relevance in greenhouses.

Humus: a dark coloured, stable form of organic matter that remains after most of plant or animal residues have decomposed.

Hybrid: a plant with parents which are genetically distinct. The parent plants may be different cultivars, varieties, species or genera but not different families.

Hybridisation: plant breeding.

Hydroculture (Hydroponics): a method of growing a plant in water containing dissolved nutrients.

Hypertufa: an artificial stone mix made from sand, cement and peat used to make alpine sinks.

Incurved: describes some flowers where the petals curve inwards to form a ball shape, e.g. Chrysanthemums.

Inflorescence: a group of flowers arranged on a stem, sometimes simply called a flower head.

Informal: a garden style which is based on curves and natural shapes rather than geometric patterns. (Opposite Formal.)

Inorganic: a chemical or fertilizer which is not obtained from a natural source.

Insecticide: a material (pesticide) used to kill or repel insects.

Internode: the part of the stem between two nodes (leaf joints).

Interplanting: the planting of one, often short-term crop amongst another crop.

John Innes Composts: a range of loam (soil) based composts made to standard mixes.

Lateral: a side shoot.

Latex: milky sap which exudes from cut surfaces of certain plants, such as *Ficus elastica* and *Euphorbia*.

Layering: a means of propagation whereby shoots are pegged down to root.

Leaching: the loss of soluble nutrients from the soil through means of heavy rain or irrigation.

Leader: the main (central or terminal) shoot in a plant.

Leaf mould: partially decomposed leaves used for soil enrichment.

Leaflet: a leaf-like section of a compound leaf.

Leggy: abnormally tall and spindly growth.

Legume: the correct name for peas and beans, all plants in the family *Leguminosae*.

Lime: calcium compounds used to raise soil pH.

Loam: a mixed soil containing sand, silt and clay. Also refers to the soil constituent of traditional potting composts and was made from stacked, matured turf.

Lute: a piece of equipment used for working top dressings into lawns.

Maiden: a young fruit tree in its first year.

Marginals: water plants that grow on the edge of a pool in shallow water.

Manure: animal excreta, stored and matured and then used as a soil improver. A form of organic matter.

Meristem: the growing point of a plant.

Microclimate: a particular small area where the climate is slightly different from the overall surroundings.

Micropropagation: multiplication of plants using tiny microscopic parts of the plant. Sometimes called tissue culture.

Micro-organisms: minute animals and plants that are too small to be seen clearly with the naked eye. Many live in the soil.

Midrib: the central vein of a leaf.

Mist propagation: propagation using a piece of equipment that keeps cuttings constantly damped over.

Monocotyledon: a plant that has only one seed leaf at germination, e.g. grasses.

Monoecious: a plant which bears both male and female flowers on the same plant. (Compare Dioecious.)

Mulch: any loose, usually organic material placed over the soil as a protective covering to reduce water loss and discourage weeds.

Mutation: a genetic change in a plant, for example the production of variegated leaves. Also called a sport.

Mycorrhizae: beneficial soil fungi that live in association with certain plants such as some conifers and orchids.

Naturalise: to establish and grow in a natural manner, for example bulbs.

Neutral: neither acid nor alkaline; pH 7.0.

Nitrogen cycle: the transformation of nitrogen from an atmospheric gas to organic compounds in the soil, then to compounds in plants and eventually the release of nitrogen gas back into the atmosphere.

Nitrogen fixation: the capture and conversion of atmospheric nitrogen gas into nitrogen compounds, stored in the soil, that can be used by plants. Particularly by peas and beans.

Nodal cutting: a cutting trimmed to just below a node.

Node: the point on a stem where a leaf or bud is attached.

Nutrients: the minerals required for plant growth.

Offset: a young plantlet which appears on a mature plant. An offset can generally be detached and used for propagation.

Opposite: leaf form, where the leaves are arranged in opposite pairs along the stem. (Compare Alternate.)

Organic: a chemical or fertilizer

obtained from a source which is or has been alive. Also a general term used for the type of gardening using no chemical or synthetic fertilisers or pesticides.

Ovary: the basal part of the flower that develops into the fruit.

Ovule: the part of the ovary that develops into the seed.

Oxygenator: a submerged aquatic plant that releases oxygen into the water in a pool.

Palmate: describing leaves, hand-like with five or more lobes arising from one point.

Pan: a hard layer within the soil often created by poor past cultivation. Or a shallow flower pot used for alpines or bulbs.

Panicle: a branched inflorescence bearing many small flowers.

Peat: partially decomposed sphagnum moss or sedges used in making composts. Valuable for its pronounced air and water holding capacity and its freedom from weeds and disease organisms.

Pedicel: the stalk of an individual flower.

Peduncle: the stalk of a flower head.

Pendant: hanging or trailing.

Perennial: a plant that lives for three years or more under normal conditions.

Perfoliate: paired leaves that fuse around the stem giving the impression of a single leaf through which the stem grows.

Perianth: collective term for calyx and corolla in many flowers.

Perlite: a mineral expanded by heating to form very lightweight, porous white granules useful in container soil mixes to enhance moisture and air retention.

Perpetual: describing plants that have a long season of flower or cropping.

Petal: one of the divisions of the corolla, generally the showy part of the flower.

Petiole: a leaf stalk.

pH: a measure of acidity and alkalinity. Scale 1–14. Below pH 7.0 is acid, above pH 7.0 is alkaline, pH 7.0 is neutral.

Photosynthesis: the production of sugars by green leaves in the presence of light.

Picotee: term applied to a narrow band of colour on a pale ground at the edge of a petal.

Pinching out: the removal of the growing point of a stem to induce bushiness or to encourage flowering. Also known as stopping.

Pinnate leaf: a compound leaf with a series of leaflets arranged on either side of a central stalk.

Pleaching: a method of training trees to form what appears to be a hedge on tall stems.

Plug: a small plant raised in a cell unit and sold for growing on.

Plunge: to place a pot up to its rim outdoors in soil, peat or ashes.

Pollarding: an outdated method of tree pruning involving hard pruning of all branches back to the main trunk.

Pollen: the yellow dust produced by the anthers. It is the male element which fertilises the ovule.

Pollination: the transfer of pollen from anthers to stigma.

Pollinator: the means by which pollination happens, e.g. an insect.

Also a cultivar of fruit which is used as a compatible partner for pollination.

Pompom: small globular flower head.

Pot bound: refers to plants growing in pots which are too small to allow proper leaf and stem growth.

Potting on: moving a plant on to a larger pot size.

Potting up: placing young plants or seedlings in pots for the first time.

Pricking out: the moving of seedlings from the tray or pot in which they were sown to other receptacles where they are spaced out individually.

Propagation: in horticulture, this refers to the many different ways of increasing plants.

Propagator: an enclosed and often heated box for rooting cuttings and raising seeds. Also a person who works in a nursery propagating plants.

Pruning: the removal of parts of a plant, usually stems or branches for various reasons, usually cultural or aesthetic.

Raceme: a type of flower stem with many smaller flowers.

Radicle: the young root that appears when a seed germinates.

Rain shadow: an area of ground near to a wall or fence that is sheltered from wind and rain.

Reflexed: flower form where the petals bend backwards, e.g. some chrysanthemums.

Renewal pruning: a method by which apples are pruned, removing old wood and encouraging new shoots.

Respiration: a process taking place

in all living organisms, all the time whereby energy is released for growth.

Reversion: generally refers to when variegated plants produce green shoots.

Rhizome: a thickened stem which grows horizontally below or on the soil surface. Acts as a storage organ.

Root: the part of the plant, normally underground that anchors it and absorbs water and nutrients.

Root ball: matted roots and attached soil within the pot of a container-grown plant. Or a tree dug up with this intact.

Root crops: vegetable with swollen roots that are edible, e.g. carrots.

Root cutting: a type of cutting made from a section of root rather than shoot.

Rooting hormone: a synthesised chemical in powder or liquid form which promotes the formation of roots at the base of a cutting.

Rootstock: a plant used to provide the root system of a grafted plant.

Rose: a perforated nozzle on a watering can, used for watering delicate plants.

Rosette: term applied to a whorl of leaves arising at the base of a plant.

Runner: a creeping stem which produces small plantlets along its length.

Sap: the juices within a plant.

Sapling: a young tree in its first few years.

Scarification: treatment of the hard seed coat on some seeds. Also removal of moss and dead grass from a lawn.

Scion: the upper half of a grafted plant. Usually refers to it during the propagation stage.

Scree: a stoney slope within a rock garden.

Self colour: a flower with single coloured petals throughout the flowerhead.

Self-fertile: a plant that produces viable seed when fertilised with its own pollen.

Self-pollination: transfer of pollen to stigma within the same flower or another flower on the same plant.

Semi-ripe cutting: an autumn cutting when the tissues are starting to harden.

Sepal: the outer whorl of the flower.

Serrate: saw-edged leaf pattern.

Sessile: applied to leaves or flowers which are borne directly on the stem.

Sexual reproduction: this refers to reproduction by fertilisation, which leads to seed production.

Short day plant: a plant that responds to the shorter days of autumn and winter by flowering, e.g. Chrysanthemum and Poinsettia.

Shrub: a woody plant with a framework of branches and little or no central stem. (Compare Tree.)

Side shoot: a shoot arising from the side of a main stem.

Simple: refers to leaves that are entire and undivided.

Single digging: cultivating the soil with a spade to the depth of one spit.

Single flower: a flower with a normal amount of petals present, arranged in a single row. Lawn daisies are a good example of this type.

Snag: a small stump left after poor pruning which is inclined to rot.

Soil polymers: super absorbent polymers recently developed that can increase water retention of soils and are primarily used in container grown plants.

Spathe: a large bract, sometimes highly coloured, e.g. *Anthurium* and *Spathiphyllum.*

Species: used when naming plants. Designates a specific type within the Genus and is best described as the plant world's equivalent to our first names.

Sphagnum moss: bog mosses often used in the past for gardening purposes. For conservation reasons should not now be used.

Spike: a narrow type of inflorescence.

Spit: a single spade's depth within the soil (approximately 30 cm/12 in).

Spore: a reproductive cell of non-flowering plants, such as ferns, fungi and mosses.

Sport: a plant that shows a marked and inheritable change from its parent, i.e. a mutation.

Spray: a flower formation with many small flowers on a branching stem.

Spur: a short branchlet bearing flowers and fruit.

Stamens: the male reproductive parts of a flower.

Standard: a plant which does not normally grow as a tree but is trained into a tree-like form with a bare stem.

Stigma: the part of the female organ of the flower which catches the pollen.

Stipule: a small outgrowth at the base of the leaf stalk.

Stolon: a horizontal spreading stem that roots as it grows.

Stool: a root of various plants such as Chrysanthemums used to produce cuttings.

Stooling: hard pruning back to ground level used with plants that are required to make vigorous growth.

Stopping: another term for pinching out.

Stove plant: an outdated term used to refer to tropical greenhouse plants.

Stratification: storage of seed of certain hardy plants outside so that the cold breaks the dormancy.

Sub-shrub: a low growing plant that has some woody growths which are not long lasting.

Subsoil: the poorer layer of soil underneath the topsoil.

Succulent: a plant with thick fleshy leaves that are adapted to store water.

Sucker: a shoot that arises from either the rootsystem of a plant or from beneath the union of a grafted plant.

Systemic: term describing pesticides or herbicides which go inside the plant and travel in the sap stream, affecting the whole plant.

Tap root: a strong deep root, sometimes swollen, which grows vertically into the soil or compost.

Tender: a plant which is vulnerable to cold weather or frosts.

Tendril: a thread-like stem or leaf which climbing plants use to cling to any nearby support.

Terminal: applied to the uppermost bud or flower on a stem.

Terrarium: a partly or entirely closed glass container used to house a collection of indoor plants. Similar to a bottle garden.

Terrestrial: a plant that grows in the soil.

Thatch: the layer of dead grass that accumulates in a lawn.

Thinning: the removal of excess seedlings, flowers or fruits to encourage those remaining.

Tilth: a fine crumbly soil surface produced by cultivation and the right weather conditions.

Tissue culture: the growth of young plants in artificial, sterile conditions. See Micro-propagation.

Topdressing: the addition of a fertiliser or other soil dressing to the surface of the soil.

Topiary: the art of clipping and training woody plants to form geometric shapes or intricate patterns.

Topsoil: the uppermost spit of soil, highly fertile and generally ideal for growth.

Trace element: a nutrient essential for plant growth but only required in minute quantities.

Translocation: the movement of dissolved materials within the plant's system, usually nutrients but can also be other materials such as herbicides.

Transpiration: the loss of water through the pores of the leaf.

Tree: a woody plant generally with a distinct central trunk. (Compare Shrub.)

True breeding: plants that give rise to offspring similar to parents.

Trunk: the thickened woody stem of a tree.

Tuber: a storage organ comprised of a swollen underground stem or root.

Tufa: a porous rock sometimes used for building rock gardens.

Umbel: a flowering stem in which all the flower stalks are of similar length and arise from the same point.

Underplanting: the use of a lower, groundcover plant underneath a taller plant to give a two level effect.

Union: the point of a graft, usually always visible even on mature plants.

Variegated: marked with various different colours. Usually refers to leaves rather than flowers.

Variety: a naturally occurring variation on a wild species. Often incorrectly used to refer to cultivars, which occur in garden or other cultivated situations.

Vegetative growth: leafy non-flowering growth.

Vegetative propagation: asexual propagation. Cuttings, layers, etc. producing plants identical to the parents.

Vermiculite: lightweight mica-like mineral in granular form, capable of holding both water and air. Used for propagation.

Weed: a plant growing in a place where it is not wanted, often crowding out cultivated plants.

Whorled: three or more leaves radiating from a single node.

Wind-break: a thick hedge or screen planned to soften the effect of wind.

Wind-rock: destabilisation of a plant by high winds. Results in a cone-shaped depression around the roots which becomes waterlogged.

PLANTS FOR DIFFERENT LOCATIONS

This section helps you select appropriate plants to grow in the various locations of your garden. So whether your garden is exposed or shady, or your soil sandy or chalky, the following information will help you decide what to plant where.

DRY SHADE
Cotoneaster horizontalis
Mahonia aquifolium
Bergenia cordifolia
Euonymus fortunei 'Sunspot'
Ilex aquifolium 'Golden King'

MOIST SHADE
Acer palmatum
Hamamelis mollis
Camellia 'Donation'
Pieris japonica
Hydrangea paniculata

COLD EXPOSED SITES
Buddleia davidii Cultivars
Cornus alba cultivars
Elaeagnus pungens 'Maculata'
Potentilla fruticosa 'Goldfinger'
Chaenomeles speciosa 'Nivalis'

FULL SUN AND DRY
Cistus corbariensis
Ceratostigma willmottianum
Hebe 'Great Orme'
Lavandula x intermedia 'Grosso'
Phlomis fruticosa

WET SITES
Cornus alba Cultivars
Physocarpus 'Dart's Gold' AGM
Spirarea japonica 'Goldflame'
Salix alba 'Chermosina'
Sambucus racemosa 'Sutherland'

FOR HEAVY CLAY SOILS
Berberis thunbergii 'Red Chief'
Hypericum 'Hidcote'
Pyracantha 'Orange Glow'
Viburnum tinus
Philadelphus 'Sybille'

FOR LIGHT SANDY SOILS
Cytisus x praecox
Rosmarinus 'Severn Seas'
Spartium junceum
Perovskia 'Blue Spire'
Artemesia 'Powis Castle'

FOR CHALKY SOILS
Ceanothus 'Italian Skies'
Escallonia 'Apple Blossom'
Fuchsia magellanica 'Aurea'
Pittosporum tennuifolium
Choisya 'Aztec Pearl'

FOR ACID SOILS
Rhododendrons in variety
Callunna vulgaris
Pierris japonica 'Flame of the Forest'
Camellia 'Donation'
Pernettya mucronata
Gaultheria 'Shallon'

FOR TINY GARDENS
Chaenomeles 'Red Trail'
Forsythia 'Fiesta'
Philadelphus 'Manteau d'Hermine'
Fuchsia ' Tom Thumb'
Potentilla 'Knaphill Seedling'

PRICKLY PLANTS FOR SECURITY
Berberis julianae
Crateagus x prunifolia
Ilex aquifolium
Ulex europaeus
Rosa moyesii 'Geranium'

INDEX